Plants for
Atlantic Gardens

Handsome and Hard-working Shrubs, Trees, and Perennials

Jodi DeLong

NIMBUS
PUBLISHING

Nimbus Publishing Limited
3731 Mackintosh St, Halifax, NS B3K 5A5
(902) 455-4286 nimbus.ca

Cover & Interior Design: Margaret Issenman
Printed and bound in China
This book contains only FSC certified paper

Map on page vii: "Plant Hardiness Zones in Canada (2000)" © Agriculture and Agri-Food Canada. The map is an official work of the Government of Canada. It has not been produced in affiliation with, or with the endorsement of, the Government of Canada.

Library and Archives Canada Cataloguing in Publication

DeLong, Jodi, 1958-
Plants for Atlantic gardens : handsome and hard-
working shrubs, trees, and perennials / Jodi Delong.
ISBN 978-1-55109-798-5

1. Gardening—Atlantic Provinces. 2. Plants, Ornamental Atlantic Provinces. I. Title.

SB453.3.C2D45 2011   635.09715   C2010-903089-3

Canadä The Canada Council | Le Conseil des Arts NOVA SCOTIA
              for the Arts | du Canada   Tourism, Culture d Heritage

We acknowledge the financial support of the Government of Canada through the Book Publishing Industry Development Program (BPIDP) and the Canada Council, a f the Province of Nova Scotia through the Department of Tourism, Culture and Herit   r publishing activities.

Contents

FOREWORD

Jodi DeLong is not an armchair gardener. She gives presentations and workshops; visits nurseries, greenhouses, and garden centres; and attends horticultural conferences. Jodi modestly states in her acknowledgements that she never "purport[s] to be an expert when it comes to plants." Well, Jodi *is* an expert. With her garden blog, magazine articles, and regional presentations and workshops, Jodi is probably the most widely known garden writer and speaker in Atlantic Canada. The gardening public, and those of us who are in the nursery industry and involved in horticultural education, all know Jodi DeLong.

In *Plants for Atlantic Gardens*, Jodi has put together a well-selected list. She has included an excellent selection of new and old cultivars of both native and non-native plants. Each plant profile provides sufficient information for the reader to get to know that plant: its hardiness rating, soil requirements, bloom period, height, and any potential problems. In recent years, one of the biggest factors affecting perennial, shrub, and tree sales has nothing to do with garden design trends, but is instead the ever-increasing deer problem. In this book, Jodi notes the deer-resistant shrubs, trees, and perennials such as barberries, ninebarks, monkshood, and lady's mantle.

Many of the plants that Jodi writes about have a story with some personal connection, and she tells that story well in just a few sentences; plants such as silver birch, horse chestnut, purple coneflower, and her bristlecone pine named "Bob," to name a few. Jodi has included common garden stalwarts such as daylily and spirea, but also less common plants and plant cultivars such as rattlesnake master, European wood anemone, Itoh peony, and 'Butterfly' Japanese maple.

She also includes some wonderful woody plants, underutilized and not nearly as well known as they should be: chokeberry, Preston lilacs, bayberry, falsecypress, staghorn sumac, and one of my favourite native plants, Canada holly. Favourite perennials of mine, such as 'Angelina' sedum, Japanese forest grass, the bugbanes—particularly 'Pink Spike' and 'Hillside Black Beauty'—lady's mantle, the masterworts, blue false indigo, and the meadow rue, *Thalictrum rochebruneanum*, are also included.

Plants for Atlantic Gardens should be in every gardener's library. It is thoroughly packed with useful and interesting information on some of the best plants for Atlantic Canadian gardens.

Lloyd Mapplebeck is associate professor of environmental sciences at Nova Scotia Agricultural College, and owner of Hillendale Perennials, both located in Truro, N.S.

Acknowledgements

No gardener, unless a hermit living in the back of beyond, is an island when it comes to plants and planting tips. I owe a huge debt of gratitude to gardeners past and present, professional horticulturists, nursery operators, garden bloggers, family and friends.

Although I'm a seasoned gardener, having been grubbing in the soil for more years than I really want to admit, I never purport to be an expert when it comes to plants. We always learn best from experience coupled with shared knowledge from other gardeners and plant people, and I'm no exception. Among the people—many of whom are cherished friends—who have been generous and wise resources for my gardening and writing adventures over the years are Alice d'Entremont, Jill Covill, Sharon Bryson and Bill Wilgenhof, Lloyd Mapplebeck, Bob Osborne, Diana Steele, Carol Goodwin, Todd Boland, Tim Amos, Jamie Ellison, Rosaleen MacDonald, Wayne Ward and Wayne Storrie, Lee and John Dickie, Jana and Frank Fejtek, Jerry Huntley, Lorraine Beswick, Melanie Priestnitz, and Flora Shaw.

My friend, fellow plant addict, and all-around outstanding nurseryman Rob Baldwin has been invaluable in helping me put this book together. Rob has an inquisitive mind and an endless fascination with plants, particularly shrubs and trees and those perennials that encourage pollinators. He patiently answered my questions pertaining to many of the woody selections found in this book, and has shared many plants with me over the years, saying, "Take this home and cold-test it!"

Since January of 2006, I have written a blog called "bloomingwriter" (bloomingwriter. blogspot.com). Through blogging, I have gotten to know literally dozens of bloggers around the world, some of whom garden in exotic locales in the southern hemisphere, others of whom are scattered across Canada, the United States, and Europe. I cannot possibly try to list them all for fear of omitting someone, but I offer huge thanks to them for sharing their knowledge, their encouragement, and in some cases, their seeds and plants, with me.

A book doesn't come together without the efforts of a tremendous group of people in the publishing house. To Patrick Murphy, the Nimbus editor who was willing to take a chance on my idea and who has been a stalwart support, bouquets of gratitude. Thanks also to designer Margaret Issenman, production manager Heather Bryan, and marketing manager Diane Faulkner.

Last in the list of gratitude but first in my heart is my family, including my mother, Joan, my sister Kelly DeLong Marcoux, and my son, Ryan Saunders, all of whom share my passion for gardening. Most of all, there aren't enough words to adequately thank my beloved "Long Suffering Spouse," Lowell Huntley. Living with a gardener who is also a writer is no mean feat, and LSS helps around the house and yard, accompanies me around the region when I go to give talks or seek out plants, and always encourages me, especially when weeds thrive and words fail. If I am any plant, I'm a lichen, and he's the rock to which I must cling to survive.

This book is lovingly dedicated to the late Captain Richard Steele, OC, the best plantsman I have ever had the pleasure to meet. His generosity of spirit and huge enthusiasm for growing plants has inspired many a gardener, including me, and I'm humbled and honoured to be considered his friend.

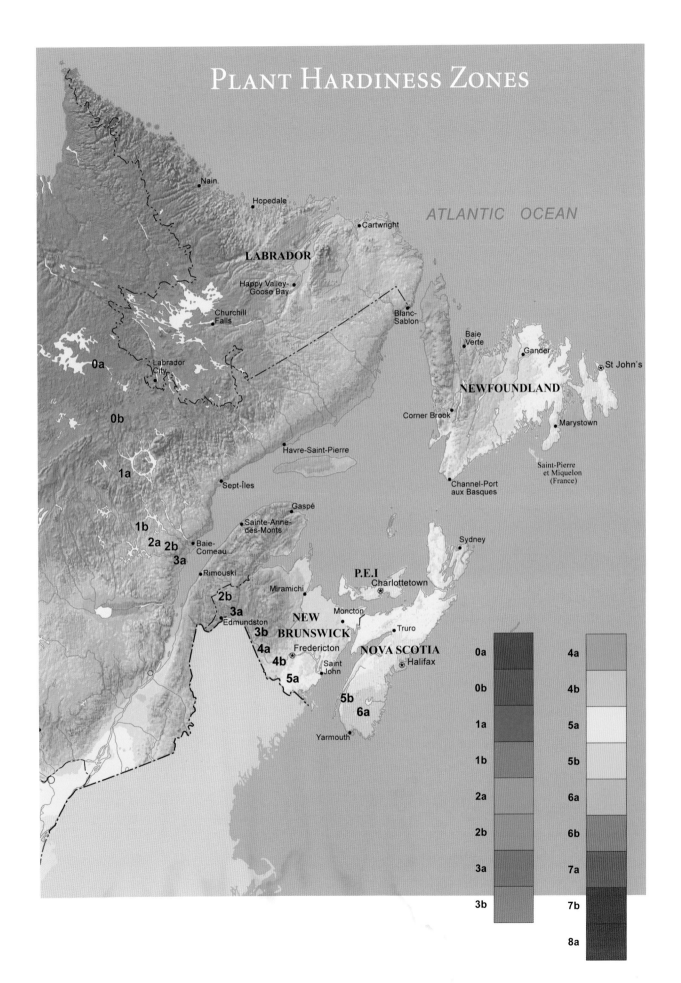

INTRODUCTION: GARDENING IN ATLANTIC CANADA

When my long-suffering spouse and I first moved to our home on the North Mountain of Nova Scotia's Annapolis Valley, overlooking the upper Bay of Fundy, I was extremely excited. Suddenly, I had all the room I could possibly need in which to develop the garden of my dreams. It was February when we bought the rural property, with icy winds swirling in off the bay, and just a few shrubs and trees and the skeletons of perennials providing some glimpse of what was, and what could be. After years of never living in one location for more than a couple of years, the plan was to "plant" myself permanently on the hill. I would plant trees, shrubs, and perennials of all kinds, have a vegetable garden, some wild areas. I'd dig out the big pond that was filled with cattails and alders, replant the edges with drifts of native plants for birds and bees and other wildlife to enjoy.

The reality is never quite what imagination brings us, but that's not necessarily a bad thing. The first spring, I came up against the first of my gardening challenges: the soil, a mixture of rock and clay. Heavy, cold, waterlogged clay, fed by an assortment of springs that cross our property. Then there was the climate, which even for Atlantic Canada was a bit daunting. Winds scour the bay, bringing bitter cold in the winter months, tearing leaves off trees before they've even had a chance to change colour in the fall, burning flower buds in a chilly spring breeze. Since our house is on top of a hill, we catch wind from all directions, and few spots are truly sheltered from wrathful zephyrs. Fog can and does show up in every month, though predominantly in spring and summer. When it is sunny here, it tends to be at least a few degrees cooler than the Valley, which can be an advantage when the Valley swelters in midsummer humidity.

Over the past twelve years I've done a lot of experimenting with garden plants on our property, finding species that tolerate the challenges of our climate. I've been amending the soil with additions of compost, building a few raised beds, getting to know the spots that stay wet and those that have relatively good drainage, the areas that are most sheltered from the winter, and the plants that can withstand almost anything that nature throws at them. I've planted hundreds of different varieties, species, and cultivars of plants all around the place. Some varieties have died a few times before I've admitted defeat. Others have languished in a semi-existence before finally going to sleep forever. Still others have thrived, in some cases too exuberantly.

At the same time as I've been field-testing plants here, I've had the privilege to get to know many gardeners around the region, in person, through email correspondence, and through gardening blogs. Gardeners are always willing to share their experiences and knowledge—along with their plants—with other gardeners, which is one of the reasons that this pastime so appeals to me and to my fellow green thumbs. It's a course in lifetime learning, a social activity, a way of giving back to the earth around us.

As one who spends a great deal of time working with, thinking about, reading about, and writing and speaking about plants, I often receive questions about what plants work well in various gardening conditions. None of us lives in a perfect climate, or has a perfect location where every plant we've ever grown from seed, bought from a nursery, or acquired in a plant swap has done well for us. There are challenges to gardening in our region. Many of our soils are heavy with clay and tend toward acidity, although there are also areas with sandy soil and even some locations that are more alkaline than acid. We can have late springs, be plagued with too much or not enough rain during the summer, and have curious winters that may include days well above freezing and other days that are Arctic-like. Some of us live near the ocean, be it the Bay of Fundy, the Gulf of St. Lawrence, or the Atlantic, and deal with salt and wind off the water. Deer, slugs, and other nuisances dine on our daylilies, taste our tulips, hunger for our hostas.

bee on heath

fruit of Cornus kousa

If you were to visit a number of gardens throughout our region, you'd probably find a mixture of native species along with introduced cultivars—old-fashioned heirloom or heritage plants as well as new, improved hybrids. Some of us stick with plants we know well, that we know will tolerate—if not thrive in—our challenging growing conditions. Others like to push the envelope, exercise zonal-denial by planting species that are marginally hardy, and experiment with new and unproven (to us, anyway) varieties.

There are hundreds, probably even thousands, of plants that do well in Atlantic Canada, so selecting plants for this book was quite a challenge. We don't all have huge, sprawling properties where we can plant copper beeches or oak trees that will eventually tower many feet in the air. Some of us like to collect particular species such as hostas, daylilies, and roses, while others specialize in shade plants, alpine gardening, rhododendrons, or species with great foliage. Still others want to use only native plants. How to decide on which species should be included? I drew on my own experience, but also on that of gardeners, horticulturists, and nursery operators around the region to come up with a list of top plants for our region.

The first step was to decide what *not* to include. There are no annuals, vegetables, or fruits included in this book. Annuals only have a short lifespan in our gardens, replanted yearly. Others have written wonderfully helpful books on food growing in our region, so there was no need to reinvent the wheel.

I have left out some plants, especially trees and shrubs, that are either so commonly used throughout the region that it seemed a waste of space to include them, had some challenges due to hardiness, disease or pest problems, or didn't have enough multi-season interest to warrant taking a space in the list of most-recommended species. These include balsam fir, yew, forsythia, deutzia, hibiscus, beautybush (*Kolkwitzia*), butterfly bush (*Buddleia*), euonymus, catalpa, caryopteris, and honeysuckle. I did the same with certain perennials that are either extremely common or else can be particularly challenging to grow, including crocosmia, kniphofia, some of the daisies and sunflowers and their relatives, gentians, forget-me-nots, and my beloved but cranky blue poppy, *Meconopsis*. In several instances, I combined a group of species together into a special section because they could be (and have been) the subject of numerous books: grasses, ferns, and alpines.

One gardener's pest is another gardener's favourite plant, but I wanted to avoid recommending any overachievers (i.e. invasive species such as goutweed, *Aegopodium*, or oriental bittersweet, *Celastrus orbiculatus*). I have included a list of plants that should come with "Plant at Your Own Risk" labels, in the section on garden thugs, page 104.

What you *will* find within the pages of this book are a variety of woody plants—trees and shrubs—as well as many herbaceous perennials. Some are native to this region, some introduced; some are beloved old-fashioned varieties, while others include interesting new hybrids and cultivars that didn't even exist when I started gardening. Each plant profile gives a bit of background information on the species and what makes it a particularly appealing plant for our region. Wherever possible, I've included a few recommended varieties or cultivars of the various plant types, but in many cases, such as with hostas, there are hundreds, even thousands of varieties. In those cases, you may want to go to reliable websites or nurseries to make your choice.

epimedium foliage

You will find a collection of appendices in the back of this book, including lists of plants that work in particular conditions (e.g. plants that are salt-tolerant, deer-resistant, good pollinators, and more). These lists include some plants that aren't profiled in this book, but that are worthwhile to check out for yourself.

Remember that plants are living beings, and even when you give them the best of care, they can sicken and die rather arbitrarily. I always say that plants can't read, and although they might be supposed to grow to a certain height or to be hardy to a particular temperature, they can

yellow foxglove

surprise us—in good and bad ways. No plant is absolutely deer-, insect-, or climate-proof; at best they are resistant to, or tolerant of, various challenges. There may be something about your soil, or about the way the wind blows around your property, that works against a plant in your garden while it thrives in a neighbour's. Don't be discouraged by plants with capricious natures; take comfort in realizing that a dead plant just means you have a ready-made hole in which to plant something else.

A NOTE ON PLANT TOXICITY

Gardening is a rewarding and popular pastime, although not without its risks. One of these has to do with the toxicity of plants. Many plants are toxic in some, if not all, of their parts, but can affect people and animals in different ways. The commonly used evergreen tree or shrub yew (*Taxus*), for example, is extremely toxic to horses—yet deer browse on it with no obvious harmful effects. By the same token, we humans eat rhubarb stalks, tomato fruits, and potato tubers, yet the leaves of all these plants are poisonous to us and to many other species. Lilies are highly toxic to cats, but dined on by any number of insects. And so on. Some plants are phytophototoxic, which means that when their sap combines with sunlight, they will produce an irritating rash or blisters on the skin. Use caution when dealing with plants. Most perennials and shrubs sold by reputable nurseries will have labels indicating any toxicity, so make sure to read such labels before purchasing.

Shrubs and Trees

PROPER PLANTING OF A SHRUB OR TREE

When I talk to gardeners about trees, one of the things I stress is to purchase young, small, container-grown specimens. Smaller trees are more adaptive to the site they're going to be planted in, they require less watering, and quite often they don't need to be staked. You'll probably have more success if you avoid purchasing trees that are in wire baskets or "ball and burlap"; so many roots have been cut off these trees when they are dug that the tree must spend the next three to five years repairing its roots, with very little growth above the ground. Many nurseries are now using large containers and getting away from wire baskets for just such reasons.

Before purchasing a tree or shrub, if at all possible check the root ball by lifting the plant carefully from the container. If the roots are tightly spiralling around inside the container, they are unlikely to ever open up and spread away from the plant without a little help. If you're unable to check the roots before purchase and get the plant home to discover that it has been "root-bound" in this way, you'll have to do what nursery operator Robert Baldwin calls "scuffing up the roots." Gently tease the roots apart with your fingers, spreading them out away from the base of the tree or shrub. If the roots are very tight and tough and you can't move them with your fingers, use pruners or a knife to slice the sides of the root ball before you plant it. It may take a season or two for the roots to spread out and the plant to start growing in earnest, but it's far more likely to thrive than one planted without tackling the root-bound problem.

Should you stake a tree or shrub? It depends very much on your growing conditions and the size of the plant. If the tree is more than six or seven feet in height, or if you live in a particularly windy spot, you will need to stake newly planted specimens. Without staking, wind can rock the root ball and allow air to get in under the roots so the tree dries out. Use stakes on your trees the way people use crutches—temporarily. If you do use a stake, make sure to remove the wires, cord, or other material used to hold the tree to the stake when you pull the support out. I often see trees with wires still on them ten years after planting, with the wire having grown into the tree limb or trunk and "girdling" it, leading to the death of the limb or the entire tree.

If you need to leave an identifying tag on a tree or shrub, remove the tag from the base of the plant where it is normally attached by the grower, and move it to a higher branch where you can see it but where it's unlikely to do damage. The other option is to map out your garden on paper, labelling each specimen on your map. (I've been meaning to do this for about a decade now.)

Step-by-step tree or shrub planting

- If possible, plant in early spring or late fall during the rainier parts of the season so you'll have to do less watering.

- Dig the hole 1–2 inches deeper than the pot and 1.5 to 2 times as wide.

- Remove the tree from its container.

- Do a trial planting to make sure the depth is correct.

- Amend the soil by mixing compost in with the local soil (up to a fifty-fifty ratio). (Don't use pure compost or too much fertilizer because the tree roots need to stretch out into the regular soil, not become dependent on the locally added fertility.) Put 1–2 inches of the amended soil in the bottom of the hole.

- Put the plant in the hole so that the soil level of the root ball is 1–2 inches higher than the surrounding soil, to allow for settling.

- Refill hole with remaining soil, mounding a little bit over the original soil (1 inch or so).

- Lightly firm the soil around the trunk.

- Flood the area with water. You can't overwater new plants unless you're living in a swamp. The water will get rid of all the air spaces and as a result the plant may settle a little.

- Mulch around the tree, but never bury the trunk, as mulching too closely around the trunk can cause disease problems in some plants. Leave a depression around the trunk to act as a little watering well.

- Use a two-stake system with wire threaded through leaky garden hose. Place the stakes outside the root ball's circumference so as not to damage the young roots.

- Do not let the tree dry out. Water regularly, especially in dry summers; many plants are potted in containers using potting mixes that dry out extremely quickly.

Acer

maple

Family: Sapindaceae
Hardy to: zone 3
Bloom period: early to mid spring
Growing requirements: full sun; compost-rich, moist, but well-drained soil
Height: 30–100 feet

Where best used: specimen tree, shade tree, street plantings, hedging
Propagation: seed
Problems: No serious pests or diseases in recommended species.
Notes: Excellent hardwoods noted for great fall colour.

Maples are at once a familiar, beloved plant and an exotic, demanding one. We are thrilled by the sight of the maple leaf on our Canadian flag, although ironically it's a representation of an introduced species, the ubiquitously planted Norway maple (*Acer platanoides*). I never recommend Norway maple because it is overused and susceptible to several diseases, including tar spot fungus and verticillium wilt, and also seeds prolifically, displacing native species by shading out undergrowth and competing for nutrients. We delight in the explosive colour displays of maple foliage in autumn, as woodlands blaze with crimson, gold, red, and copper. And of course many of us make an annual, late-winter trip to a sugarbush to enjoy freshly made maple syrup on pancakes or maple taffy made on snow.

Numerous maple species are used in home gardening situations, with species ranging in size from largish shrubs to magnificent trees. The larger maples make marvellous shade trees, and of course provide that burst of rapturous fall colour. It can be a challenge to find plants that will grow under these trees, both because they cast such a large shade canopy, but also because they take up a lot of moisture and nutrients from the soil. With a little creative thinking and planning, you can grow ground covers and other shade-tolerant plants under maples, providing

mature sugar maples

flowers of red maple

you water these sites and mulch around the perennials.

The flowers of maple trees are inconspicuous when compared to the showier flowers of trees such as magnolias. However, maple flowers are very important as nectar and pollen sources for bees, especially in the early spring when few other trees and shrubs are yet in bloom. Interestingly, the red maple (*Acer rubrum*), which is one of the first native trees to flower, also releases its seeds early (late June to early July) as a survival mechanism.

Unless otherwise noted below, maples are best planted in moist but freely draining soils. While some are more tolerant of wet soils, most do not handle drought well at all, and are best avoided in consistently dry conditions. Choose your species carefully: a sugar maple can grow very large over the years and can dwarf a yard, shading out everything else growing there.

Recommended species

Acer ginnala: Amur maple is a smaller species, useful for providing privacy and screening areas. It is tolerant of some shade. Hardy in zones 3 to 8, with rich plum and scarlet fall colours, often holding seeds through much of winter. Mulch heavily underneath to reduce seedling germination.

Acer griseum: The paperbark maple is best known for its winter interest, as its bark exfoliates to reveal cinnamon or russet-coloured new bark underneath. Hardy only to zone 5—not recommended for colder parts of region.

Acer pennsylvanicum: The striped or moosewood maple is best suited for growing in shelterbelt areas on farms and other rural properties, along streams or other wet areas. In nature it's an understorey species and is not majestic like red or sugar maples. Zone 3.

Acer rubrum: The native red maple has reddish-tinged leaves in spring, and often (but not always) excellent red fall colour. One of first hardwoods to flower in spring, and very tolerant of wet, even swampy, locations. Hardy in zones 3 to 9, the red maple has a greater north-south range than any other tree in North America.

Acer saccharum: The sugar maple (often referred to as rock maple in parts of the region) is a slow-growing tree that can reach great heights. Magnificent fall colour but best planted in large yards or on rural properties. Zone 3.

fall foliage of sugar maple

Acer palmatum

Japanese maple, cut leaf maple

Family: Sapindaceae

Hardy to: zone 5 with winter protection

Bloom period: April–May

Growing requirements: sun to partial shade, compost-rich soil, good drainage

Height: 10–20 feet

Where best used: specimen tree

Propagation: seed, cuttings

Problems: Some cultivars very cold- and wind-sensitive. Protect from sunscald in winter.

Notes: Truly spectacular foliage texture and fall colour.

I include this separate profile on Japanese maples with apologies to all those who don't live in the more southerly ranges of Atlantic Canada. If you can't grow a Japanese maple, you are missing out on one of the most stunning of maples, perhaps of all trees. There is so much to love about these shrubby, small trees, from their palmate, colourful, cut-patterned leaves to their smooth bark and graceful, bonsai-like growth habits. The seeds of some cultivars are beautiful, and the fall foliage colour is on a par with the best sugar and red maples.

new growth of 'Osakazuki' seedling

All that beauty comes at a price: Japanese maples can be a challenge to grow for many of us. Heavy snowfalls can break delicate branches, cold winds can cause winter damage, and late spring frosts can kill off tender new shoots and leaves. Because I face all of these situations in any given year here on my North Mountain property, and because Japanese maples are a higher-end investment for the garden, I had been reluctant to invest in a tree of any more than seedling size until this past summer, when I was given a three-year-old sapling grown from seeds of the Osakazuki cultivar to cold-test here. A neighbour a kilometre or so up the road from me has had the Bloodgood cultivar for a number of years, and there are people having good success with the hardier cultivars across the region. So it's well worth giving a Japanese maple a try.

If you *are* in a location that is open to a lot of wind, situate a new maple so that it is sheltered from the worst of prevailing winter winds. Often the east side of a house is a good choice, where some shade protection is also offered. Japanese maples like morning sun but

cascading growth habit of a Japanese maple

also do best with some shade from hot afternoon sunlight. Planting near larger trees that will shade your maple is often a good way to solve these challenges.

Japanese maples like moisture but also need good drainage; you may wish to amend the soil with sharp sand and compost to improve its drainage before planting your tree, and you should mulch generously following planting. Several reputable nursery operators tell their customers not to feed a Japanese maple with conventional commercial fertilizers, but to instead add compost or sheep manure and bone meal to the planting hole before adding the tree. In subsequent years, topdressing with a generous layer of compost will be sufficient. If you're blessed with a sandier soil, make sure to water your tree well at least twice a week, especially in drier summers.

If you handle the cultivation requirements for your tree, it should do well for many years and have few pest or disease problems. Winter sunscald can be a problem, particularly with trees in a southern exposure: wrapping the trunks of young maples with burlap before winter will protect the bark until it becomes strong enough to deflect the sun. Japanese maples can be prone to certain fungal diseases, including botrytis and fusarium wilt, but good air circulation and adequate drainage will go a long way in preventing such problems.

Recommended species and cultivars

Although many Japanese maples have red or wine-coloured foliage throughout the growing year, all of them put on an amazing display of colour when autumn arrives. Newly emerging leaves are delicately coloured pastels, and of course the weeping varieties provide winter interest with their graceful shapes.

'Inabe Shidare': A deep purple red in the summer with large, finely cut leaves and a weeping habit.

'Butterfly': Graceful upright habit and white-edged green leaves.

'Osakazuki': Green foliage with bright red flowers in spring, blaze orange fall colour.

'Waterfall': A green cut-leaf weeping variety with a cascading shape.

'Bloodgood': Among the hardiest of choices for our region, with consistent deep wine leaves and stems, red fall colour.

flowers of golden full moon maple

'Sango kaku': An upright green variety with gorgeous red bark and golden fall colour.

***Acer shirasawanum* 'Aureum,'**
Golden full moon maple: This tree has somewhat large yellow leaves and is upright in growth habit. It gets greener as the season progresses, but it still offers great contrast in the landscape.

Aesculus

horse chestnut, buckeye

Family: Sapindaceae (formerly Hippocastanaceae)
Hardy to: zone 3 or 4
Bloom period: mid-May–June
Growing requirements: Moist, well-drained soil is preferred. Tolerant of clay, acid soil.
Height: 50–100 feet at maturity
Where best used: Excellent shade trees. Can grow very large over time.

Propagation: seed or grafting
Problems: Leaf blotch in late summer; leaf scorch, especially in drier conditions. Caterpillars and borers sometimes apparent.
Notes: Deer-resistant. Flowers attract hummingbirds. Ohio buckeye (*A. glabra*) one of first trees to leaf out in spring.

When my long-suffering spouse was a child, he helped his grandfather plant several horse chestnut trees on the family farm in rural Kings County. To celebrate and continue that legacy, the first tree I bought and gave to him when we moved to our place was a small horse chestnut. Although it's only been planted for just over a decade, it is turning into a handsome and nicely shaped tree, and has been flowering for about five years.

My love for horse chestnut trees goes back to my own youth spent in St. John's, Newfoundland. A favourite pastime in late summer was collecting the prickly seed pods

Ohio buckeye new foliage

that fell on sidewalks around the city, and removing the large, shiny, and deep brown seeds from within. Articles on horse chestnuts often mention that little boys like to put these seeds on strings and play "conkers" with them, trying to break one another's seeds. (From experience I can report that it is not only little boys who like to play that game.)

Aesculus species make beautiful shade trees for home gardens, public parks, and street plantings, although not everyone is as enamoured of the seed pods as are little boys and garden writers. The species are distinctive with their easily recognized palmate leaves, and their flower heads are spectacular, candelabra-like stems holding many pink-and-white, red, or yellowish flowers.

flower buds of horse chestnut

open flowers, horse chestnut

Horse chestnuts and buckeyes prefer rich soil and adequate moisture, but they are extremely hardy and tolerant of many growing conditions. Leaf scorch and leaf blotch can appear in late summer, especially if the trees are planted in crowded conditions, but neither problem is fatal. Fall foliage is unremarkable, as the leaves simply turn yellowish and drop off.

Planting under horse chestnuts can be a challenge, as most produce such shade and extensive root systems that there's little light, moisture, or nutrients available for other plants. It's thought that the bottlebrush buckeye has alleleopathic properties, producing chemicals that deter germination or growth of other plant seeds.

Recommended species

Aesculus hippocastanum: Common horse chestnut is the most common of the species to be planted in our region. Bark sometimes exfoliates to display bright orange new bark underneath. Zone 3.

A. glabra: Ohio buckeye. This is an unusual species because it leafs out in late April when temperatures can routinely dip below freezing. The spring foliage is beautiful, bronze-red in colour, and the seed pods are smooth. Michael Dirr writes that cultivars of the Ohio buckeye are usually grafted onto standard horse chestnut root stocks, so be careful that the plant doesn't revert. Zone 3.

A. x carnea: Red horse chestnut. Hybrid with pink to red flowers, showy during bloom. Smaller tree than common horse chestnut (30–40 feet tall) and more drought tolerant. Zone 4.

A. parviflora: Bottlebrush buckeye. Shrub-sized, maturing to a maximum of 12 feet. Seed pods are smooth, unlike common horse chestnut. Tends to be free of leaf blotch/scorch problem seen in other species. Zone 5a.

Amelanchier

serviceberry, shadbush

Family: Rosaceae

Hardy to: zone 3

Bloom period: April–May

Growing requirements: Grows in poorest of soils; good tree for small yards.

Height: 15–20 feet, occasionally taller.

Where best used: Excellent small tree or large shrub for front yards, mixed borders, wildlife plantings.

Propagation: remove suckers from base of shrub; hardwood cuttings

Problems: No serious pests or diseases. Occasional caterpillars.

Notes: Naturally found in wet, boggy habitats. One of earliest showy flowering plants in spring.

If ever there was an ideal example for using botanical names when talking about a plant, *Amelanchier* is it. Common names vary with regionality, but include shadbush, serviceberry, chuckly pear, Indian pear, saskatoon, and juneberry. But if we refer to amelanchier, we know we're all talking about the same plant: a small, multi-trunked tree, native to Atlantic Canada, and a valuable addition to any garden.

You may be out driving or hiking in mid-spring and notice a small tree or tall shrub along the edges of woodlands, covered in white blooms that resemble apple or cherry blossoms. Chances are, what you're seeing is an amelanchier, one of the plants tracked by citizen scientists involved in PlantWatch, part of the national NatureWatch program monitoring ecological activity in our environment (www.naturewatch.ca).

A number of species of amelanchier grow in the wild throughout Atlantic Canada, and are also offered as ornamental shrubs from nurseries. However, as with hawthorns (*Crataegus* spp.), the plants hybridize freely, which makes it difficult to definitively identify a specimen in the wild by species. In the horticultural trades, you'll often see the plant sold as *Amelanchier canadensis* unless the garden centre is specifically selling saskatoonberry, which is *A. alnifolia*. (The city of Saskatoon actually takes its name from a Cree word for the berry of *A. alnifolia*.)

A. canadensis *flowers and spring foliage*

unripe fruit, late June

The versatile amelanchier is a lovely tree for small yards or for creating nature habitats on larger properties. It's highly ornamental, with smooth greyish barks accented with white striations, and its spring foliage is bronzy green in colour. This tree flowers before its leaves are even finished unfurling and is beloved by pollinating insects. Newly formed berries are white, turn pink, and are deep purple-blue when ripe, and while they're very tasty, you may find you're competing with a host of songbirds for your tree's berries. The berries look and taste something like a blueberry, but have larger seeds. In autumn, amelanchier trees show off their fall finery with brilliant scarlet, purple, and gold colours in their foliage. The bark shows up well in winter, particularly if the plant has been pruned so that it looks more like a tree than a multi-stemmed bush.

If you have wet spots in your garden and yard, amelanchier will do well there provided it has full sun. You may choose to let your amelanchier develop suckers and shoots so that it forms a more shrubby thicket of growth, or prune it so that it looks more like a small tree. Whatever the case, amelanchier transplants and adapts very easily to most garden conditions, making it a good option for any gardener.

Planting under shade trees

Garden writers regularly are asked what plants will flourish under shade trees. The answer to the question depends on what you, the gardener, are prepared to do to amend conditions under your trees. Many trees have large roots that grow near the surface, making it difficult to find any spaces where you can dig into the soil to add plants. Others produce such heavy shade that most flowering perennials don't do well. Trees by their very size require a lot of moisture and nutrients, and their eager roots thus leave little behind for other plants to use.

Where you have large roots near the surface, you will often find there are pockets of space where you can add soil and then plant ferns, hostas, and other shade-loving species.

While many plants are happiest with moist shade, there are few that thrive in dry shade, such as that found under large trees. In order to keep perennials healthy, you may have to water them regularly. Mulching heavily around your plants will help reduce water evaporation and keep soil cool and moist, but you may still need to water, especially during hot, dry spells.

One other option that requires less work is to put shade-loving annuals and perennials into container plantings and place those under your shade trees. You can rearrange the containers as you please (providing they aren't too large and unwieldy), moving them into less-shaded spots for a change in growing conditions.

Aronia

Family: Rosaceae
Hardy to: zone 3
Bloom period: May to early June
Growing requirements: full sun to partial shade
Height: 6–12 feet

Where best used: Native plantings, roadside and parking lot adaptable. Will naturalize.
Propagation: Division of suckers is easy.
Problems: No serious pests or diseases. Deer may nibble shoots in spring.
Notes: Salt-, pollution-, and drought-tolerant. Attractive to pollinators.

Choke*berry* is often mistakenly referred to as choke*cherry*, which is an entirely different plant, *Prunus virginiana*. Just to make it fun, however, some taxonomists classify chokeberries in the genus *Pyrus* (pear), while others consider it a stand-alone genus, *Aronia*. There are two species in the genus *Aronia* native to eastern North America: the red chokeberry, *Aronia arbutifolia*, and the black chokeberry, *A. melanocarpa*. Of the two, I personally prefer the black species because the fruit is attractive in late summer and autumn, but both species are important for songbirds and pollinators.

I've seen writers refer to chokeberry as an old-fashioned plant, but I'm not entirely sure what that means. That term can sometimes seem derogatory, but I love chokeberries because they are stalwart workhorses of the native or wildlife garden. As long as they have adequate sun (light shade to full sun) they will tolerate any growing conditions: swampy, dry, clay, sandy. In the spring, the shrub is covered in delicate clusters of petite, white and pink flowers that resemble miniature cherry blossoms, followed by glossy clusters of red or black fruit. Summer foliage is deep green, brightening to salmon, gold, and burgundy in the autumn.

The chokeberry is a good choice for a naturalized planting or a border, although if you don't want it to spread you'll have to remove its suckers. It's a good back-of-border choice because its leggy shape (no low branches or leaves) means you

black chokeberry fruit in early autumn

flowers of black chokeberry

can plant spring bulbs and medium-sized perennials in front of it without them being crowded out, and without the shrub looking cramped.

The fruit of black chokeberries has high concentrations of phytochemicals such as anthocyanins (which give the berries their dark colour) and is being researched for its strong antioxidant properties. Researchers at the University of Illinois are studying compounds from the species as possible aids in the fight against cancer and heart disease. Of the two species, the red chokeberry is the more palatable as a fresh fruit, and is sometimes used in jam and pemmican (a dried food developed by the native peoples of North America, consisting of bison, moose, or deer meat mixed with melted fat and berries). The black chokeberry fruit has a more bitter taste, but is used in making products that include wine and jam.

What's a shelterbelt?

You may see the term "shelterbelt" used with regards to farming, gardening, or landscaping, usually with reference to native species of trees and shrubs. Also known as windbreaks, shelterbelts are areas planted to help protect a property from wind damage, from snowdrift formation, and in some cases to develop microclimates. Most commonly used in rural properties, shelterbelts can also provide important habitat for wildlife, particularly when native species of shrubs and trees are chosen.

A simple row of trees isn't sufficient to create a shelterbelt. What is generally needed is as many as four rows, beginning with fast-growing species of shrubs, followed by fast-growing trees (such as poplars), and then followed by slower-growing small deciduous trees (such as Manitoba maples), and slow-growing, densely foliaged conifers (such as pine and spruce). Although shelterbelts are particularly common in the Prairie provinces to help reduce erosion, they can be useful anywhere around dwellings located in open sites.

Berberis

Japanese barberry

Family: Berberidaceae
Hardy to: zone 4
Bloom period: May–mid-June (depending on location)
Growing requirements: Partial shade to full sun; dry to medium soil. Can tolerate clay as long as there is some drainage.

Height: 12 inches–6 feet
Where best used: hedges, specimen plants
Propagation: seed or cuttings
Problems: No significant pests or diseases. Can be tricky to prune.
Notes: Drought- and deer-resistant. True four-season shrub; berries appealing to birds.

When it comes to distinctive four-season shrubs, I always include the Japanese barberry in my list of recommended plants. In winter, its distinctive branches remain festooned with brilliant red berries, which birds dine on; in spring, fresh new green, red, gold, or purple foliage is followed by small yellow flowers beloved by bees; autumn sees the barberries explode into foliar fireworks as their leaves turn a host of brilliant shades. Yes, the shrub is highly thorny, making it tricky to plant or prune, but on the upside, it's one of the more deer-resistant shrubs you can add to your garden.

For many years, barberries dealt with a knock to their reputation because the common or European barberry (*Berberis vulgaris*) is one of the alternate hosts for a fungus that causes stem rust in wheat plants. As a result, all barberries were regarded with a suspicious eye, with the common species being mostly eradicated from cultivated areas. Japanese barberries do not spread the wheat rust, and are approved for use as garden plants.

Nana Aurea

fall colour on green form

various cultivars at a nursery

Barberries range in size from tidy dwarf specimens less than two feet tall to more rangy varieties that top seven feet. They can have various forms, from globular to creeping and spreading to columnar and upright—a more open, fountain-like structure. The taller forms can be planted as a hedge and either left to their natural shape or pruned; shorter cultivars make good specimens for mass plantings or as striking additions to a rock garden or other display garden. There is a gold-foliaged form at the Nova Scotia Agricultural College's rock garden that is a real showstopper, and a number of large hedges of barberries are seen in the south end of Halifax.

Recommended cultivars

There are numerous cultivars of Japanese barberry; some might say too many. A good number of them are cultivars developed from the purple-leafed form (*var. atropurpurea*), many with deep wine or rich purple foliage but with varying growth habits and sizes. One of my favourites, however, is the standard green form barberry, which puts on a display of autumn colour as spectacular as a burning bush or sugar maple, with fluorescent red, orange, and gold foliage.

'Rose Glow': Foliage mottled with pink, white, and red. Arching, fountain-like form as it gets larger. 5–6 feet.

'Concorde': super dwarf (18 inches); round form; good purple colour that doesn't fade in heat.

'Royal Burgundy': Rich purple colour, low mounding form. Water droplets stay on leaves much like they do on *Alchemilla mollis*, lady's mantle.

'Aurea': Early summer growth is luminescent, holds gold colour well through season unless planted in shade. Doesn't burn in hot sun conditions. 3–5 feet.

'Helmond Pillar': Unusual form in that its growth habit is columnar and very upright, to 8 feet tall while only 2 feet wide. Deep red foliage.

Betula

birch

Family: Betulaceae

Hardy to: zone 2

Bloom period: May and June. Insignificant flowers (male and female catkins).

Growing requirements: full sun to light shade; moist, rich soil

Height: 50–70 feet

Where best used: winter interest tree for white or gold bark on older growth; not recommended for small yards

Propagation: seed; cuttings; grafted varieties

Problems: A variety of disease and insect problems can occur. Easily damaged by mechanical injury (mowers, string trimmers) or extreme drought.

Notes: Birch is often made into fine furniture.

On our living room wall, there are two framed prints by Wallace MacAskill (1890–1956), a famed Nova Scotian photographer best known for his images of sailing ships and landscapes. They had hung in my parents' homes for as long as I can remember until my mother gave them to me some years ago. One of them is called *Silver Birches, Antigonish*, and this old photograph explains why birches were one of the first hardwoods I learned to identify.

the glowing white bark of a birch

Birches are a part of our landscape, and sometimes we take them for granted. Who, as a child, didn't peel the bark from white or yellow birches, using it as makeshift paper or to create works of whimsy? It's funny how we so often take plants for granted until someone allows us to see them with fresh eyes. A friend of mine told me about students visiting here from Asia who were fascinated with the white-barked birch trees, which they had never seen before.

Birch is a pioneer species, meaning birch trees are among the first to dominate a site, and generally have a lifespan of about a century in the wild. Several species are native to the

wire birches bent by ice

yellow birch foliage

region, all of which do well in areas with good drainage and ordinary soil. These aren't trees for small yards, because they will get quite tall over time, but if you have the space for them, they're wonderful.

Although you'll see a variety of birches offered for sale, this is one genus where I strongly recommend staying with the native species. Certain diseases and pests are especially problematic in some non-native birches, especially the sweet birch (*B. lenta*) and European white (*B. pendula*), making them species to avoid. These species are particularly susceptible to the birch borer, which will eventually kill the tree. Even the often-sought-after Young's weeping birch, (*B. pendula* 'Youngii') should be avoided, because along with susceptibility to the birch borer, it is intolerant of wet soil, yet wants cool roots and a sunny site. In the right situation it is a striking weeping specimen tree, but is usually not worth the investment when other weeping tree species are more dependable.

Recommended species

Betula allegheniensis: Yellow birch is a stunning tree when mature—its bark has a wonderful golden sheen, while lumber from the species is highly valued for furniture and cabinet-making.

B. papyrifera: The canoe, white, or paper birch is reasonably resistant to the bronze birch borer. Its striking white bark is a highlight of winter landscapes.

B. populifolia: The grey birch has white bark (that doesn't peel easily) and smaller leaves than the white or yellow species. It is highly susceptible to leaf miner, which will turn foliage brown, but otherwise is an attractive and sturdy tree. Ice damage will cause the trees to bend over, but those on our property have never broken significant limbs unless wind has accompanied an ice storm.

Buxus

boxwood, box

Family: Buxaceae

Hardy to: zone 4–6

Bloom period: insignificant blooms, but fragrant and bees love them

Growing requirements: moist, well-drained and fertile soils; full sun to light shade

Height: 2–30 feet; usually shorter forms in Atlantic Canada

Where best used: hedging; topiary; walkway edging; winter colour

Propagation: cuttings

Problems: windburn; sunscald; lack of fertility

Notes: highly adapted for shearing; deer-resistant

At the risk of scandalizing gardeners everywhere, let me get this confession out right now: I've never grown box. I'm no fan of topiary or overly clipped, sheared shrubs, and box has traditionally been used to create just such curiosities.

However, the more I talked to nursery people about this broadleaf evergreen, the more fascinated I became with box. Did you know that its wood is very finely grained and dense, and that it's used in croquet balls, wood blocks for engravings, chess pieces, and other products that require a hard, high-quality wood?

Although somewhat temperamental about its growing conditions, box is deer-resistant, which makes it highly appealing to those gardeners who are plagued by Bambi. The trick is

formal clipped hedge in a public garden

the tiny flowers of box in spring

to site it correctly, which primarily has to do with soil fertility and protection from winter weather. Choose a location that has good drainage and partial to full sun, and be prepared to wrap your box shrubs in winter if they're in a particularly exposed site or they may burn.

Box is a heavy feeder, so when you first plant it you'll need to fertilize with a good shot of triple-20 if you use traditional fertilizer formulations, or a heavy application of compost or seaweed fertilizer if opting for the organic route. When the plant is in need of fertilizer, its foliage turns a yellowy-bronze colour, beginning with the lower leaves.

Some literature and websites list *Buxus* as being quite toxic, with its leaves containing steroidal alkaloids that can cause stomach upset if ingested and mild dermatitis if the sap gets on skin. Perhaps this is why deer tend to favour other, more delectable offerings in your garden.

One observation for those who like the clipped appearance of box in hedges or topiary: if you're going to buy a sheared, topiary-formed plant, know that you're going to have to keep shearing to maintain the plant's shape.

Recommended species and cultivars

Buxus microphylla: Japanese, or littleleaf, box is less hardy than its European cousin, and is best suited only for the mildest parts of Atlantic Canada (zone 6 with winter protection).

B. sempervirons: Common, or European, box is much taller, growing to 20 feet tall and wide, and is hardy to zone 5 with winter protection from wind and sunscald.

Sheridan Nurseries in Ontario is well known for having developed a number of dwarf *Buxus* hybrids, known as the Sheridan hybrids, that are particularly cold hardy (zone 4) while also having excellent green leaf colour. Look for 'Green Gem', 'Green Mountain', 'Green Mound', and 'Green Velvet.'

Calluna and Erica

Family: Ericaceae

Hardy to: heaths to zone 3 or 4, heathers to zone 4 or 5 with protection from dry cold

Bloom period: spring for heaths, summer for heathers

Growing requirements: full sun to light shade; well drained, acid soil

Height: under 1 foot

Where best used: massed displays; edging pathways; container plantings

Propagation: cuttings

Problems: winter protection often necessary

Notes: Deer-resistant; great pollinator; shear after bloom to promote growth.

Often when people talk about heathers they are referring to two different genera, *Erica* and *Calluna*. These are similar in appearance, with low, creeping growth forming into tidy mats, tiny scale-like or needle-like leaves, and flowers in shades of rose, lavender, magenta, and white. Both can have colourful foliage that becomes even more colourful in autumn through to spring. Both are beloved by bees—and by those of us with Scottish ancestry—and both are a bit demanding in their needs. Give them what they need, however, and they'll reward you with years of colourful blooms and attractive foliage.

The easiest way to remember the difference between heathers and heaths? Heath (*Erica*, various species) loosely rhymes with Easter, and plants bloom in late winter through to spring. Heathers (*Calluna vulgaris*, many cultivars) bloom from midsummer into fall.

One of the gardening axioms I learned years ago from my friend Jill Covill is the wisdom of digging a twenty-dollar hole for a two-dollar plant. This means that

Erica *'Irish Lemon'*

preparing the soil and planting the hole properly will pay you big dividends. It's not enough to simply scoop a trowel-full of soil out of the ground and stick a plant in—this is especially true with heathers and heaths (and I made this mistake on my first attempt to grow them). While they don't need particularly rich soil, heaths and heathers will sulk and die if they don't have good drainage and an acid soil.

Calluna *'Con Brio'*

In order to know whether your soil is suitable, it's recommended that you have a soil test done at a provincial government laboratory, which will tell you the soil's pH as well as its type and nutrient level. A soil acidity of between 5 and 6 pH is considered suitable for most heath and heather cultivars. If your soil is alkaline (pH 7 or above), a yearly application of aluminum sulphate will lower the pH; mulching with conifer needles will also help increase acidity.

If your soil has the right pH but a lot of clay, you'll need to add plenty of organic matter, and possibly some sand, to improve the drainage conditions. Just to make it interesting, heathers and heaths need that good drainage but their fine roots are also susceptible to drying out at all times of the year. If it's a dry winter with little snowfall, you may actually need to water in late March or early April to prevent your plants from drought damage. Both species prefer to be protected from cold, desiccating winter winds, so it's a good idea to provide some sort of wind break or winter mulch, especially if there is little snow cover.

Recommended cultivars

Heaths (*Erica* species)
'Alba Mollis': White flowers with silver-green foliage.
'Foxhollow': Pink flowers; yellow foliage tinted bronze at the tips; turns bronze-orange in winter.
'Golden Starlet': White flowers; luminous gold foliage that turns lime-green in winter.
'Springwood Pink' and 'Springwood White': These are the two hardiest heaths, with pink and white flowers respectively.

Heathers (*Calluna vulgaris*)
'Boskoop': Lavender flowers with gold-salmon foliage; turns orange with red tinges in winter.
'Con Brio': Magenta flowers; contrasting yellow-green foliage; changes to bronze-red in winter.
'Silver Knight': Lavender flowers; silvery grey foliage deepens to purple-grey in cold weather.
'Wickware Flame': Mauve flowers with gold summer foliage; deepens to copper-orange and then deep red winter colour.

Calluna *'Silver Knight'*

In order to make the greatest impact when creating a heath and heather bed, plant multiple specimens of the same cultivar together in a mass planting, so you do not end up with a polka dot effect from having one or two plants each of a dozen different varieties.

Cercidiphyllum

katsura, katsuratree

Family: Cercidiphyllaceae

Hardy to: zone 4

Bloom period: inconspicuous flowers and fruit

Growing requirements: Fertile, moist, but well-drained soil; full sun to partial shade. Will tolerate a range of soil types and acidity.

Height: 40 feet

Where best used: large ornamental tree for good-sized yards

Propagation: seed; grafted cuttings

Problems: No serious insect or disease problems.

Notes: Dioecious, requiring male and female trees in order to produce fruit.

I am willing to bet that you remember the first time you ever saw a katsura, if you've ever seen one. You might not remember the botanical name, but that graceful tree with the heart-shaped leaves catches and holds the eye. My first encounter was in horticulturist Tim Amos's yard, where I stood transfixed by the delicate foliage with its bronze-red highlights. I bought a katsura the next week, and have been charmed by it ever since.

As suggested by its species name, the katsura is a native of Japan and China. The genus only consists of one species, although some taxonomists are arguing that a variety known as *C. japonicum* var. *magnificum* deserves to be labelled as a species. Even though Michael Dirr lists several cultivars in his *Manual of Woody Landscape Plants*, including a weeping form and one with golden foliage in summer, chances are you'll only ever see the standard species offered for sale locally.

The katsura is not a tree for a small yard, as it can easily reach 40 feet or even taller in milder climates. Nor is it a tree for a site where it won't get adequate moisture, especially for the first three or four years while it is establishing itself. While katsura likes good drainage, it also requires plenty of moisture, so you need to be prepared to water it regularly if the growing months see low rainfall totals. My katsura is planted in clay amended with plenty of compost and has been doing fine for five years. If you're not watering the tree enough, it will drop

bronze colour on spring foliage

its leaves in response to drought conditions. The roots of the katsura tend to run quite close to the soil surface, especially if planted in compacted soil.

Unlike some trees, the katsura is relatively fast-growing, at least in its early years, and will grow in full sun to partial shade. New foliage growth is a lovely shade of reddish plum, turning to a pale bright green as the leaf matures. Its flowers are not showy, but if you have both male and female trees and they produce fruit, the 3/4-inch-long brown seed pods will stay on the tree for much of the winter.

Although I love the appearance of the Eastern redbud (*Cercis canadensis*), which has similar heart-shaped leaves but also very attractive flowers, I've been hesitant to try one in my garden because it has disease and hardiness issues. I find the katsura to be a satisfying substitution for the gardener who likes a variety of deciduous trees in the garden for fall colour. In autumn, the katsura erupts into its full glory, with varying shades of orange, yellow, and red in its leaves. Curiously, autumn foliage will give off a fragrance variously described as resembling brown sugar, toffee, or crème brûlée.

The katsura isn't bothered by significant problems with pests or diseases, but does come with several mechanical and cultural caveats. If your site is particularly hot and dry or prone to a lot of wind, it would be a good idea to plant your specimen in a sheltered place, as the foliage has been known to scorch in hot, dry, windy conditions. Young trees should be pruned so they develop a strong structure that will reduce branches breaking from wind or snow.

Standard trees and shrubs

In the wonderful world of tree and shrub production, unusual specimens known as "standards" are often for sale at nurseries. These are very formal-looking plants, highly pruned and popular in some public gardens and parks. The standard shrub or tree will generally have a single bare trunk for at least 4–5 feet (from the soil line), crowned with a shrubby growth at the top of the trunk. Roses are sometimes made into "rose trees," which are standards, but a number of other flowering shrubs, Japanese maples, fruit trees, and evergreens are also made into standards.

Generally speaking, standard trees are created either by grafting one type of plant onto another, or by careful pruning of a shrub to develop one central stem to produce the desired shape of plant. Sometimes called "lollipop" trees (because that's what they look like), standards can be very expensive—it takes time to graft, prune, and train a plant into the desired shape. They can also be more fragile than normal shrubs and trees, usually at the graft point. Care should be taken to situate standards where they will not be damaged by mowing, trimming, excess snow buildup, and other yard-care activities.

cascading form of a mature tree

Chamaecyparis

falsecypress, white cedar

Family: Cupressaceae

Hardy to: varies with species

Bloom period: insignificant bloom (early summer); some have interesting cones

Growing requirements: well-drained but moist soil

Height: several inches to over 100 feet

Where best used: hedging, miniature conifer display, mixed borders, alpine/rock gardens

Propagation: cuttings and seed (seed produces huge genetic variety)

Problems: Some burn in hot sun. Some species attractive to deer.

Notes: Huge variety of forms, sizes, foliage colours. Prickly-foliaged types are deer-resistant.

When I was a student at agricultural college, I had several friends who were in what was then called the ornamental horticulture program. I can still remember the frustration one friend expressed as he struggled trying to remember the names and forms of literally dozens of *Chamaecyparis* species and varieties, and his exasperation at trying to remember the correct spelling of the genus name.

He may have been exasperated back then, but I'm sure he would agree that *Chamaecyparis* is one of the best evergreen

golden threadleaf

genera for gardeners because of the plethora of species, hybrids, forms, shapes, textures, sizes, and colours. When garden writers suggest there is a form of "X" plant for every garden, they are often being overly optimistic, but when it comes to the falsecypress, it's true. Whether you're a gardener with only a small condo-plot, or one with acres of space, you can find a chamaecyparis that suits your tastes.

In his entry on the falsecypress family in his *Manual of Woody Landscape Plants*, Michael Dirr observes, "It is easy to confuse *Thuja* (cedar) with *Chamaecyparis*." It's a great relief to find this coming from an expert of Dirr's calibre, because I still have problems deciding

cones of 'Nootka' falsecypress

dwarf 'Hinoki' cultivars in containers

which family some ornamental evergreens belong to, especially at first glance. Both can have scaly leaves that are almost reptilian in nature, but the cones are very different. Cones of the falsecypress don't resemble cones of other evergreens like fir and pine: they are small, berrylike fruit that almost look like they came from another planet.

For landscape purposes, there are four main species of *Chamaecyparis*, each of which can have dozens of cultivars. This is where the gardener can get confused, and where it's important to purchase specimens from a reputable nursery whose owners and employees know their plants. Some falsecypress are dwarf, very slow-growing, and susceptible to burning from wind and sun. Others can grow 75 to 100 feet, or even taller. Some are deer-resistant—others are not. Most have complex names that can sound variously like you're sneezing or swearing.

To keep falsecypress happy, plant them in full sun with rich, moist, but well-draining soil. Most appreciate a spot where they can be sheltered from the worst of winter winds, so try to situate yours away from full exposure to prevailing gales.

Recommended species and cultivars

Chamaecyparis nootkatensis: Recent taxonomic reclassification has changed the genus of this species to *Callitropsis*, but it is often still listed as a *Chamaecyparis*. The most beloved are the weeping forms such as 'Glauca Pendula.'

C. thyoides: A particularly attractive cultivar is 'Heatherbun,' the foliage of which turns a handsome plum colour in winter. Avoid 'Ericoides' as it's very appealing to deer.

C. pisifera: Look for 'Plumosa Aurea,' which has golden, prickly, plume-type foliage and is deer-resistant. The threadleaf cultivars, like 'Filifera Aurea,' are particularly attractive with their distinctive weeping foliage.

C. obtusa: This is the species referred to as the Hinoki cypress, native to Japan. There are dozens of cultivars, varying in size from dwarf forms less than a foot tall to massive trees towering many feet in the air. Choice specimens include 'Tetragona Aurea,' a gold form with unique foliage; 'Gracilis,' a slender tree that grows to 20 feet; the compact little mound known as 'Juniperoides,' which works well in rock gardens; and the unique dwarf 'Torulosa,' which has contorted, twisted limbs and is also a good rock garden choice.

Cornus

dogwood

Family: Cornaceae

Hardy to: zone 2

Bloom period: late spring to early summer

Growing requirements: sun to light shade; moist, rich soil

Height: 2–20 feet

Where best used: specimen plants, hedgerows, winter colour

Propagation: cuttings; *C. kousa* is grafted only

Problems: twig blight; canker; sawfly borers

Notes: Edible, showy fruit is very attractive to birds.

The dogwoods are a group of versatile and beautiful deciduous shrubs and small trees, some of which are particularly eye-catching when they bloom. The botanical name *Cornus* derives from the Latin word for horn, which *Roland's Flora* indicates refers to the hardness of the wood. Other references say that the name refers to the horned, or branching, growth habit of many of the species.

In Atlantic Canada, a number of native and introduced species are popular with gardeners, some for their handsome, brilliant twig colour in winter, others for their showy spring blooms. The flowering dogwoods, which include the Japanese dogwood (*C. kousa*) as well as the flowering dogwood of southeastern North America, (*C. florida*), have gorgeous blossoms that can completely cover the tree during peak bloom period. What many observers mistake for flower petals on the showier flowering dogwoods are actually bracts, or modified leaves, which may be greenish,

'Satomi' dogwood

white, or pink depending on the species and cultivar. These bracts last for a long time before dropping away from the forming fruit, which are edible and a source of fat for migrating bird species.

The showy dogwoods are good choices as specimen trees for smaller gardens, although you need to check the hardiness zone when making a choice. Being a pragmatic gardener, I have stayed away from the pricier *Cornus* species and cultivars, primarily because I have been concerned about their winter hardiness in my windy, chilly garden. However, other

Cornus sericea *berries*

fruit of C. kousa

gardeners on the Annapolis Valley floor have had success with both *C. kousa* and *C. florida*, so the secret is to site these more marginal species in a somewhat sheltered location where they are less likely to be damaged by cold winds.

If you are developing your garden with an eye to winter interest as well as other attributes, the red osier dogwood and the Tatarian dogwood are great choices with their blazing red or gold twig colours throughout the winter months. Both have a tendency to spread into thickets, so make sure you have space for them. These are hardy choices and ideal for moist areas such as beside ponds and ditches.

The sub-shrub bunchberry (*Cornus canadensis*) is a wonderful ornamental ground cover and profiled in the perennial section on page 129.

Recommended species and cultivars

***Cornus alba*:** Tatarian dogwood is native to Siberia and other northern areas of Asia. It can have brilliant red foliage in autumn, which contrasts beautifully with its white berries and brilliant red twigs, which are particularly showy in winter. Zone 2.

***C. alternifolia*:** The pagoda dogwood is native to eastern North America, and is a lovely small tree with a distinct horizontal structure to its branches. Small, white, fragrant flowers appear in clusters from mid-June to July. The cultivar 'Argentea' is variegated and makes a good specimen plant. Zone 4.

***C. florida*:** A beautiful specimen tree but susceptible to several diseases and pests. Winter cold may kill flower buds. Hardy to zone 5 with proper site selection.

***C. mas*:** The Cornelian cherry isn't the showiest of dogwoods, but it is an interesting choice for smaller yards because its fragrant though unostentatious flowers appear very early in spring. These become olive-shaped, edible red fruit in mid- to late summer, although you may need to race the birds to eat them. Zone 4.

***C. kousa*:** The kousa, or Japanese dogwood, is another showy species and has good fall colour as well as showy flowers with bracts. Fruit are described as resembling large round raspberries and are showy but not particularly tasty. A number of cultivars exist, many hardy to zone 5 with protection from chilling winds. Most available cultivars are grafted, so check trees before purchase to make sure the graft looks strong. Zone 5.

***C. sericea* (syn. *stolonifera*):** The native red-osier dogwood is a great shrub choice for erosion control, and provides excellent winter interest with its brilliant red twigs. The variety 'Flaviramea' has bright yellow twigs in winter; 'Silver and Gold' has variegated foliage. Zone 2.

Corylus avellana 'Contorta'

corkscrew hazel, European filbert, Harry Lauder's walking stick

Family: Betulaceae

Hardy to: zone 4

Bloom period: catkins in late April to early May

Growing requirements: rich, moist soil; sun to partial shade

Height: 6–8 feet tall, 4–6 feet wide

Where best used: specimen plant with excellent winter interest

Propagation: all grafted

Problems: Because *C. avellana* 'Contorta' is grafted, watch for shoots coming below the graft, and remove them carefully.

Notes: Spectacular winter interest and early spring display of catkins.

There are two questions people usually ask when they see a Harry Lauder's walking stick, also known as the corkscrew hazel, for the first time. The first question, naturally, is "What on earth is *that*?!" Once told the most popular name of the shrub, the second question is, "Who is Harry Lauder and why would his walking stick look like a corkscrew?" Sir Henry (Harry) Lauder (1870–1950) was a Scottish comedian and singer, who often used a crooked walking stick in his stage performances. So now you know.

The corkscrew hazel is a sport (or genetic mutation) of the true hazel or filbert, but isn't grown for nut production.

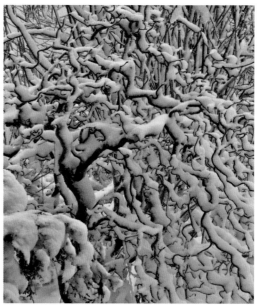

snow on branches

Discovered in an English hedgerow in the late nineteenth century, it is widely sought after by gardeners with a passion for creating winter interest in their yards. The gnarled, twisted limbs are especially handsome when dusted lightly with snow or festooned with ice, although you will want to do a little selective pruning to show off the limbs to their best appearances.

In early spring, the corkscrew hazel produces yellowish catkins that droop from the branches, drawing even more attention to their distinctive structure. Once the shrub leafs out, the foliage obscures many of the branches. Don't be alarmed and think that you have insect damage when you see the leaves for the first time; they also have a gnarled and twisty appearance, giving the plant a sort of lumpy effect during the summer and autumn. Autumn colour is an undistinguished yellow, except in the cultivar 'Red Majestic.'

Harry Lauder's walking stick is always grafted onto a rootstock of another type of filbert, *Corylus colurna*, so make sure to watch for suckers coming up around the plant's base in the spring and summer and remove them promptly. Spring pruning to remove rubbing twigs or overly crowded branches will help show the shrub off to its best shape.

A recent cultivar of *C. avellana* is 'Red Majestic,' which has rich burgundy foliage in spring. This deepens to a coppery green in summer (although new summer growth still comes in burgundy red) and then returns to wine colour for autumn. It doesn't grow as large as the original, but its catkins are also purple-tinted, and the occasional nuts have a purple-red hue as well.

catkins in spring

leaves with their twisted foliage

GROUND COVERS

Despite our best plans, we don't all have perfectly designed properties on which to garden. Some of us have problem areas like slopes, very dry or wet sites, areas under trees where many things refuse to grow, or spots where rain creates erosion problems. We want something that's attractive and easy to care for, but don't want to have to mow or fuss with it.

The answer to many of these problem areas is to plant some sort of ground cover. Most plants in this category spread relatively quickly to cover a substantial area of earth, and some—but not all—are even durable enough to be walked on. What you choose to plant will depend partly on the site's conditions, and of course on your own tastes. Under trees with large roots that grow close to the surface, you'll want to plant a species with some drought resistance and a shallow root system.

Before planting ground covers, prepare the soil well, adding some compost and removing all the weeds you see; it can be tricky weeding through a ground cover with its tangle of roots and runners. If you have a large area to plant, you'll need to purchase a number of plants of the species you choose. Plant these closer together than you might in a garden bed: recommended spacing ranges from 6 inches to 2 feet, depending on the species and how fast they grow. Plants like pachysandra and vinca often take a couple of years to get growing in earnest, and you'll need to keep the weeds under control by mulching and probably hand-weeding until your cover is well established.

The main thing to remember about ground covers is what their name suggests: they cover ground—sometimes, more than we might want. If you have a small spot in a perennial bed and tuck a bugleweed (*Ajuga*) or a deadnettle (*Lamium*) in, don't expect those plants to stay in a polite clump. Most ground covers spread by sending out underground roots, rhizomes, or stolons, from which new plants arise. Although many are well behaved and easy to remove if they do spread beyond where you want them, others are not so good.

The classic example of a ground cover gone bad is my personal nemesis, and that of many other gardeners (as I've ranted many times before, including in the section on invasive plants): *Aegopodium podegraria*. Goutweed, bishop's weed, snow-on-the-mountain, ground elder…whatever you call it, it's probably the most noxious plant to ever take hold in a garden. I'm not alone in feeling this way. The most common question I get asked in emails or during garden talks is how to get rid of this stuff. Some nurseries have elected not to even sell it, and my gardening hat is off to them. Others ought to follow suit. For those readers who don't have goutweed in your gardens; please don't plant it thinking you're saving yourself some work. Trust me—and the thousands of others who rue the day they accepted a green-and-white-foliaged plant thinking, "Oh, it's so pretty…"

Ajuga: Bugleweed is a low-growing relative of mint featuring attractive leaves, often variegated with other colours. Spikes of blue or pink flowers appear above the foliage in mid- to late spring. A variety of cultivars are available.

Asarum: Wild ginger forms a low mat of glossy, heart-shaped foliage, with curious wine or dark brown flowers hidden under the leaves.

Epimedium: (See profile page 148) Barrenwort, or bishop's cap, is a spring flowering perennial with lovely heart-shaped leaves. It prefers moist and partly shaded areas.

wild ginger

Gallium odoratum: Sweet woodruff is a delicate-looking ground cover that quickly forms a low mat, with sweetly scented starry white flowers.

Hosta: (See profile page 172) We often think of hostas as plants for beds and borders, but they also work well as ground covers around the base of trees and other shaded sites.

Houttuynia cordata: Chameleon plant is an unusual-looking ground cover, with ivy-like leaves splashed in pinkish-red, cream, yellow, and green. The foliage smells like orange marmalade. In some parts of Canada and the U.S. this plant is considered invasive.

sweet woodruff

Lamium and **Lamiastrum**: Deadnettle and archangel are closely related, and usually feature variegated leaves and attractive flowers in white, rosy pink, or yellow. The best-behaved lamiastrum is 'Herman's Pride,' which doesn't creep but forms a tidy mound of attractive green and silver leaves and yellow flowers.

Lysimachia nummularia 'Aurea': Golden creeping Jenny is beloved by some gardeners and despised by others. Its golden foliage lightens up shaded areas.

Pachysandra: Pachysandra is often planted under trees and flowering shrubs. It can be very slow to settle in and start growing well and is not overly interesting to look at.

yellow archangel 'Herman's Pride'

Phlox subulata: (see profile page 205) Creeping, or moss, phlox produces brilliant patches of flowers that arise in mid-spring in shades of purple, rose, magenta, and sometimes bicolour. Best for well-drained soils.

Sedum: (see profile page 224) A number of sedums are low-growing and work well as ground covers, especially in hot, dry areas like the side of a south-facing hill.

Thymus species: Thymes are particularly popular used along walkways or stepping-stones. There are many different varieties, with different flower colours, fragrances, and foliage colours.

Vinca: Whether you call this periwinkle, vinca, or myrtle, it's a tried-and-true performer under trees. The variegated types, which come in gold and green or cream and green, are slower to spread but more interesting and brighter in shaded areas. A new double-flowered form also looks quite promising.

Crataegus

hawthorn, mayhaw, thornapple

Family: Rosaceae

Hardy to: zone 4

Bloom period: late April to May (after *Amelanchier*)

Growing requirements: full sun; well-drained soils

Height: 20 feet

Where best used: specimen trees, hedgerows; good in small yards and will work under power lines

Propagation: suckers, seeds (slow to germinate); ornamental forms are often grafted

Problems: Similar pests and diseases as apple trees, including apple or cedar rust. Beware of thorns!

Notes: Drought-tolerant once established. Fruiting varieties produce berries that are loved by birds.

There are more than one hundred species of hawthorns throughout north-temperate regions of the world. What I remember distinctly about hawthorns comes from my days as a student at the Nova Scotia Agricultural College in Truro. The late Dr. Albert E. Roland, author of *Flora of Nova Scotia* and by that time a professor emeritus who still came in daily to his office, told me that hawthorns were a promiscuous lot with a maddening tendency to hybridize even in the wild. Ten species are found growing wild throughout Nova Scotia alone, often

'Paul's Scarlet'

around old homesteads, edging pastures, fields, and alongside streams.

As their common name suggests, members of this genus have vicious thorns but include a number of valuable ornamental species. Along with being handsome shrubs or trees when in bloom, hawthorns are food plants for numerous butterfly and moth species that feed on the foliage. The fruit, which resemble miniature plums and are red or orange in colour, are an important food source for many songbirds, including waxwings.

Hawthorns have a host of uses to humans as well as wildlife. The wood is extremely hard and rot-resistant, with a fine grain that polishes beautifully, lending to its use in making

'Crimson Cloud'

walking sticks, tool and knife handles, and turned-wood fine art pieces. The wood burns extremely hot, and as a result, hawthorn is sometimes used in making charcoal. Horticulturists occasionally use hawthorn as a rootstock for grafting other species, including pears and the medlar, a lesser-known pome fruit similar to a quince. The fruit of some hawthorn species are referred to as mayhaws (because the species so often blooms in May) and can be made into jellies. The fruit and leaves are also used in traditional herbal medicines in various cultures.

No plant is pest-free, and in the case of hawthorns there are a number of potential problems. Despite the thorniness of some species, the young shoots can be eaten by rabbits and deer, while mice will often cause damage to the bark. Some of the moths that feed on the foliage can be huge nuisances, including the gypsy moth and the white tussock moth. Some hawthorns can be host plants for the fungal cedar/apple rust disease or may suffer from leaf blight, but breeders are developing resistant cultivars. Aphids may be a problem with some trees but can be controlled easily by hosing the plant with a blast of water.

Recommended species and cultivars

Hawthorn nomenclature can be confusing. At least two species, *C. laevigata* and *C. monogyna*, are referred to as English hawthorn. For the purpose of this book I'm following the lead of Michael Dirr in his *Manual of Woody Landscape Plants* in referring to these two species.

Crataegus crus-galli: The cockspur hawthorn can have vicious thorns, as its common name suggests, but also makes a handsome tree for hedging or screening. The natural variety *inermis* is thornless and sometimes sold as 'Cruzam.'

C. monogyna: The singleseed hawthorn grows wild throughout Atlantic Canada. It is particularly thorny and susceptible to leaf blight, but is the species most often used in hedgerows throughout the United Kingdom, explaining one of its names: English hawthorn.

C. laevigata: Several particularly showy forms of the true English hawthorn are popular as small ornamental trees in commercial as well as home plantings. 'Paul's Scarlet' has lovely double blossoms that are rose-red in colour; although it is listed as susceptible to hawthorn leaf spot, I have not seen this problem in my tree or in others throughout my area. 'Crimson Cloud' has single rose-red flowers with white 'eyes' and is disease-resistant; 'Toba' and 'Snowbird' are two white-flowered cultivars developed at Morden agricultural station in Manitoba and are promoted as being leaf spot–resistant.

Fagus sylvatica

European beech

Family: Fagaceae

Hardy to: zone 4

Bloom period: Flowers in early May, but blossoms are insignificant. Fruit is a triangular nut encased in a spiky seedcase.

Growing requirements: Full sun; rich, moist soil. Doesn't like continuously wet soil.

Height: 30–40 feet wide, 100 feet tall

Where best used: large yards or properties

Propagation: grafted or from seed

Problems: woolly aphids and powdery mildew

Notes: Winter interest. Resistant to beech bark disease that has been killing the native species, *Fagus grandifolia*.

When I look at a handsome beech tree, I often wish that I had planted one when I was a child, or even better, that someone had planted several a century ago on what is now our property. These majestic trees are glorious year-round, and they make a wonderful memorial tree because they will live for three hundred years. This also means that it takes a while for a young one to gain some size, but I'm patient.

Outside the south window of my office there is a young copper beech (cultivar 'Riversii') that I planted about five years ago. In the spring, its long bronzed buds unfurl into coppery pink leaves that eventually deepen to burgundy, making it an eye-catching specimen in the summer garden. Even in the winter, it's beautiful to look at because the beech is one of a handful of tree species that holds onto its leaves throughout much of the winter, a process known as marcescence.

Unless you're opting for one of the smaller cultivars, you need ample room to grow a beech. Many of them grow as wide as they are tall, so they aren't suited for a small yard. The green-leafed species will show yellow fall colour before the leaves fade to bronze, and the tree bark is smooth and attractive.

Although there is a native species of beech

'Riversii'

found throughout the region (*Fagus grandifolia*, the American beech), it is being decimated by a number of pests and diseases, including beech bark disease, which is caused by combined assault of a fungus following wounds made by the beech scale insect. Work is being done on developing disease-resistant forms. European beech is resistant to the disease.

'Tricolor'

new growth on 'Riversii'

Recommended cultivars

'Dawyckii,' also seen as 'Fastigiata': This form has a columnar shape and is much more narrow than the usual spreading shape of the species.

'Pendula': The weeping branches of this cultivar make a lovely silhouette in a large yard or park setting. Grows to 50 feet tall and wide.

'Purple Fountain': Similar to 'Pendula' but with purple foliage. Very slow-growing.

'Riversii': The so-called copper beech grows to 50 feet tall and has gorgeous, deep purple leaves.

'Tricolor': a slow-growing, smaller tree (30 feet) sometimes sold as 'Roseomarginata.' Striking foliage is purple with cream or pink edging, brightest in colour during the spring. This cultivar's leaves will burn in hot sunlight, so it does well in light shade. Tends to be a pricey plant, not to be purchased on a whim.

'Tortuosa': A dwarf, green-leafed form that grows to 15 feet, with twisted branches somewhat similar to the twisted hazel (*Corylus avellana* 'Contorta').

When is a beech not a beech? When it's a hornbeam. The very handsome tree commonly called "blue beech" is actually a hornbeam, *Carpinus caroliniana*. It's a lovely ornamental tree with no serious pests or diseases, good fall colour, and interesting winged seeds. Hardy to zone 3, it generally grows to 30 feet tall and wide.

Ginkgo biloba

ginkgo, maidenhair tree

Family: Ginkgoaceae

Hardy to: zone 3

Bloom period: Late April to May, not conspicuous.

Growing requirements: full sun; well-drained but moist soil with ample organic matter

Height: 60–100 feet or more but takes many years to reach mature size

Where best used: large yards; street tree

Propagation: seed or grafted (for cultivars)

Problems: Virtually pest free. Large females that produce ample seed crop results in rotting fruit that causes a stench.

Notes: Salt-tolerant and relatively pollution-resistant. Dioecious species.

Everything about the ginkgo appeals to me: its prehistoric origins (it is estimated to have originated between 150 and 200 million years ago), its handsome foliage, and its golden fall colour. It's not native to North America—or at least hasn't been since we were all a part of the supercontinent Pangaea—but I've never been a native-only sort of gardener, and always knew I'd have a ginkgo as soon as I had a place with room for a large, handsome tree. The common name of maidenhair tree comes from the notion that ginkgo leaves are similar in shape to the fronds of the maidenhair ferns (*Adiantum* species).

closeup of ginkgo foliage

My only exasperation is that it is a slow-growing species, taking at least a generation to reach flowering size, and tending to sulk for several years after transplanting. The biggest specimen I can think of is on the campus of Acadia University, right in the middle of the native-plant Harriet Irving Botanical Gardens. It was there long before the gardens were developed, and no one wanted to cut the magnificent tree down, so it remains an iconoclastic statement among a host of native trees, shrubs, and perennial species.

Gingko bonsai

Perhaps because it has survived for millions of years, the ginkgo is a pretty tolerant tree, wanting only full sun and decent drainage to make it happy. It's salt-tolerant, drought- and pollution-resistant, and blithely free of pests and diseases. The only thing you need other than the above-mentioned growing requirements are adequate space for what can eventually become a very large tree, and the patience to let it do just that.

Book and magazine articles often claim that the female ginkgo bears foul-smelling fruit, and to avoid this you should only buy named cultivars that were cloned or grafted from male trees. I have no idea of the gender of my small ginkgo out in the backyard, but even if it is a female, I'm not concerned about the potential for smell if there are ever fruits, as I live on a substantial acreage rather than a suburban plot.

mature ginkgo tree at Acadia University

Recommended cultivars

The most common ginkgo sold at nurseries is the regular species, but you can also find several with different growth habits, whether weeping, more upright, or even (relatively) dwarf forms that have been developed from witches brooms. 'Autumn Gold' has particularly good fall colour, while 'Pendula' has drooping or weeping branches. 'Fastigiata' is a very upward-branching form with a columnar shape.

Hamamelis

Family: Hamamelidaceae
Hardy to: zone 4–5
Bloom period: autumn, late winter to spring
Growing requirements: sun to partial shade
Height: 5–15 feet

Where best used: massed plantings, wildlife gardens, specimen plants
Propagation: cuttings, grafting
Problems: No serious pests or diseases.
Notes: Some species and cultivars highly fragrant.

'Arnold Promise'

Some years back, my long-suffering spouse and I were traipsing through Pine Grove, a marvellous park established and maintained by Bowater Mersey in Milton, near Liverpool on Nova Scotia's south shore. It was still late winter or early spring; ice on the pond provided a convenient place for a host of ducks, and there was snow in shaded areas of the park. We were coming across a clearing when I caught a fragrance on the air, sweet as honey. We couldn't figure out where it was coming from until I discovered a modest shrub, leafless of course, but festooned with spidery flowers that had stringy orangish-gold petals. At the time, I didn't recognize the shrub for what it was, a witch-hazel, but I was immediately taken with it.

Witch-hazel belongs to the genus *Hamamelis*, and there are five species, with only one, *H. virginiana*, being native to eastern Canada. What's interesting about our native species is that it flowers in autumn, usually between October and December, with curious flowers that are generally yellow but occasionally tinted with red or orange. The petals look like crumpled streamers of crepe paper, and while they aren't beautiful, they often have a lovely fragrance. You may notice that scent when out walking in autumn woodlands and wonder where it's coming from; look for shrubs with largish, somewhat toothed leaves, turning to yellow fall colour, and you should see the flowers on closer examination of the plant.

fruit of H. virginiana   *new growth in 'Arnold Promise'*   *flowers of 'Jelena'*

If you plan to add one of the hybrids to your garden, plant it in sun to partial shade and in rich but freely draining soil. Unlike the native species, the hybrids are more resentful of heavy clay soil that doesn't drain. If your soil does tend to clay, amend it with compost before planting your new witch-hazel. Aside from that planting caveat, witch-hazels are easy-care shrubs, seldom bothered by diseases or insects. They require minimal pruning other than to remove suckers if you don't want your plants to spread or if they are grafted onto hardier rootstock. Whatever pruning you do, make sure to wait until the plant has flowered, which isn't difficult as they bloom so early.

Although not often used in the horticultural trade, *H. virginiana* is an easy-care shrub that will accept almost any growing conditions, and the fall-flowering behaviour makes it a nice curiosity for the native garden. If you need to find water on your property, diviners prefer forked branches of the witch-hazel as their divining rod, which explains why these individuals are often referred to as "water witches" or are said to be "witching water." Witch-hazel is also the source of an extract used in various cosmetic and pharmaceutical compounds, from aftershave to hemorrhoid treatments, as well as for wounds and itchy, dry skin.

The more commonly used shrubs in ornamental situations come from other species in the witch-hazel genus. *Hamamelis mollis* is the Chinese witch-hazel and is said to be the most fragrant species. It is used in gardening and landscaping in milder climates but generally isn't reliably hardy beyond zone 5b or 6a, because buds can be killed by too cold a winter.

H. mollis is valuable for Atlantic Canadian gardeners as a cross with the Japanese witch-hazel, *H. japonica*, resulting in hybrids generally classified as *H.* x *intermedia*. These are wonderful landscaping plants, and include several very popular cultivars, including 'Arnold Promise,' 'Diane,' 'Ruby Glow,' and 'Jelena' (sometimes labelled 'Copper Beauty').

The *Intermedia* hybrids tend to flower in late winter to early spring: as early as mid-January in warmer zones but more commonly from late February into April throughout most of Atlantic Canada. The fall foliage display can be quite spectacular depending on the cultivar as well as weather conditions, with red-flowered cultivars often displaying more red foliage in their fall finery. 'Arnold Promise,' a yellow-flowered variety, also displays beautiful ruby and purple tints in new leaf growth.

Hippophae rhamnoides

sea buckthorn, sea pineapple

Family: Eleagnaceae

Hardy to: zone 3

Bloom period: Not significant, but berries are orange, egg-shaped, and persist into April.

Growing requirements: full sun, sandy soil, good drainage

Height: 12–30 feet

Where best used: seashore; hedging; winter colour; privacy hedge

Propagation: seed; division of suckers

Problems: No serious pests or diseases.

Notes: drought- and salt-tolerant; deer-resistant

You're probably not alone if you've never heard of sea buckthorn. It is an underutilized shrub that doesn't yet command the same sort of attention as fancy-flowered hydrangeas, rhododendrons, or weigelas. Yet Michael Dirr refers to this as one of the best plants available for winter colour, and Rob Baldwin put me onto sea buckthorn for its many positive attributes. I saw a collection of sea buckthorn shrubs at Rob's nursery in late autumn, their orange berries glowing in the dreary November light, and was completely smitten.

The botanical genus name *Hippophae* refers to the horse, and this shrub's foliage was apparently used as fodder for horses in ancient Greece, as it helped them gain

glossy foliage

weight and promoted a shiny coat. Sea buckthorn is not to be confused with the highly invasive glossy buckthorn (*Frangula alnus*), the purging buckthorn (*Rhamnus cathartica*), or any other plant in the so-called buckthorn (*Rhamnus* or *Frangula*) genus.

Sea buckthorn is a native of Europe and northern Asia, where it is often used in roadside plantings, but it is also popular in western Canada as an effective windbreak or shelterbelt species. Whether you call it a large shrub or a small tree, sea buckthorn makes a handsome shrub all year long, with its grey green, willow-like foliage that shows silver undersides in a breeze. Because it is decidedly thorny, it works brilliantly as a privacy or barrier hedge, and because it is highly salt-tolerant, it works well along seashores and highway medians. Its tendency to produce suckers, or additional shoots, from its roots or stem, makes it valuable in stabilizing sloped sites, including along beaches, and it is quite deer-resistant to boot. Like lupins, clovers, and some other plants, sea buckthorn also contains nitrogen-fixing bacteria, which help to improve soil fertility. It does require regular moisture when it is newly planted or if you have female, berry-producing shrubs, but once established sea buckthorn is reasonably drought-tolerant.

There is one drawback to purchasing sea buckthorn shrubs as young plants: when they are grown from seed, the sex of the plants cannot be determined until they flower (which they do before leafing out, though the flowers are not showy). This is a drawback since, like hollies and northern

berries on female glow in autumn

bayberry, this species is dioecious, so only the females will bear the brilliant orange fruit. The berries will stay on the plant throughout winter, because birds don't usually get at them due to the plant's thorns. Literature suggests that one male plant produces enough pollen to adequately fertilize at least seven female shrubs.

Researchers have been working with the fruit of the sea buckthorn for years, because it is rich in vitamin C, Omega-3 oils, and carotene. A few commercial plantings of sea buckthorn, grown for their berries, are available in other parts of Canada, but harvesting the fruit is labour-intensive. Breeders are at work developing thorn-free varieties, but around Atlantic Canada you'll probably only find the standard species.

Hydrangea

hydrangea

Family: Hydrangeaceae
Hardy to: varies with species
Bloom period: late June to September
Growing requirements: moist, rich, well-drained soil; morning sun, afternoon shade
Height: 2–10 feet

Where best used: in mixed borders or as specimens
Propagation: softwood cuttings
Problems: Must choose right species for your climate. Very susceptible to drying out in summer.
Notes: Some types may be used as dried flowers.

Hydrangeas are one of the most beautiful and valuable of landscape shrubs, in part because of their striking flower heads, but also because they have a long period of bloom. Some species flower later in the year, adding an extra burst of late summer and autumn colour.

There is a hydrangea for almost any garden, providing you choose a species and cultivar hardy for your zone. Those of us in cooler areas of Atlantic Canada will have trouble growing the lacecaps and mopheads, which are generally hardy to zone 5, but the white-flowered *arborescens*

'Blue Billows' lacecap

and the splendid *paniculata* ("Peegee-type") cultivars are hardy to zones 3 or 4. It may take several years for them to settle in well and really begin blooming with vigour.

Hydrangeas have both sterile and fertile flowers, or florets. Sterile florets are large and colourful, and are actually sepals, or modified leaves, while "perfect" or fertile flowers, containing both male and female parts, are located in the centre of the blossom cluster. Mopheads are generally composed of all sterile florets, but if you examine a lacecap closely you can easily see the difference between sterile and perfect florets.

Hydrangeas do best in a loamy, well-drained soil rich in organic matter, preferably with morning sun and some shade during the heat of the afternoon. In our region, there's little danger of too much heat, but if you do plant hydrangeas in a full-sun site, make sure to

a purple mophead hydrangea

keep them watered. Too much dryness or irregular moisture can prevent the plants from flowering; if it's a dry season, remember to water and mulch around your plants to keep them happy.

Hydrangeas are well known as greedy feeders, but you can use a slow release fertilizer or an organic product to keep them in the pink (or in the blue). In our garden, newly planted hydrangeas receive compost, liquid seaweed fertilizer, and bone meal, and usually a handful of dried seaweed meal once or twice during the growing season.

One of the most common laments that nursery operators hear about hydrangeas is that they fail to flower, or fail to flower profusely. There can be a number of reasons for this. Often, the gardener has inadvertently pruned away too much wood and pruned the flower buds at the same time. The best way around this? Avoid pruning at all, especially if you aren't sure whether your hydrangea blooms on old or new wood. Other causes of flower failure can be too cold a climate (which has killed the flower buds), too much shade, or inadequate soil.

Another common question about hydrangeas is how to get those spectacular blue blooms on some mophead and lacecap varieties. The answer has to do with the soil pH; acid soil causes blue flowers, alkaline soil will cause pink. However, bear in mind that not all species or cultivars will turn blue or pink. White-flowered forms are white and nothing is going to change that.

Recommended species and cultivars

Hydrangea anomala: Climbing hydrangea is slow to start, gorgeous once established and in flower. Favours light shade; older stems exfoliate like *Acer griseum* or *Physocarpus*. Zone 4.

H. arborescens: Usually white; mophead-type flowers will not change colour regardless of acidity; plants will sucker. 'Annabelle' is a beloved cultivar. There is now a newly released pink-flowered hybrid, 'Invincibelle Spirit,' which is equally hardy. Zone 3.

H. macrophylla: Classic mophead flowers often can be blue in acid soil, pink in alkaline soil. Look for 'Nikko Blue' and 'Preziosa,' as well as the reblooming series from Endless Summer ('Bailmer' and 'Blushing Bride'). Zone 5b. *H. macrophylla normalis* includes the lacecap hydrangeas, my personal favourites and more reliably hardy than the mopheads. Flower heads are flat rather than ball-shaped, but can have white, pink, blue, or reddish flowers. 'Blue Bird,' 'Blue Billows,' and 'White Dome' are popular choices. Zone 5.

H. paniculata: Often referred to as "Peegee types" because of abbreviating of species name with one cultivar, 'Grandiflora.' Also known as the graveyard tree because it is often planted in cemeteries around the region. More tolerant of clay than others. Flower from new growth rather than old wood. Try 'Limelight,' which has soft green flowers. Zone 3.

H. querquefolia: Oakleaf hydrangea tolerates more sun and drier soils but hates too wet a soil, particularly in winter. Gorgeous fall colour. Zone 5b–6 with good drainage and winter protection.

Ilex verticillata

winterberry, Canada holly, sparkleberry

Family: Aquifoliaceae
Hardy to: zone 3
Bloom period: summer (but insignificant); highy attractive berries appear in late summer and last until birds eat them
Growing requirements: sun to part shade, good moisture

Height: 3–10 feet
Where best used: native plantings, sloped areas, wet sites
Propagation: suckers, cuttings
Problems: No serious pests or diseases.
Notes: Must have male and female plants for pollination and berry production.

For those of us who love plants, there are always certain species or varieties that make us instantly happy. Sunflowers are one such plant in my gardening world, because they look like big floral smiles. But January finds us with very few sunflowers in bloom, at least in our neck of the woods.

My instant-smile plant for the dark days of winter glows with brilliant scarlet, orange, or red berries on an artistic sculpture of branches scoured bare of leaves. Whether you call it winterberry, Canada holly, coralberry, sparkleberry, or by the curiously unrelated name of

berry colour can vary

black alder, *Ilex verticillata* is a terrific plant for generating winter interest in the Atlantic gardenscape. This deciduous shrub is native to eastern North America and can often be found growing in large thickets, which are particularly noticeable once autumn winds have stripped away the leaves so the berries can be seen.

If you're a bird or wildlife gardener, you'll plant winterberry to draw in fruit-eating songbirds such as waxwings and overwintering robins. These birds will strip the berries away from your shrubs by mid- to late winter, but you'll enjoy the displays of brilliant berries until that time, and the winged visitors are irresistible.

First Nations people referred to winterberry as "feverbush," because they used a solution made with the plant's bark as a potion for reducing fever, as well as for an antiseptic solution in cleaning wounds and injuries. Plants for a Future (www.pfaf.org) reports that a herbal tea can be made from dried leaves, but the berries are not rated as desirable for human consumption.

Like their showy relatives the evergreen hollies, winterberry is dioecious and requires both male and female plants in order to produce fruit. There are ongoing discussions in the botanical world about how close the male plant needs to be to females, and the appropriate ratio of each. Most gardeners will plant several females to one male.

Winterberry is naturally found in moist areas where the soil is rich in organic matter. Because the plants sucker, they're ideal for creating a mass planting along a pond or other suitable location. The shrubs tend to be slow growing for a few years until well established, and normally will mature to a height of 6–10 feet. If you keep suckers pruned you can limit the shrub's spread, but I am waiting patiently for mine to form thickets, such as those that delight residents and visitors to the southwestern parts of Nova Scotia's shoreline.

If you have a damp area where you want to secure the soil, such as a slope leading into a wetland, ditch, or garden runoff, consider planting Canada holly, because it works brilliantly to reduce erosion. The plant is best suited to soils that are acid, which is a condition that most Atlantic gardeners experience. Alkaline soils will cause leaves to yellow and often to drop off.

Although Dirr's *Manual of Woody Landscape Plants* lists a dizzying number of winterberry cultivars, these are often very regional in nature and not available outside the particular part of the United States or Canada where they were hybridized. *I. verticillata* has been successfully crossed with other deciduous species of *Ilex*, generally with *I. serrata*, but that latter species is marginally hardy for much of Atlantic Canada. If you do manage to locate named cultivars of winterberry, make sure that you find males and females that will bloom at the same time of the season, or else pollination will be a failure. *Ilex* will cross-pollinate with other species (including broadleaf evergreen holly), although the best fruit set will come from having two plants of the same species.

ripening berries with summer foliage

Juniperus

Family: Cupressaceae
Hardy to: varies with species
Bloom period: not significant
Growing requirements: full sun, good drainage
Height: some low-growing creepers; others up to 15 feet

Where best used: collections, mixed borders, ground covers, compact species good for rock gardens
Propagation: seeds and cuttings
Problems: A variety of pests and diseases, depending on cultivar. Snow breakage can be problematic in some varieties.
Notes: Very cold-tolerant, some salt-tolerant, and most are deer-resistant.

'Dream Joy'

Back when I was a child in Newfoundland, one of the first evergreen shrubs I learned about was the common native juniper (*J. communis*). I came home with a small dish of bright blue berries and asked my father if these were blueberries. He had taught me never to eat any wild plant without knowing exactly what it was, and to his credit, didn't laugh when I presented him with the juniper berries. He did, however, take me blueberry picking not long after that and pointed out the difference between the two plant species.

If you aren't a conifer fan, you're still probably aware of junipers the way you are of maples: they exist, there are many of them, they're often used—or overused—in landscape plantings, and some are great and some not so great. The main thing to remember about junipers is that they prefer conditions that are "high and dry": provide them with full sun and decent drainage and they'll grow in any soil.

There are dozens of species of junipers, and hundreds of cultivars within the species most commonly used in gardening and landscaping. One of the interesting—and confusing—characteristics of junipers is that they have two different types of foliage. Juvenile foliage is always needlelike, while mature foliage can be either needlelike or scaly.

One of my favourite lines about junipers comes from Michael Dirr, who writes, "If you cannot grow junipers, do not bother planting anything else." This is true even though several diseases and pests can attack junipers. Juniper webworm is a real problem in some

a creeping juniper on a wall

species, and the damage it causes may not be noticeable right away because of the dense growth habit of most junipers. The pest can be controlled using organic insecticidal soap or dormant oil sprays, but follow recommendations for the use of these and any other pesticides. Juniper tip blight, a fungal disease that can kill the entire plant if left untreated, is controllable by pruning out diseased tips, ensuring good air circulation, minimal fertilization, and avoiding mechanical damage to the plant.

Recommended species and cultivars

Junipers come in many varieties, so your best option is to look around a nursery to find what you want. Here are a few to look for:

Juniperus chinensis: Chinese junipers are usually larger species, useful in low hedges or open beds and borders. Look for 'Aurea,' 'Gold Star' (Bakaurea), 'Plumosa Aurea,' or 'Saybrook Gold' for gold-foliaged forms. 'Blaauw' is an upright form with fountaining sprays of foliage and is very salt-tolerant.

J. communis: Common juniper can grow to ten feet, and often have cone-shaped growth habit. 'Compressa' is a dwarf, slow-growing form; 'Gold Cone' has a narrow shape with gold foliage in spring and grey-blue growth during the rest of season.

J. horizontalis: Creeping junipers are excellent for ground covers or use on rock walls and sloping banks. The blue rug variety ('Wiltonii') is an old-fashioned standby that is salt-tolerant and common throughout the region; other varieties to look for include 'Blue Chip,' 'Bar Harbor,' and my favourite, 'Icee Blue,' which turns purple-blue in the autumn. 'Mother Lode' is a yellow sport of 'Wiltonii' that turns bronze-orange in winter.

J. virginiana: This species, native to eastern North America, sometimes goes by the bizarre common name of "eastern red cedar," but is more accurately called eastern juniper. It can grow into a large tree, very pyramidal in shape. 'Grey Owl' is a shade-tolerant form with upright, blue-grey foliage.

J. squamata: The flaky juniper is native to China and the Himalayas, and includes several very popular blue-foliaged forms. 'Blue Star' is a slow-growing, low-mounding cultivar, useful in rock gardens but can be flattened by snow cover; 'Blue Carpet' has a more spreading, ground cover behaviour.

Magnolia

Family: Magnoliaceae

Hardy to: varies with species

Bloom period: mid May–July; some will rebloom

Growing requirements: moist, fertile, well-drained soil; full sun to part shade

Height: varies with species and cultivar

Where best used: specimen tree or shrub; shade-tolerant, but slower growing and fewer blooms

Propagation: cuttings and seeds

Problems: No serious pests or diseases. Late frosts can kill flowers.

Notes: Many species are deer-resistant.

For many of us the magnolia suggests the balmy climate of the southern United States, where many different species grow to statuesque proportions and bewitch with their gorgeous flowers. Happily for most Atlantic Canadians, however, there are cold-hardy magnolias that can be grown here with a little care and planning. The first time I saw a magnolia blooming in this region was in Wolfville, Nova Scotia, more than thirty years ago. Someone mistakenly called it a "tulip tree" (which is the common name for a different genus, *Liriodendron*), but even then, long before I had a family and a property of my own, I knew I'd be adding one to my garden someday.

The magnolia genus is ancient and interesting, with more than two hundred species native to various regions of the world, including North, Central, and South America. Some species are evergreen, others deciduous, and they can vary in size from tidy shrubs to massive trees many feet high. The flowers themselves have very tough reproductive parts as well as the shiny tepals (petal-like leaves) that make them so attractive—magnolias evolved before bees, and were pollinated by beetles, so they had to be tough to withstand the weight of beetles climbing over them.

The secret to success with a magnolia is to pick the right species or hybrid for your growing conditions. These trees appreciate full sun but will tolerate some shade, although

'Betty'

M. sieboldii

'Leonard Messel'

Magnolia stellata: The star magnolia is the most hardy, and flowers before it leafs out in spring. Can be highly fragrant. 'Royal Star' is a popular cultivar. Zone 4.

M. x loebneri: Hybrids with the appearance of a star magnolia but with more fragrance. 'Merrill' has many petals and pure white blooms; 'Leonard Messel' are pink to pinkish white. Zone 5.

M. x soulangiana: The saucer magnolia is hardy to zone 4 with winter protection. Flowers are cup-shaped and pink, purple or white.

M. sieboldii: The pendulous and beautiful flowers of Siebold magnolia face downwards; plant near a patio or other site where you can sit nearby and enjoy the blossoms. Reblooms sporadically. Zone 5.

M. acuminata: The cucumber magnolia is one of the cold-hardiest (zone 4) and isn't particularly ornamental. However, it is used in hybridizing with other species (including the saucer magnolia) to produce yellow-flowered varieties such as 'Elizabeth,' 'Yellow Bird,' and 'Butterflies,' all of which are hardy to zone 5 with some winter protection.

"The Girls": These are a collection of eight named hybrids developed at the U.S. National Arboretum in Washington, D.C. They grow to a maximum of 20 feet and produce flowers that can have red, purple, lavender, and cream shades in their petals. "The Girls" are 'Ann,' 'Betty,' 'Jane,' 'Judy,' 'Pinkie,' 'Randy,' 'Ricki,' and 'Susan'; availability varies at nurseries around the region. Zone 5.

they won't bloom as profusely. A rich, moist soil, well amended with organic matter, will make them very happy. Try to plant your specimen so that it won't be buffeted by the worst of prevailing winds: a late frost or cold wind can kill the flower buds, and too much snow piling up around a young plant will easily break limbs. However, don't plant a magnolia on a southern exposure where buds might be prompted to open too early and be lost to frost.

Magnolias have shallow root systems and are susceptible to drought damage. Be prepared to mulch well around the base of your magnolias, and if you wish to underplant, use perennials that don't need to be divided regularly, rather than annuals or perennials that require division. Ground covers such as periwinkle (*Vinca*) or creeping bleeding heart can be effective as a living mulch.

In southern climates, magnolias can be troubled by a number of pests and diseases, but they are seldom bothered by any in our region. Deer tend to avoid them, so provided you have a proper site, mulch well, and don't disturb your plant's roots, you should be able to enjoy magnolias for many years.

'Yellow Bird'

Metasequoia glyptostroboides

dawn redwood

Family: Cupressaceae
Hardy to: zone 4
Bloom period: not significant; cones are small but attractive
Growing requirements: full sun; rich, moist to wet soil
Height: 70–100 feet

Where best used: specimen tree, street tree
Propagation: cuttings and seed
Problems: No serious pests or diseases.
Notes: Deer-resistant, good fall colour, interesting bark; critically endangered in the wild.

I still remember the day Captain Dick Steele called me to ask if I'd ever seen or heard of the dawn redwood. At that time I hadn't, and he told me the story of this unique plant, discovered in China in the early 1940s as fossil material, found as a live plant in 1945, and officially named in 1948. It is the sole living species of the genus and is related to the coast redwood. Like the bald cypress and larch, it's a deciduous conifer, losing its needles in the autumn.

A friend of mine refers to the *Metasequoia* as a great lawnmower tree, because the trunks are extremely tough and aren't easily damaged like some trees. The tree is fast growing and rapidly develops a thick, flaring trunk with a "muscled" appearance.

'Ogon,' also known as 'Gold Rush'

Dawn redwood isn't a tree for small yards, given that it grows fairly quickly and can reach 70 feet or more. Mine has been planted for about five years now and has settled in nicely, so I'm hopeful I'll see its curious, boxy little cones in the next couple of years.

Metasequoia likes a soil that is moist, even wet, which explains why it does well in my spring-fed clay soil. It will falter if your soil is dry unless you commit to watering regularly, and you should mulch well around its base to help retain soil moisture. My specimen has never shown any sign of pest problems, and deer aren't enamoured of it like they are with some conifers.

A couple of interesting varieties are now available, but be aware that they are not inexpensive. 'Gold Rush' (also called 'Ogon') has golden yellow needles that are absolutely luminescent when they first appear in spring. The gold-needled varieties are slower growing, and won't attain quite the height of the standard species.

M. 'Jack Frost' and 'White Spot' are both variations having light green needles accented with white and are also slower-growing than the species. I have only seen photos of these cultivars, and haven't been overly impressed, but some gardeners might like them for the curiosity factor. Reports are that these cultivars don't burn in the sun despite their white-accented needles.

'Sheridan Spire' was introduced by Sheridan Nurseries of Ontario, and is both more narrow and shorter than the species, topping out at around 50 feet.

'Sheridan Spire' in late winter

Myrica pennysylvanica

northern bayberry, candleberry, bog myrtle

Family: Myricaceae
Hardy to: zone 3
Bloom period: flowers insignificant; fruit a waxy, blue-grey berry
Growing requirements: Doesn't like too much heat, otherwise tolerant of most any growing conditions.
Height: 4–10 feet

Where best used: small hedges, mass plantings, wildlife plantings
Propagation: seed and root cuttings (females)
Problems: No serious pests or diseases.
Notes: Salt-tolerant native plant with great versatility.

Depending on where you live in Atlantic Canada, you may see wonderful stands of northern bayberry growing along roadsides, in ditches, and in open meadows. You may not have realized that this plant is native to all of eastern Canada and is a remarkable addition to any garden. I would venture to say it's one of those great native plants that has been overlooked for years but is about to become highly popular for its beautiful and hardworking versatility. Its fragrant foliage is semi-evergreen, often turning shades of rose and burgundy before dropping in late autumn to reveal its waxy berries. Tolerant

fall colour in young plants

of poor soil and almost any growing conditions, northern bayberry is also salt-tolerant and deer-resistant. It makes an attractive hedging or specimen plant, and its leafless structure provides good winter interest. What's not to love about a low-care and versatile shrub with so many great features?

Northern bayberry can grow to about ten feet in height over the years, and also suckers slowly, producing small thickets of plants if left undisturbed. A dioecious shrub, you need both male and female northern bayberry plants to produce the blue-grey, waxy berries from which bayberry candles are made. The berries appear only on the female plants, as with any dioecious species. While it's not evergreen, it can be effective clipped for use in an edging or privacy hedge (if you like a clipped appearance in shrubs) in areas where *Buxus* (box) is not reliably hardy. I prefer the unclipped look of most any plant, so my bayberries just grow as they wish.

Although you may dig up wild bayberries from roadsides, the easier option is simply to purchase plants from local nurseries that include native plants in their inventory. Make sure that plants come from sources in Atlantic Canada or (if availability is a problem) the northern United States, so that the plants are best adapted to our growing conditions.

berries appear on female plants

Like many Atlantic Canadians, I've made garlands, swags, and wreaths using branches of myrica and have enjoyed using berry-laden twigs in festive floral arrangements. Tradition says that a bayberry candle burned on Christmas Eve will bring good health and fortune to the house.

bayberry fruit

Physocarpus

Family: Rosaceae

Hardy to: zone 2

Bloom period: early summer; bladder-shaped, hollow fruit through fall

Growing requirements: sun to partial shade; moist, well-drained soil

Height: varies with cultivar; most no taller than 8–10 feet

Where best used: mixed borders, specimen plants, wildlife gardens

Propagation: softwood cuttings, or by removing suckers from main plant

Problems: No serious pests or diseases.

Notes: Pruning of twiggy growth after flowering will help to display handsome, peeling bark.

When gardeners ask me to recommend a shrub that has good foliage colour and is almost foolproof, I invariably suggest that they try a ninebark. The species is not native to Atlantic Canada, but is native through Quebec and parts of the southeastern United States. A member of the rose family, ninebark is a deciduous shrub, with multiple stems in its native form.

What makes the ninebark so desirable as a garden shrub? To begin with, it's decidedly easy to grow, very hardy, and untroubled by any significant pests or diseases. There's likely a spot in any garden for a ninebark, because the shrub will grow in full sun to partial shade, providing it has moist, well-

'Coppertina'

drained soil that is a little bit acid, which is usually not a problem in Atlantic Canada. It's also drought-tolerant, which is a bonus for those summers with sporadic rainfall.

Numerous cultivars are available featuring gold, copper, or purple foliage that deepens in colour in autumn. Pinkish-white flowers are borne in clusters in early summer, and look something like spirea flowers or tiny roses. You'll find that bees, butterflies, and other pollinators will flock to your ninebark while it blooms over a period of at least several weeks. Depending on the cultivar, the shrub will produce bladder-shaped, red- or wine-

flowers of 'Diabolo'

'Nugget'

coloured fruit that are quite attractive and are used as a food source by overwintering birds. The generic name *Physocarpus* actually means bladder-fruit, referring to the hollow, saclike appearance of the fruit capsules.

Speaking of winter, this is a season when ninebarks will shine, especially if they've been pruned to open up their dense, twiggy growth habit. The bark on older branches and stems of ninebarks peels away in papery strips, revealing cinnamon-coloured bark underneath. Supposedly, the shrub has nine layers of bark, which explains its common name.

Ninebarks are deer-resistant and aren't troubled by any major insect pests. Occasionally the leaves will develop leaf spot or powdery mildew, but neither of these problems is widespread or fatal to the shrub. All parts of the shrub are toxic, so while birds will eat the fruits of ninebark, don't try them yourself.

If you want your ninebark to be able to display its peeling bark during winter, prune out some of the twiggy branches after flowering has finished in midsummer. This will open up the shrub's appearance during growing months, and make it easier to see the bark once its leaves have dropped. Don't prune the shrub in the spring, or you'll have minimal flowers.

The ninebark has been the subject of interesting hybridization over the past decade or so, resulting in a number of very good cultivars. Of these, perhaps the most well known is 'Diablo' (sometimes seen as 'Diabolo'), which has deep purple foliage that holds its colour well throughout the growing months. There are two popular yellow-foliaged cultivars, 'Nugget' and 'Dart's Gold'; in warmer parts of the region (and where the shrub is in full sun) the foliage may lose its gold colour as summer progresses, though it will turn yellow again in autumn. Both of these yellow-foliaged cultivars are more compact than 'Diablo,' growing to 5–6 feet rather than 8–10.

Two newer cultivar introductions have become quite popular in the past several years. 'Summer Wine' has a more compact and arching growth habit than some of the older cultivars and features rich burgundy-coloured foliage. My personal favourite, however, is 'Coppertina,' which as the name suggests boasts coppery coloured foliage that deepens into shades of wine or purple when autumn arrives.

Picea

spruce

Family: Pinaceae

Hardy to: zone 2

Bloom period: Insignificant flowers; pollen release end of May–early June. Cones last for months on trees.

Growing requirements: Full sun to light shade; moist rich soil is ideal, but adaptable to most growing conditions.

Height: Varies with species. White spruce can reach 50–70 feet; Alberta spruce 5–8 feet.

Where best used: specimen trees, hedging, windbreaks, wildlife plantings

Propagation: seed; dwarf Alberta from cuttings

Problems: spruce gall aphids, red spider, beetles

Notes: deer-resistant; some species salt-tolerant

Our property has a number of large white (*P. glauca*) and red (*P. rubens*) spruces growing along its perimeters, and their tall, sweeping silhouettes draw my eye whenever I glance out a window, especially in winter. Several species are native to our region, easily recognizable in the wild by their more or less symmetrical, pyramidal growth habit. Spruces are pioneer trees, being among the first to colonize an area, and are known for their durability and salt-resistance. The native white and black spruce are the northernmost tree species found in North America, growing to the arctic treeline (which can vary from 56°–69° north depending on geographical

blue spruce

influences). These are important wildlife trees, as many species of birds nest in them and their cones and seeds are a source of food for birds as well as squirrels.

Our native spruce species are often used in commercial lumber and forestry, but they are also important as cultivated landscape plants. Often you'll see hedges of spruce, sometimes clipped into shapes, other times simply topped and allowed to fill in, in rural maritime communities where they are used as windbreaks due to their tolerance for salt. But there are a number of wonderful cultivars derived from native and introduced species that are

blue spruce 'Hoopsii'   cones of Norway spruce

especially popular. What we call the dwarf Alberta spruce was actually a witch's broom on a white spruce that was discovered in 1904 and propagated to make a popular dwarf cultivar.

The keyword with spruces is durability: given full sun or very light shade, they can be planted in many different locations, although you will need to site the more fragile cultivars with a bit more care than the native species. They may prefer a moist, well-drained and moderately rich soil, but grow quite happily in clay and even in ditches along our property. Cultivars such as dwarf Alberta spruce may need some protection from harsh winds; the first year I planted one its foliage was damaged on the west face of the shrub, but in the five years since, it has developed an indifference to whatever our weather throws at it.

Spruces are sometimes subject to infestation by a variety of pests, including red spider, aphids, tussock moths, and others. Most of these have natural predators, or if it's a population boom year, can be controlled by organic controls such as insecticidal soap or B.t. (*Bacillis thurengiensis*) spray. Although natives are salt-resistant, be careful not to get driveway or walkway salt onto the lower limbs of dwarf or blue spruces, as it can cause needle death.

Recommended species and cultivars

Picea abies: Norway spruce is an important forestry tree but is also used in landscapes.

P. abies 'Pendula': Naturally ground-covering, but can be trained into an upright, weeping shrub.

P. glauca 'Conica': Dwarf Alberta spruce is one of most popular spruces used in gardens and landscapes. Will eventually reach 12 feet (after twenty-five years).

P. omerika: Serbian spruce matures to 60 feet, but dwarf forms are slow-growing options, eventually maturing at 6 feet tall and wide.

P. pungens 'Glauca': Blue spruce is one of the most desirable conifers in horticulture and can be found in many different forms and growth habits, from globe to weeping, some dwarf and others reaching 60 feet. The best seed sources are trees in the Kaibab forest of Arizona, which is why you will sometimes see 'Kaibab' in the spruce's name. Varieties to look for include 'Hoopsii,' one of the bluest forms; 'Fat Albert,' a semi-dwarf; 'Thomsenii,' a symmetrical tree with silver-blue foliage; and 'Iseli Foxtail,' with a tight columnar form.

Pieris japonica

Japanese pieris, Japanese andromeda

Family: Ericaceae

Hardy to: zone 4b with winter protection

Bloom period: mid-May

Growing requirements: well-drained, moist, organic soils; takes some shade

Height: 4–5 feet, occasionally to 8 feet

Where best used: smaller specimens in rock gardens; specimen plant or in shrub borders

Propagation: cuttings

Problems: may need winter protection

Notes: Very deer-resistant. Can force stems indoors for late winter blooms.

When I was finalizing a preliminary list of plants to include in this book, I wanted a second set of eyes on the shrubs and trees section, so I asked nurseryman Rob Baldwin his opinion. It's a good thing I did, because he looked at the list, nodding at some, raising his eyebrows at others, and then looking up at me with a frown.

"Where's pieris?" he demanded. "What would Dick say if you left that out?"

What, indeed? In front of our house, in the corner garden most sheltered from the worst winter winds, is a pieris given to me some years ago by friend and beloved plantsman, the late Captain Richard (Dick) Steele.

containers of 'Mountain Fire' showing new growth

"Take this home and see how it does," he remarked one day when I was visiting him at Bayport Plant Farm. Never one to argue with Dick, especially when it came to plants, I did just that, though it took me well over a month to decide on a good spot for the shrub. It settled in and thrived nicely, and was just emerging from a winter's worth of snow drifted over it, its pink buds jewel-like in the March sunlight of 2010, when we learned that Dick had passed away. Now, forever, that shrub will have an even more precious place in my heart.

For those of you who didn't know Captain Steele, why might you want to include pieris in your plantings? If you're a fan of ericaceous plants (members of the heath

cascade of flowers　　　　　*seedheads in late summer*

family, including rhododendron, azaleas, heaths and heathers, andromeda, cranberry, and blueberry), you'll love pieris for its gorgeous flowers, which resemble clusters of lilies of the valley both in appearance and in fragrance. Some cultivars have spectacular colour in their early spring foliage, which can be bronze to ruby red in colour before deepening to rich green. In winter, the foliage shines against snow, while the terminal clusters of flower buds are pink in colour.

It is said that early horticulturists gave pieris the common name Andromeda because the flower clusters had a fanciful resemblance to chains. In Greek mythology the Ethiopian princess Andromeda was chained to rocks beside an ocean, from which the hero Perseus rescued her. Just to make nomenclature more entertaining, there is a separate genus of ericaceous plant, bog rosemary, which bears the botanical name of *Andromeda polifolia* and is native throughout Atlantic Canada. To be on the safe side, I always refer to the plant in this profile as pieris.

Pieris is very shade-tolerant and accepting of clay soil provided it's well drained, which can be achieved by adding compost or leaf mould to the ground around the shrub every spring and fall. Those of you who are plagued by deer will love this: when Bambi has gnawed your rhododendrons to nubbins, your pieris will remain unscathed and lovely.

Although most references list pieris as hardy to zone 4b with winter protection, I stress that site selection is crucial. Site this shrub with the same care that you would a Japanese maple, and be prepared to protect it from winter winds if it's in any sort of exposed location.

A number of cultivars are sold in the region, the most reliably hardy of which are 'Prelude,' which is very dwarf at under two feet in height, and 'Mountain Fire,' which has snow white flowers and especially brilliant colour on new spring growth. If you live in the milder parts of the region (zone 6) or have microclimates and good shelter, you can look for 'Katsura,' which has pink flowers, or 'Valley Valentine,' with deeper rose to red flowers.

Pinus

pine

Family: Pinaceae

Hardy to: varies with species

Bloom period: Not significant, though pollen release in June may cause allergies.

Growing requirements: full sun; tolerant of most soils; most prefer good drainage

Height: varies with species

Where best used: hedging, specimen trees, windbreaks, shelterbelts

Propagation: seed; grafting for unusual varieties

Problems: various insects and diseases but not usually a large problem

Notes: A few pines are salt-tolerant, but most are damaged by road salt or sea spray.

There's something irresistible, even romantic, about pines. Maybe it's their long, graceful needles, or the way the wind whispers through them, or their pungent scent, but seeing a group of pine trees immediately makes me happy. We have several different species on our property, from a supposedly dwarf Mugo that is spreading much further than I want it to grow, to a white pine dug up years ago alongside a road, to a small but sturdy bristlecone pine named "Bob" because it was given to me by a friend of the same name (and it seemed to require a name).

Pines are easily recognizable by their needles, which are longer than any other conifer and appear in clusters of two, three, or five needles, depending on the species. Authorities argue over just how many species of pines there are, but it's safe to say there are over one hundred, many of which are used in commercial and home landscaping.

young cones and new growth on Mugo pine

needles of bristlecone pine

Often you'll see pines alongside roads and highways showing reddish, dying needles; these are usually due to damage from highway salt, so make sure to plant your own pines away from sites where they may be sprayed by salt. If you're planting near the shore, your best options are the Austrian, Jack, and Mugo species. Porcupines find Scots pine particularly tasty, but deer tend to avoid the trees due to the needles, which can be quite sharp. Most of the pests and diseases affecting pines are not problematic, but the exception is the white pine blister rust (see sidebar, page 62).

Pinus aristata: Bristlecone pine is one of the oldest living plants on earth, with some species recorded at over four thousand years old. Interesting white resinous speckles on needles. Extremely slow growing. Zone 4.

P. banksiana: Jack pines are tough as nails, and are particularly useful in poor, sandy, or gravelly soil. Foliage may yellow somewhat during winter. Mature to 50 feet. Zone 2.

P. cembra: Swiss stone pine is a handsome specimen tree though slow growing. Matures to 40 feet. Zone 3.

P. mugo: Mugo is a low, broadly spreading pine, with many dwarf cultivars available. Useful in mass plantings and mixed borders. Check cultivars for mature heights as can range widely. Cultivars include 'Mops,' 'Gnom,' 'Sherwood Compact,' 'Aurea' (gold foliage in winter). Zone 3.

Pinus nigra: Austrian pine has rich dark green to green-black needles, in groups of two, which are very stiff in texture, sharp on tips. Salt-tolerant. Good for windbreaks, matures to 60 feet. Zone 3.

P. ponderosa: Ponderosa, or western yellow pine, is used in shelterbelts or mass plantings. Height to 100 feet. Zone 3.

P. resinosa: Red pine is native throughout the region and very tolerant of exposed settings and poor soils. Needles in groups of 2, height 80 feet at maturity, hardy to zone 2.

P. strobus: Eastern white pine is very long-lived, prefers moist, even boggy soil, but will tolerate dry conditions once established. Hugely important in the Maritimes as a lumber tree, and native throughout all of Atlantic Canada. Needles in clusters of five, grows to 80 feet tall. Zone 3.

P. sylvestris: Scotch pine has been introduced from Europe but is found growing wild as an escape from cultivation throughout Atlantic Canada. Popular cultivated as a Christmas tree, although there is great variation in needle colour from yellowish-green to a rich blue-green. Grows to 60 feet. Zone 3.

new growth on tips of pine branches

a young columnar Scotch pine

White Pine Blister Rust

Introduced from Asia around 1900, white pine blister rust is a fungus that affects white pines but spends part of its life cycle on an essential alternate host, plants of the *Ribes* species, which are more commonly known as currants and gooseberries. The fungus begins as small spots on needles and progresses to swellings on branches that ultimately turn into large cankers that can kill the tree. The rust doesn't spread from pine to pine but must have gooseberry or currant bushes for part of its life cycle, which has led to numerous attempted eradications of these plants throughout North America in an effort to control the fungus. Some varieties of *Ribes* are now bred to be rust-resistant, and work is being done to develop rust-resistant white pines, in part by hybridizing them with other species, in part by propagating cuttings from existing trees that show natural resistance to infestation from the fungus.

Research done in Canada indicates that pruning lower branches of trees in commercial plantings helps to reduce the appearance and spread of the disease. If you're growing white pines only as an ornamental species you probably don't have a lot to worry about, but if you're growing currants or gooseberries for their fruit and also have white pines growing nearby, make sure to choose cultivars that are rust-resistant.

Rhododendron

deciduous azalea

Family: Ericaceae

Hardy to: zone 3

Bloom period: late April–June

Growing requirements: moist but well-drained, acidic soil; sun to light shade

Height: several inches to 15 feet

Where best used: mixed beds; mass plantings

Propagation: seed or cuttings

Problems: Deer like them. Root rot can be a problem. Must be careful to select the right cultivars.

Notes: Some are fragrant.

All azaleas are rhododendrons, but not all rhododendrons are azaleas. Confused? We'll put the blame on those taxonomists again. Azaleas used to be classified under the genus *Azalea*, but reorganizing of the rhododendron genus allowed numerous subgenera to be added, including two that comprise the azaleas: those in the *Pentanthera* subgenus are deciduous, while those in the *Tsusuji* subgenus are evergreen. In general (and with plants there are always exceptions), azalea leaves tend to be smaller than those of rhododendrons, and their flowers have five stamens while the flowers of rhododendrons have ten.

In Atlantic Canada, we grow members of the *Pentanthera* subgenus as hardy azaleas, leaving the evergreen types (like the grocery-store azaleas) to those who garden in warmer climates. Azalea blooms come in a range of jewel-like colours, including brilliant reds, yellows, scarlets, and pinks.

Because I'd had trouble growing those evergreen azaleas as houseplants, I was initially skeptical about growing their relatives in my garden. That is, until I got to know Bill Wilgenhof and Sharon Bryson, who live just outside Antigonish, Nova Scotia. They grow a variety of rhododendrons and azaleas and gave me several of their own seedlings to try. Sharon told

'Fireball'

'Golden Lights'

me that azaleas are essentially idiot-proof—far more forgiving of all sorts of garden issues than are rhododendrons. Azaleas are also impervious to wind, cold, and sun, as long as they have well-prepared soil, decent drainage, and adequate sunlight. She made her point, which is why I add more azaleas to my gardens every year.

The biggest mistake gardeners make with azaleas is planting them in too much shade; they like plenty of sun. If your soil, like mine, is on the heavy side, amend it with generous amounts of compost and chunky (not finely powdered) peat moss. Good drainage is crucial, because in nature these are plants of mountainous regions, where sloped terrain helps to drain away excess water.

When selecting an azalea or rhododendron at a nursery, make sure that the plant's root system is not root-bound, as these plants will never do well. Slide the pot off and look at the root system, which should be showing white root tips, not simply a circular mass of roots that have grown around and around inside the pot. You can bring around a pot-bound plant (see page 2), but instead of going through this tedium, buy from reputable growers who don't allow their plants to become pot-bound.

(see page 2)

Recommended species and cultivars

If you're fortunate enough to belong to the Atlantic Rhododendron and Horticultural Society, you have access to seeds and plants via the club's membership, and this will include hybrids not seen anywhere else. For those with limited ability to attend meetings, here are some more commonly available and interesting azaleas to look for.

Rhododendron mucronulatum: The Korean or snow azalea has excellent cold hardiness, although a late frost will damage its flowers, which appear in mid-May. Flowers are magenta in the species, but you can also find Cornell Pink, which is quite hardy and has rose pink flowers. Zone 4b.

R. schlippenbachii: When I first saw the royal azalea, it was displaying its fall foliage, which is a neon blaze of orange, yellow, and pink; it stopped me in my tracks and I have been raving about it ever since. The flowers are a pale, unexciting pink, but I grow it purely for the almost oakleaf-shaped foliage, which is tinged with bronze during the spring and summer before really turning on the colour in autumn. Zone 4.

R. 'Arneson Gem': Magnificent, large yellow-orange flowers. Zone 4.

Northern Lights series: This series of cold-hardy azaleas was developed at the University of Minnesota and are hardy to zone 3. There are at least eight named cultivars, all fragrant and having "Lights" in their names, including 'Golden Lights,' 'Mandarin Lights,' 'Orchid Lights,' and 'Northern Hi-Lights.'

'White Lights'

Rhododendron

rhododendron

Family: Ericaceae
Hardy to: varies with species and cultivar
Bloom period: late April–June
Growing requirements: moist but well-drained, acidic soil; sun to partial shade
Height: several inches to 15 feet
Where best used: Miniatures for front of border or rock garden and small lots. Larger species as specimens or mass plantings.

Propagation: seed or cuttings
Problems: Deer like them. Root rot can be a problem. Must be careful to select the right cultivars. Protect from winter wind.
Notes: Good winter interest. Huge range of flower colours and bicolours.

Rhododendrons are nothing if not versatile. At the same time that cultivated species and varieties can be a bit challenging to grow and get to flower, we have wild species and relatives that thrive throughout the region. You've probably seen rhodora, which puts on a showy display along roadsides, beside streams, and lakes throughout the region; rhodora was formerly in its own genus but now has been moved to genus *Rhododendron* (which has a number of subgenera and sections, just to make our heads hurt). The toughest species I know of is the tiny Lapland Rosebay, *R. lapponicum*, which I saw growing both on a windswept plateau in Labrador and on the inhospitable terrain of the Tablelands in Gros Morne National Park. For most people, however, the rhododendron means those ornamental, evergreen-leafed plants that put on a colourful display of flowers in the late spring and early summer throughout much of the region.

R. russatum

The main thing to remember about rhododendrons is that they demand excellent drainage: plant them in soggy soil at your peril, as a stressed rhododendron will be more susceptible to attack from diseases. They do well on a hillside with full sun to dappled

R. catawbiense *'Boursault'*

shade, and if you're growing some of the less-hardy species and hybrids, you need to protect them from wind damage, which can kill the blooms while still in bud. Like all members of the Ericaceae family, these plants like an acid soil, which most of us in Atlantic Canada have in abundance. If your soil does lean towards a more alkaline pH, you can amend it with ammonium sulphate (available at garden centres) or with aged manure, woodland litter or humus, pine needles, and peat moss.

Often plants that are sold at nurseries have been grown in containers for several years, and may be pot-bound. Before planting a newly purchased rhododendron, loosen the root ball so the roots will spread out around the plant, and take care not to plant too deeply. The top of the root ball can actually be left exposed, and you shouldn't tamp down the soil too firmly around your plant. You may also want to mulch the shallow-growing root systems with bark or pine needles to protect against drying out in summer and excessively cold winter weather.

One definite drawback to growing rhododendrons—even for those who can grow them well—is that deer love them. There are no easy cures for this, because what works for one property owner seems to deter the animals not a bit at other locations. A variety of homemade as well as commercial deer repellents are available, most having to be reapplied after rain. (See Appendix A: Deer-resistant plants, page 242.)

When it comes to choosing rhododendrons for your garden, make sure to buy from a reputable nursery or from collectors who have a passion for these plants and know which ones do well in our region. Some big-box stores bring in cultivars that have been propagated in Florida and other warm-climate areas, and these plants aren't acclimatized for growing here, and may not even be cold-hardy enough to withstand our winters. It's always best to go to experts when investing in a pricey plant such as a rhododendron.

I could more than fill this book with discussions on rhododendron species, subspecies, and such, but for our purposes I'm dividing them into two sections: the lepidotes, or small-leafed varieties, and the elepidotes, which are the large-leafed types.

Lepidotes:

'PJM': Fragrant foliage, mauve or magenta flowers, deep burgundy foliage in autumn and winter. One of most popular lepidotes. Zone 4.

'April Rose': Pale purple, double blooms. Zone 4.

'Olga Mezitt': Hot bubblegum-pink flowers; leaves are bronze-copper in winter. Zone 4b.

'Ramapo': Tiny, purple flowers, great edging shrub (grows to 3 feet over many years), foliage green-black in winter. Zone 5.

R. russatum: A species that is underutilized but gorgeous, with flowers that are lavender-blue in colour. Zone 4b.

'Ginny Gee': Pink and white flowers fade to white as they mature. Zone 5.

Elepidotes:

'Capistrano': Lovely yellow flowers, grows to 4 feet. Zone 5.

'Nova Zembla': First "red" flowered rhododendron but actually a light red fading to pink. Zone 4.

'Francesca': Deep red, good hardiness, grows to 6 feet. Zone 5.

'Mist Maiden': Pink buds open to pale pink fading to white. Grey-orange indumentum on leaf undersides. Zone 4b.

'Ken Janeck': Pink with beautiful indumentum on leaf undersides. Zone 5.

'Purple Passion': Incredible deep-purple buds open to a royal purple. Zone 4.

'Catawbiense Boursault': One of most common older rhododendrons around the region; magenta-pink flowers. Can grow to 10 feet and more over time. Zone 4.

'Capistrano'

Labrador tea, sometimes listed as Rhododendron groenlandicum

Rhus

staghorn sumac, sumac

Family: Anacardiaceae

Hardy to: zone 3

Bloom period: June

Growing requirements: Any soil, from pure sand to clay; good drainage. Full sun to part shade.

Height: 15 feet

Where best used: native and bird gardens, bank and hillside stabilization, fall colour

Propagation: suckers, cuttings, seeds

Problems: No serious pests or diseases, though deer will eat tips of new growth.

Notes: Dioecious species with striking fall colour. Excellent species for wildlife.

The staghorn sumac gets its common name from its branches, which look like velvety deer antlers. Interestingly, this family consists of some not-so-desirable species that were formerly classified as *Rhus* species, including poison ivy (now *Toxicodendron radicans*, formerly *R. radicans*), but the rhus we use as ornamentals are not toxic.

'Tiger Eyes' sumac

The common sumac (*R. typhina*) found throughout this region spreads from root suckers, and you'll often see thickets or colonies of the shrubs growing along roadsides. Adaptability is the sumac's middle name, as it's very cold hardy, grows in full sun to partial shade, and on just about any type of soil other than pure gravel or swampland. It has a striking, easily recognizable form, with a flat, spreading silhouette, pinnately compound leaves, and tight, cone-shaped spikes of fruit composed of many small, hairy, red berries. The plant has long been cherished for its fall foliage but has a variety of other uses. The bark, fruit, and foliage have been used for tanning hides, while the fruit is sometimes used to make a refreshing, lemonade-like drink. Many species of birds and other types of wildlife also enjoy the fruit, which is only found on female plants.

Although you need to be careful where you plant the common sumac because of its propensity to run, several better-behaved cultivars have been bred for their delicate foliage and remarkable fall colour display. If you have a hilly area that needs erosion control, a thicket of sumac will fit the bill nicely. The shrubs are also salt- and wind-tolerant, but do not do well in overly soggy soil.

Recommended species and cultivars

Rhus aromatica: The fragrant sumac gets its name from the lemon-like scent emitted from crushing its foliage and stems. 'Gro-Low' is an interesting cultivar that reaches only to about 24 inches in height but works well as a ground cover because it can spread as much as 8 feet in length. This species can be monoecious or dioecious.

R. typhina 'Tiger Eyes' (also seen as 'Bailtiger'): This well-behaved cultivar burst onto the gardening scene around 2006, and gardeners continue to rave about it. It's much smaller than the species and boasts chartreuse-gold foliage that turns spectacular red and orange shades in the fall.

R. glabra 'Laciniata' (also seen as *R. typhina* 'Laciniata'): The cutleaf sumac's background causes some confusion, but authorities agree that it is an all-female cultivar, so you will always get the stalks of red berries on your plant. Its cutleaf form makes it particularly attractive, and it has the fine fall colour of its parent plants.

sumac fruit

Rosa

rose

Family: Rosaceae

Hardy to: zone 3

Bloom period: spring to autumn frost

Growing requirements: rich, well drained soil; full sun to light shade

Height: 6 inches to 15 feet

Where best used: hedges, specimens, arbours and trellises

Propagation: cuttings, grafting, seed

Problems: Deer, aphids, blackspot, and rose sawfly—among other diseases and pests.

Notes: Rose hips are great feed for birds; very ornamental.

Roses are perhaps the most quintessential of garden plants, although they are not the easiest to grow or care for. I do not recommend hybrid teas or any other grafted roses to those who live in Atlantic Canada: grafted roses are most fragile at the graft union, are often marginally hardy and subject to a host of diseases, and require a lot of coddling to get them through.

If you can get a copy, I highly recommend Robert Osborne's book *Hardy Roses*, which goes into the detail for care that can't be included here. He also profiles dozens of roses suited to our climate, and he should know—as owner

'Topaz Jewel' rugosa hybrid

of Cornhill Nursery near Petitcodiac, New Brunswick, Bob grows a number of rose species and cultivars in his zone 4 garden. The Canadian Rose Society (www.canadianrosesociety. org) also lists dozens of roses according to zone-hardiness.

Roses will thrive best in full sun and rich, well-drained soil with plenty of organic matter worked into it. Many will tolerate a few hours of shade, but won't bloom as heavily as they do with 6–8 hours of sunlight.

Many of the species of roses or hybrids available now are quite resistant to various diseases. Blackspot, for example, can be a huge problem in red- or yellow-flowered roses, but breeders have been selecting for disease resistance in recent years and have made good inroads with some of their newer cultivars.

There are also insects that can be problematic for rose-fanciers. Aphids cluster around the tips of branches and on flower buds: these can be controlled by hosing them off with a stream of water. Rose sawflies spend the larval stage of their lives as voracious little green worms that can skeletonize rose leaves, but are controllable with insecticidal soap.

'Polareis' rugosa hybrid

Recommended species and cultivars

The world of roses is one of plentitude—there are choices in a whole range of sizes and flower colours, and you simply need to select according to your tastes. Two lines of hardy roses have been bred in Canada: the Explorer series and the Parkland series, which were developed by breeders at the Ottawa and Morden, Manitoba, research stations, respectively.

Explorer series: These are predominately pink- or red-flowered roses, with a couple of yellows. Look for 'Champlain' (deep red), 'J. P. Connell' (pale yellow, good fragrance), 'Henry Hudson' (white rugosa type, great fragrance), and 'John Davis,' a climber that reaches 8 feet and covers itself with brilliant pink flowers.

Parkland: These are particularly winter hardy and disease-resistant varieties bred in Manitoba. The cultivars include 'Morden Sunrise' (yellow-orange blend), 'Hope for Humanity' (deep red), 'Morden Snowbeauty' (pure white), and 'Adelaide Hoodless' (red).

Species roses: Certain rose species have been cultivated and hybridized for years, and include some desirable traits, such as unusual colour or high fragrance. These include:

Rosa spinosissima syn. *Rosa pimpinellifolia*: Although the burnet species roses' name is cumbersome no matter which you choose, these are delightful roses with delicate, fern-like foliage. Some, like 'Harison's Yellow' and 'Scotch Rose,' are once-flowering; 'Stanwell Perpetual,' as its name suggests, is a repeat bloomer.

R. gallica: Once-flowering but highly fragrant roses, including 'Charles de Milles' and the bicolour 'Rosa Mundi.'

R. rugosa: Sometimes called the saltwater rose because it is often seen growing along beaches. Extremely tolerant plants, very thorny, highly fragrant, some sucker a great deal. Many excellent hybrids: 'Topaz Jewel' is a pale yellow; 'Polareis' is white with pink edging; 'Rosarie de la Haie' is a rich carmine red. The 'Pavement' series is a low-growing, mildly suckering line designed for use in median and sidewalk plantings and includes some of the top-scented rugosas, such as 'Snow Pavement.'

Modern Shrub: This is a catch-all category and includes a variety of free-flowering and usually quite disease-resistant roses. Some of the more popular are 'Golden Wings' (single, yellow), 'Robusta' (single, deep red), 'Bonica' and 'Super Bonica' (pale pink, double, highly floriferous), and 'Sally Holms' (apricot-white).

Salix

willow

Family: Salicaceae
Hardy to: zone 2
Bloom period: spring catkins
Growing requirements: moist soil, full sun to partial shade
Height: 2–100 feet

Where best used: specimen tree or shrub, hedging, standard
Propagation: cuttings
Problems: A variety of diseases and pests plague some willows.
Notes: Huge variety of species and uses. Important to pollinators in spring.

For many of us, the weeping willow is the epitome of stately, graceful trees, with its pendulous branches that wave in the slightest wind. Few people in Atlantic Canada haven't celebrated the arrival of spring by picking pussy willows (stems of male catkins) to use in floral arrangements or wreaths. My earliest knowledge of willows was somewhat romanticized, as I had a miniature set of Blue Willow china when I was a child and was a bit disappointed to find out that the willow trees in our neighbourhood weren't that shade of blue. (The fable behind the china

weeping willow

tells the tale of two star-crossed lovers who would meet under a willow tree, and whom the gods turned into a pair of lovebirds so they would always be together.)

Between seventy-five and one hundred species are native to North America, including a significant number found in our region, although it can be confusing to identify some species in the wild because of their proclivity to hybridize. Even without hybridizing, the variety in species is astonishing, ranging from ground covers that never grow more than a couple of inches tall to those magnificent weeping willows that can live for hundreds of years.

Some of the willows have their drawbacks, including the fact that they can grow very quickly and be quite aggressive. Some areas ban the growing of golden weeping willow (*Salix alba* 'Tristis') in small communities and yards because of its aggressive root systems,

'Nishiki' (dappled) willow

a bee seeking nutrients on willow catkins

Salix alba: Golden weeping willow requires a large yard or else must be kept rigorously pruned to keep it under control. Its bright golden twigs in late February and early March are a harbinger of spring. Zone 2.

***S. elaeagnos* 'Angustifolia'**: The rosemary willow is a shrub growing to 10 feet tall and features silvery foliage that moves beautifully in the slightest breeze. Best pruned yearly in late winter to promote long, slender shoot growth. Zone 3.

***S. integra* 'Hakuro Nishiki'**: The Japanese dappled willow is the biggest thing to hit the willow business, a wonder of colourful foliage. Small green leaves splashed with white and accented with pink, on pink twigs, make this a delightful choice for a small yard. Shear it yearly to promote the brightest new growth. Excellent for hedging, specimen, and sometimes grown as a standard. Zone 3.

S. matsudana: The curly or corkscrew willow is a native of China grown for its interesting, twisted twigs, which are particularly attractive in winter. Good for smaller yards as its maximum height is 30 feet. Zone 4.

S. repens* var. *argentea: Creeping willow is quite delightfully different, growing only 2–3 feet tall and spreading to a maximum of 5–6 feet. Its foliage is silvery blue and rounded like mouse ears. Excellent as a ground cover or at the front of borders. Zone 4.

***S. purpurea* 'Nana'**: Dwarf arctic blue-leaf willow isn't so much dwarf as it is a medium-sized shrub. It has a mounded growth habit, to 7 feet tall and wide, and boasts purplish stems with blue-grey foliage. Shear yearly to keep it from getting leggy. Disease-resistant and sturdy. Zone 3.

which have been known to invade wells and septic systems in search of moisture. However, the willow is also famed for its uses in both conventional and herbal medicine as a source of salicin, the precursor of acetylsalicylic acid, better known as aspirin. It has also been the choice of wood for water dousing, and is used to make woven, living fences (wattling) as well as other types of woven twig sculpture.

With the exception of golden weeping willow, the species recommended here are smaller, shrubby types that work well in most garden settings. All are fairly disease-resistant, although some are susceptible to damage from deer feeding on shoots or voles feeding on roots or the bark of young branches.

Sambucus

elder, elderberry

Family: Caprifoliaceae

Hardy to: zone 3

Bloom period: Late spring–early summer. Berries persist until autumn or until birds consume them all.

Growing requirements: sun to light shade, moist soil

Height: 10–20 feet

Where best used: native plantings, bog gardens, specimen shrub

Propagation: cuttings, suckers, seed

Problems: No serious pests or diseases. Native form is stoloniferous so watch for suckering.

Notes: Attracts birds such as waxwings; edible fruit.

Those who promote new cultivars of plants are sometimes prone to hyperbole. I remember when 'Black Lace' *Sambucus* was released on the market; some advertising material proclaimed it was "almost like a Japanese maple!" I love this shrub, but it doesn't look anything like a Japanese maple, especially when it produces its clouds of pale pink flowers.

The elder genus includes the native shrub *S. canadensis*, which is curiously called the American elderberry rather than the Canadian elder. You have probably seen this plant or the red-berried elder, *S. racemosa*, growing wild throughout parts of Atlantic Canada.

Its foliage is pinnate, with each leaf composed of many smaller leaflets growing on either side of a central stem (pinnately compound). Flower clusters are composed of many white to pink florets, and these give way to small red or black berries, which are voraciously consumed by birds and other types of wildlife.

Until plant breeders got busy hybridizing elderberries, developing

'Black Lace' sambucus foliage and flowers

new foliage colours and leaf textures, I think many of us North American gardeners had a sort of "familiarity breeds contempt" attitude towards the shrub; it was so common in the wild that we scarcely saw it. Happily, that isn't the case now, and the various species and hybrids of elderberry are taking their rightful place in many gardens.

Elderberries prefer rich, moist soil, so if yours is a more average soil, add generous amounts of compost to the planting hole and mix more in with the soil before you bury the plant's roots. Elderberries have shallow root systems so mulch generously to keep the soil moist and protect the roots from excessive heat or cold, and water the plants regularly, especially during the first season while they're settling in.

Although the standard species of *Sambucus* are rated as hardy to zone 3, some cultivars may kill back in cold winters. They have somewhat brittle wood, so don't plant them where they will be subject to drifts of snow or piled snow from shovelling or plowing walks and driveways. You may wish to trim your shrubs back every spring, both to shape them and to remove branch tips that might be damaged by a late spring frost.

Sambucus canadensis: American elder is multi-stemmed and grows quickly, up to 12 feet. Cultivar 'Aurea' has golden foliage that holds its colour well throughout the summer, but should be pruned hard every spring to keep it vigorous. 'Variegata' has green foliaged edged in cream to yellow; may be hard to find but worth locating. Hardy to zone 3 or 4.

S. nigra: Black elder blooms in mid-spring, weeks ahead of other species, and doesn't sucker. Cultivar 'Aurea' holds its bright yellow leaf colour very well. (You'd think the breeders could find another name that indicates it has gold foliage!) 'Black Lace,' developed in England, has deep wine foliage that is finely cut and holds its colour all season long. The species can reach 20 feet and is hardy to zone 4; cultivars may be a little less hardy depending on winter conditions. Pruning these varieties will reduce the number of blooms or fruit clusters, but they are grown primarily for their fancy foliage.

S. racemosa: European red elder matures at 12 feet tall, will sucker. 'Plumosa' is a cultivar with finely serrated leaves; 'Plumosa Aurea' has similarly serrated foliage that starts out gold and fades to a medium green by midsummer. 'Sutherland Gold' is similar in appearance but holds its colour better, although it may burn in hot weather and doesn't seem to be as vigorous as other gold-leafed cultivars. Species hardy to zone 3; cultivars to zone 4.

waxwings feasting on native American elderberries

Spirea

Family: Rosaceae

Hardy to: zone 3

Bloom period: May–July (depending on cultivar)

Growing requirements: full sun to light shade, any soil except extremely wet

Height: 2–5 feet

Where best used: hedges, specimen plants, mixed borders

Propagation: cuttings; *S. japonica* may self-seed

Problems: Aphids; occasional diseases but overall very tough plants. Some cultivars don't bloom for very long.

Notes: Deer-resistant. Bees love them. Colourful foliage, good fall colour in some cultivars and species.

I confess to a bit of a love-hate relationship with spireas. I love the wild species, which were the first spireas I came to know. Those cultivars in my garden were all selected because of particularly interesting foliage, as opposed to flowers, although pollinators love them. I find that in late spring, far too many of the so-called bridal veil type spireas are in bloom around the region, and after a week or so of show, those plants are just uninteresting green leaves that don't bring much of anything to the garden.

'Lemon Princess' showing fall (red) and summer (gold-green) colour

However, many terrific spireas are on the market, most of them touted for their interesting foliage colour during the spring, summer, or fall. Some have attractive flowers in shades of pink or white, and it's fun to see the bees and butterflies flocking to those. Spireas are also easy-care plants with good deer resistance, and those are the features that carry the day for me where this genus of plants is concerned.

A nice feature of spireas is their versatility. I've seen hedges created of one of the taller, cascading forms like

'Shirobana' spirea often shows multiple colours in flowers

'Snowmound' or *S. x van houttei*, or lower mounding types like 'Goldflame.' In my garden, I've selected them to be outbursts of colourful foliage to contrast or harmonize with

lilies, daylilies, and other strong-coloured bloomers that can hold their own with the bright foliage of 'Neon Flash' or 'Lemon Princess.' I grow one cultivar, 'Tor,' for its spectacular autumn foliage and tidy growth habit. They will take full sun to partial shade and are tolerant of anything but absolutely soggy soil. If the bushy forms get straggly, just take the clippers or shears to them in early spring and give them a good haircut, and they'll usually rebound marvellously. With the cascading types like 'Snowmound' or bridalwreath, thin out the branches like you would extra canes on a rosebush.

For those of us who enjoy getting to know our native plants, we have several choices, although they are not used as horticultural plants: *S. alba*, the meadow-sweet or hardhack, has white flowers; *S. tomentosa*, steeplebush, has rose pink flowers. Both tend to be found in moist, acid soils, often along roadside ditches or beside streams and marshy sites.

In terms of ornamental cultivars, there are dozens, and I do mean dozens. It can get confusing, especially since there are a number of cultivars with 'Gold' in their names. If you're unsure of which spirea you want, take a photograph with you to the nursery for help.

Recommended species and cultivars

'Crispa': A variety unlike the many other forms of spirea because of its deeply serrated foliage that is tinged red as it emerges. Flowers are a rich hot pink and 'Crispa' is a butterfly magnet that reblooms if deadheaded.

'Goldflame': Popular cultivar with bronze spring foliage that mellows to pale gold and finally to green. Pink flowers.

'Magic Carpet': Very low-growing (to 18 inches) with orange-red spring foliage that matures to gold.

'Lemon Princess': A true gold-foliaged cultivar that I grow only for the foliage. I had to look up the flower colour (pink) as I have been known to clip them off before they appear.

'Neon Flash': Reddish new growth, matures to deep green, with rose-red flowers.

'Shirobana': Sometimes labelled 'Shibori,' this unique cultivar can have white, pale pink, and richer pink flowers all on the same shrub.

Spirea betulifolia **'Tor':** Birch-leaf spirea has rounder leaves than most species, and pristine clusters of white flowers. The foliage turns a riot of reds, roses, and golds in autumn.

S. nipponica **'Snowmound':** If you want a high-quality, bridalwreath-type variety, this is one of your best choices, far superior to the original bridalwreath spirea, *S. prunifolia*.

Syringa

Family: Oleaceae

Hardy to: zone 2

Bloom period: mid-spring to early summer; repeat bloom on some types

Growing requirements: full sun, good drainage, average soil that is slightly acid to slightly alkaline

Height: 2–12 feet

Where best used: borders, hedges, specimen plants

Propagation: cuttings, suckers

Problems: powdery mildew, leaf spot, lilac blight

Notes: Butterflies, bees, and hummingbirds love lilacs.

Late spring always brings a heady fragrance to the air as the lilacs open their blossoms to the great delight of hummingbirds, butterflies, and human beings. Thanks to the work of breeders around the world, lilacs are even more popular today than they have been in days past.

Whether you have a large rural property or a small condo with limited yard space, there's a lilac for you. Breeders have developed dwarf varieties that grow no more than a couple of feet tall, and these are also sometimes grafted or pruned to create a standard which some gardeners find especially attractive.

With lilacs, it really is all about the flowers; the shrubs are somewhat nondescript once blooming is complete, so you'll want to plant them in a

Preston lilac 'Miss Canada'

mixed border, or else underplant them with bulbs and perennials to increase the season of interest. We have a delightful young bicoloured lilac, 'Sensation,' which we underplant with spring bulbs, pulmonaria, and hosta. The bulbs bloom before the shrub leafs out, and the attractive foliage of the two perennials look great until well into fall.

Often we see overgrown lilac bushes, towering 15 feet in the air with a cluster of flowers only on the top. Although it takes time, these can be rejuvenated. The general recommendation is to remove a third of the suckers and old stems branches each year until you have a manageable-sized shrub of a pleasing shape. Some gardeners will cut

'Beauty of Moscow'

old overgrown shrubs drastically, to about a foot high, and then thin out subsequent new growth to select a few strong stems. Be aware that it can take three years or longer before a shrub begins to flower after such treatment.

Lilacs are susceptible to a bacterial blight (*Pseudomonas syringae*), sometimes known as shoot or blossom blight. All types of lilacs are susceptible and researchers believe white-flowered varieties are the most susceptible. Symptoms include spots on leaves and stems, with increased infection resulting in blackening of the tissues, dropped leaves, and shoot wilt. The disease is most present in plants that have been stressed by improper fertilization, drought conditions, or wounds to bark by pruning or animal and insect damage. Many cultivars are resistant to infection by the pathogen, but if you have a plant with blight problems, prune out the infected area to at least 8 inches below any signs of spots or dieback, and burn or otherwise destroy the prunings. To prevent the spread of disease to healthy plants, remember to sterilize your tools after pruning any infected plant.

What you choose for species and hybrids depends on your garden size and your preference in colour and flower form. Lilacs come in a host of shades from white and cream to pink, mauve, various shades of purple, and even one bicolour! If you have a small garden, don't worry: there are compact varieties, including the dwarf Korean lilac ('Palibin') and 'Miss Kim,' neither of which get more than a few feet tall.

No discussion about lilacs in Canada is complete without mentioning Isabella Preston (1881–1965), the first Canadian woman to work as a plant hybridizer. Miss Preston worked at the Central Experimental Farm in Ottawa for many years and developed a number of hybrids, including the lilacs that bear her name. Preston lilacs are extremely winter hardy, and bloom later than other species with drooping clusters of fragrant blossoms. They tend to grow to a substantial sized shrub (10–12 feet high and

Recommended cultivars

'Sensation': A bicolour with white edging on its red-purple blossoms.

'Beauty of Moscow': Double white, with pink buds.

'Primrose': Softly yellow buds opening to creamy flowers tinted with pale yellow.

'Katherine Havemeyer': Old-fashioned variety; lavender pink and very heavy bloom.

Preston lilac cultivars:

'Miss Canada': red buds open to hot pink flowers.

'Donald Wyman': deep pink flowers.

'Isabella': highly fragrant pink.

'Nocturne': deep lilac-coloured flowers.

Why won't my lilac bloom?

Although given the right conditions, lilacs are pretty easy and rewarding shrubs, they can be cantankerous if they're not happy. Here are the most common reasons for non-flowering lilacs:

'Sensation' bicolour lilac

1. The plant isn't mature enough. It can take as long as five years for a young lilac to begin flowering after you plant it. Lilacs need to develop strong root systems, and while they may have started that in a container, they still need time to settle in once planted out. Patience is a virtue with lilacs.

2. Not enough sun. Site your lilacs where they will get a minimum of six hours of sunlight, and more if possible.

3. Too much fertilizer. Lilacs don't need a lot of fertilizer—in fact many gardeners never fertilize their lilacs, and often we see old varieties growing around abandoned homesteads, where they have had no care for years. If you plant your lilacs near a lawn, which you feed with a high-nitrogen fertilizer to promote vegetative growth, you may find that your shrubs have great foliage but no flowers. In this case you'll have to either move the lilac or stop fertilizing the lawn near it. A little compost shovelled around the base of your plant in the spring is sufficient fertilizer.

4. Soil is too dry. Lilacs like a generous amount of water, but don't want soggy feet. If it's a dry summer, mulch well around your plant's roots, and water it well at least once a week.

5. Incorrect pruning. Lilacs form next year's flowers after they finish blooming this year, and if you wait too long to deadhead or prune your plant, you may be cutting off the flower buds. If you want to deadhead, do so immediately after the flowers are past and before seeds begin to develop.

6. Wrong soil acidity (pH). Lilacs are a bit picky about soil acidity—if it's below 6 on the pH scale, it's too acid to suit them and they won't flower. Generally a soil that is slightly acid to a little bit alkaline is suitable. If none of the other factors are a problem, have a soil test done, and follow the lab recommendations to amend your soil and raise its pH.

wide) but seldom produce suckers. Numerous Preston hybrids are available, and while some were developed by later breeders using Preston's original crosses, they are always labelled as *Syringa* x *prestoniae* or Preston lilacs –a fitting legacy for a woman who pioneered horticulture in this country.

For those who want something a little different and later blooming, look for the Japanese tree lilac, *Syringa reticulata* 'Ivory Silk.' This species makes a small tree (to 25 feet) with a rounded shape, and covers itself with cream or white fragrant flowers. It is hardy to zone 3 and resistant to mildew and other problems that afflict the more common species.

Thuja occidentalis

arborvitae, thuja, eastern white cedar

Family: Cupressaceae

Hardy to: zone 3

Bloom period: not significant

Growing requirements: full sun

Height: varies with species and cultivar

Where best used: hedges, specimen shrubs, winter interest, wildlife gardening

Propagation: cuttings or seed

Problems: Some pests including bagworm and spider mites. Deer find some types delicious.

Notes: Birds like to nest in them and use cones as source of food.

It may scandalize some readers to know that one of the first things I did when we moved to our property was to rip out five nondescript *Thujas* (probably 'Emerald') and plant other species instead. My dislike for some of the arborvitae stems from the fact that several of them tend to be overused in commercial and home landscape plantings, and rank up there with Norway maples as being the most uninteresting plants sold at every big-box store in the country. That being said, some of my favourite conifers are cultivars of *Thuja*, but all are selections that feature interesting foliage colour.

'Sunkist' showing winter foliage

Apparently, the common name arborvitae (tree of life) was given to the tree by explorer Jacques Cartier, as the species *T. occidentalis* (eastern white cedar) was one of the plants eaten to treat scurvy. *Roland's Flora* claims that this was the first North American tree to be grown in Europe, brought back to Paris by an explorer to the New World before 1553. Learning these bits of history improved my opinion of this tree, which is native in parts of Atlantic Canada although not overly common in the wild. It is often (and mistakenly) called cedar, but is not a true cedar (*Cedrus*, various species). True cedars have needles rather than scaly foliage, and are not hardy in our region. The tree that we value for its fragrant wood used in furniture making, western red cedar, is actually *Thuja plicata*. (Don't you love plant taxonomy?)

In its natural form, *T. occidentalis* forms a tree up to 60 feet tall, although it more frequently grows to half that in cultivated situations. There are dozens of cultivars, and in the words of Michael Dirr, "Some of worth, about 90 percent deserving of trash heap status." He does note that there are some fine dwarf forms valued by collectors and good for landscapes and alpine gardening.

Thujas require full sun and a well-drained but moist soil. Planted in shade, these trees and shrubs will get spindly and ugly looking; in too dry soil they are apt to turn brown.

Smaller varieties are subject to breakage from snow buildup, so you may wish to protect your arborvitae over the winter. Although many sources note that arborvitae are susceptible to winter burn, the varieties that I grow seem quite tolerant of the harsh winds that blast in off the Bay of Fundy.

Unfortunately, although birds love to nest in them and enjoy their cones as a source of winter food, deer also regard most arborvitae as a salad buffet, so you may want to plant something else if they're a problem in your area.

Recommended cultivars

'Nigra': Good choice for hedging, keeps its dark green colour throughout the winter.

'Sherwood Frost': An interesting shrub, maturing to 6 feet, with white tips to its foliage. Especially showy in spring and autumn. Hardy to zone 4.

'Rheingold': A globe-shaped variety, with distinctly coloured foliage. In the spring, new growth flushes gold and bright, almost lime, green; through autumn and winter it bronzes to copper or even orange, and is an excellent winter-interest shrub. Matures at 5 feet wide and tall; hardy to zone 4.

'Sunkist': A better golden-foliaged choice than 'Golden Globe' because it holds its golden colour throughout the summer, flushing to bronze in the winter. Height 4–8 feet. Hardy to zone 4.

Thujopsis

Related to *Thuja* is the unique and interesting *Thujopsis*, which is sometimes called false or Hiba arborvitae but more often simply referred to by its genus name. There is only one species in this genus, *T. dolobrata*, although there are apparently two varieties that are slightly different morphologically. Commonly planted around temples in Japan, where it

Thujopsis *branch with cones*

is native, it's perhaps best described as looking like a swollen *Thuja*: its foliage is glossy and scaly like an arborvitae, but larger in size and almost braid-like in texture.

I had to have one because it is so unusual, even primitive, looking. It is slow-growing but doing well in my zone 5 garden. *Thujopsis* will grow in sun to partial shade, likes a moist, compost-rich soil that is a bit acid in pH, and should be protected from harsh winter winds. It has a pyramidal shape when well grown. In winter, the foliage can take on tints of bronze and copper-red.

Viburnum

Family: Adoxaceae (formerly Caprifoliaceae)
Hardy to: varies with species
Bloom period: mid-spring to midsummer
Growing requirements: sun to partial shade; rich, moist, but well-draining soil
Height: varies with species

Where best used: bird gardens, fall colour, fragrance gardens, specimen plantings
Propagation: seed or cuttings
Problems: A variety of insects can be problems, including viburnum leaf beetle and aphids.
Notes: Many species have showy fruit. Good bird plants.

V. *'Mariesii'*

One of my earlier wild-botany memories is of seeing the witherod, or wild raisin (*V. nudum* var. *cassinoides*), growing in the woodlands on Mount Scio in St. John's, Newfoundland. My father always told me that the berries, which were white, then pink, and then blue, were poisonous, so I admired them from afar but never touched them. To this day, the witherod is an important shrub in my gardening lexicon and several of them grow on our property.

However, there are so many delightful and choice viburnums that you couldn't expect me to have just one species! In late spring and early summer, the heady fragrance from several scented viburnums wafts in my office window. The elegant, pagoda-like structure of 'Mariesii' *V. plicatum* var. *tomentosum* delights me all year long. The highbush cranberry (*V. trilobum*) in our back garden provides us with a visual feast of flowers, fruit, and autumn foliage colour, just as it provides our feathered friends with a literal feast well into winter.

With all this versatility in characteristics, as well as an impressive versatility in tolerance for growth conditions, and a huge range of species and cultivars, it's easy to see why viburnums are so popular as shrubs and small trees, especially in small city gardens with limited space. Because there are so many choices for gardeners, books can be written on viburnums (and have been, including a wonderful one by Michael Dirr). Viburnums can be great choices whether you want native species to encourage birds and other wildlife, or more cultivated varieties with fragrant or otherwise highly appealing flowers. Dirr says "a garden without a viburnum is akin to life without music and art," and I agree with him.

For the most part, the secret to success with viburnums is picking the right species or cultivar for your hardiness zone. The North American natives are especially tolerant of all kinds of conditions, and for the most part, all the species we can grow here are easy to care for. Give them good air circulation, moderately fertile, moist soil with good drainage and they'll perform quite happily with minimal disease problems. The Asian species, which include the fragrant varieties, tend to be less hardy, usually to zone 5 only with winter protection.

Several pests affect viburnums, with aphids being quite common on a number of species. An introduced pest from outside North America, the viburnum leaf beetle, is showing up in our region and is particularly problematic on the highly overused snowball bush, *V. opulus*, which can be completely

'Chicago Luster' arrowwood viburnum showing berries and fall foliage colour

closeup of 'Summer Snowflake' flowers

Native to North America:

Viburnum nudum var. *cassinoides*: Common names include witherod, wild raisin, swamp viburnum. Native, with bright coloured berries, good fall colour. Height is usually 5–6 feet. Zone 3.

V. dentatum: Native arrowwood viburnum has brilliant blue berries, pink-orange fall colour. 'Chicago Luster' is a particularly attractive cultivar with glossy foliage. Height: 6–8 feet. Zone 2.

V. lantana: Wayfaring tree has creamy white flowers, black berries. 15 feet. Zone 3.

V. trilobum: Highbush cranberry (not related to true cranberries), excellent fall colour, brilliant red berries loved by birds. Height: 10 feet. Zone 2.

Fragrant flowers:

V. carlesii: Korean spice viburnum gloriously fragrant. Height: 8 feet. Zone 4 with wind protection.

V. x burkwoodii: Very fragrant hybrids, with varieties that include 'Anne Russell' and 'Mohawk.' Height 8–10 feet. Zone 4 if sheltered from cold wind.

V x juddii: Judd viburnum highly fragrant. Height 6–8 feet. Zone 4.

Special recommendations:

V. plicatum var. *tomentosum*: The gorgeous doublefile viburnum, with horizontal branches, pure white flowers, black fruit loved by birds. Cultivars include 'Mariesii' and 'Summer Snowflake.' Height: 8–10 feet. Zone 5.

V. sargentii 'Onondaga': Showy lacecap flowers with red fertile flowers, white fertile flowers, gorgeous red-tinged foliage. Height: 8–10 feet. Zone 3.

berries of witherod or wild raisin

defoliated by the pest. This beetle was in our highbush cranberry one year, but I ignored them and birds took care of them quite nicely. For those who aren't so passive in dealing with pests, applying minimally toxic treatments, such as horticultural oil or insecticidal soap, can be effective in curbing the ravages of these beetles.

flowerhead of a fragrant viburnum

Weigela

weigela

Family: Caprifoliaceae
Hardy to: zone 3–4 (depending on cultivar)
Bloom period: late spring to early summer
Growing requirements: sun to light shade; compost-rich, moist, but well-drained soil
Height: 2–10 feet

Where best used: specimen shrub, hedges, mixed borders
Propagation: cuttings
Problems: No serious pests or diseases.
Notes: Hummingbirds and other pollinators love them.

No doubt the first thing we need to say about weigelas is how to pronounce their genus name, which also happens to be their common name. Horticulturists will probably say this is one of the most mispronounced plant names out there. The correct pronunciation is "why JEE lah."

Weigela is a wonderful shrub that is currently enjoying a bit of a renaissance as plant breeders turn their attention to developing new forms. I've always liked this plant for its cascading shade and the way it utterly smothers itself in flowers during its main bloom period, which usually begins in mid-June and continues for several weeks. Some cultivars will bloom sporadically throughout the summer, and

old-fashioned floriferous variety

their trumpet-shaped flowers are always a magnet for hummingbirds and other pollinators.

Generally speaking, weigelas are one of the easiest shrubs to grow: they like sun, moist but well-drained soil amended with compost, and they require little pruning other than to trim out deadwood. If you do want to shape them, prune right after flowering so that none of the next season's flower buds are destroyed.

Weigelas are often planted as specimen shrubs, but in earlier years this was a bit of a drawback because once finished with bloom, they are unremarkable shrubs, with ordinary green leaves and no fall colour. However, one of the traits that breeders have been selecting for has been colourful foliage: you can now find cultivars with wine, gold, or bicolour

'French Lace'

Recommended cultivars

'Bristol Ruby': Popular old variety with deep red flowers. Grows to 7 feet tall. Zone 5.

'Tango': Upright growth habit (2 feet at maturity), purple flushed green foliage, cherry-red flowers. Zone 3.

'Variegata': One of the variegated-leaf varieties, with light pink flowers and green-and-white foliage. Zone 5.

'Wine and Roses' (a.k.a. 'Alexandra'): Deep purple foliage, rose-purple flowers, grows to 5 feet. Zone 4.

'French Lace': A striking, upright variety (to 6 feet) with gold-and-green variegated foliage and dark red flowers. In my garden, the cultivar is a popular pupating site for monarch caterpillars to rest before turning into butterflies. Zone 4.

'Briant Rubidor': Another eye-catching variety with golden foliage and ruby-red flowers. Very showy. 6 feet tall. Zone 5.

'My Monet': A mutant (or sport) of 'Tango' and is called the first dwarf variegated weigela. It has a very compact growth habit, grows to under 24 inches and has green leaves variegated with white and tinged with pink, similar to the 'Nishiki' dappled willow. Flowers are medium pink but it's the foliage that sells this variety. Plant in partial shade to prevent browning of leaf margins. Zone 4.

(green and gold or green and white) leaves. Additionally, a number of cultivars have been developed that are more compact in size, making them ideal for mixed borders or low hedges and perfect for the gardener with a small property.

Dozens of weigela cultivars are available, including some bred at the agriculture research station in Ottawa by Felicitas Svejda and named after dance steps, including 'Tango,' 'Rumba,' 'Samba,' and 'Polka.' These and most other cultivars available are hybrids derived from *W. florida*, although there is one unique exception. *W. middendorffiana*, the Middendorf weigela, is a compact species with unique yellow flowers accented with orange speckles on the lower petals. It blooms a little earlier than do the *W. florida* hybrids and is hardy to zone 4 with protection from harsh wind.

PLANTING A POLLINATOR-FRIENDLY GARDEN

One of the happiest events of spring is when I first notice bees—native bumblebees, as well as the imported but so-useful honeybees—tumbling around in the centres of flowers, collecting nectar to bring back to their hives and nests. At the same time as these gentle creatures are feeding themselves, they are helping to feed other species, including humans, as they pollinate flowers that will turn into food crops.

Bees are part of an important group of creatures known as pollinators, which include butterflies, wasps, some species of flies and beetles, and certain bat and bird species. Without pollinators, many plant species, including many vital food crops, will not set fruit or seed. With concerns over food security and supplies generating more and more attention, there has also been a rising voice of concern over pollinator populations in recent years. Changes to local climates, eradication of natural habitat, overuse of pesticides and other agrichemicals, introduction of sterile hybrids—all are factors thought to be contributing to a drop in bee populations. What can we as gardeners do to help pollinators?

bee on inula blossom

- Don't use pesticides on your lawn or garden. Even so-called "organic" pesticides can be particularly lethal to bees.
- Plant pollinator-friendly species, including native and heritage varieties.
- Plant a wide variety of blooming plants so as to have bloom from spring until late autumn. Red, purple, orange, and blue are particularly attractive colours for many pollinators.
- Create sheltered locations, such as no-mow areas or "wild" spots, where pollinators may rest and nest.
- Urge politicians to ban pesticides for cosmetic use.
- Encourage schools, churches, and other community groups to create pollinator-friendly gardens.

Several good sites for more information include the Xerces Society for Invertebrate Conservation (www.xerces.org) and the Canadian Wildlife Federation's Wild About Gardening site (www.wildaboutgardening.org).

For a list of some recommended plants for attracting pollinators to your garden, please see Appendix B, page 242.

Perennials

DESIGN IN THE GARDEN

I always make it clear to other gardeners that I'm a plant person, not a designer or landscaper. I describe my own garden as ruthlessly eclectic, because it doesn't adhere to any particular style of planting other than to have lots of plants. Some might call it a cottage garden, others a series of mixed borders, as trees, shrubs, perennials, herbs, ornamental grasses, some annuals, and even the occasional vegetable are planted everywhere. Each year I sneak back a little bit more of the grass that my long-suffering spouse calls the lawn, planting new borders or adding size to already-existing beds.

There *is* some rhyme and reason to where I locate new plants around our property. I try to match them to the site as much as possible, so shade-lovers don't get planted in a full-sun location, and drought-tolerant plants aren't struggling to survive in the areas that stay wet throughout the summer. Those that are marginally hardy get tucked away in the most sheltered spots, not planted out where the full ravages of our winds can cause damage to tender stems or branches.

Actaea 'Black Negligee,' Monarda 'Raspberry Wine,' and Hemerocallis 'El Desperado' in a perennial bed

One of the most important things to remember when selecting a new plant, be it a shrub, perennial, or tree, is to learn how large it will be at maturity. Those with small yards or gardens can't plant trees that mature at a hundred feet or perennials that would take over the lawn due to their spreading skills. That lovely shrub you purchased in a one-gallon pot may be just the right size now, but in five years' time when it's ten feet tall and wide, crowding out other plants, you'll feel bad when you have to cut it down or dig it out.

Achillea

yarrow, all-heal

Family: Asteraceae
Hardy to: zone 2–3
Bloom period: late spring to autumn
Growing requirements: full sun, average but well-drained soil
Height: 1–3 feet

Where best used: sunny borders, pollinator gardens, cutting gardens
Propagation: division in spring; some will self-seed
Problems: powdery mildew an occasional problem
Notes: Beloved by pollinators. Drought-tolerant and deer-resistant.

I love yarrow, but most of them hate my gardening conditions. This is because, with one or two exceptions, they like better drainage than I can provide in much of my garden. Being a stubborn gardener, however, I celebrate the ones that grow well for me, buy inexpensive pots of the more finicky types, treat them as annuals, and hope for the best. Interestingly, the wild, weedy varieties manage to grow in my garden without any difficulty.

Yarrows originated in Europe, but *A. millefolium* is a common wild plant, having escaped from gardens years ago and

'Paprika'

spread across the region. Normally, the wild plants have white blossoms, more occasionally pink or magenta. Achillea's name comes from the Greek mythological warrior Achilles, whose use of the plant as a medicinal herb is documented in Homer's epic poem the *Iliad*.

Full sun and average, even poor, garden soil with excellent drainage is the secret to success with most of the yarrows. Too much moisture will cause them to rot off at the roots, especially where there is winter wet; too rich a soil makes them prone to sprawling. Where they are happy, they will spread out, but you will need to divide them regularly to keep them healthy, as the centre of the clump tends to die out after two or three years.

Yarrows are now available in a wide range of bloom colours, some of which fade as the flowers mature. The flat-topped heads of tiny, daisy-like florets are highly desirable to

yarrow, all-heal

Achillea 'Gold Plate'

butterflies and bees, while their pungently scented foliage keeps deer and rabbits from bothering them. Deadheading the spent flowers will help to extend the bloom period. Aside from their drainage needs, yarrows are a trouble-free perennial with a long bloom period, and can be a star in a butterfly garden.

Recommended species and cultivars

Achillea filipendulina: Fern leaf yarrow is the tallest of the species, reaching 5 feet in ideal conditions. I've had 'Gold Plate,' a variety with mustard-yellow flowers, in a better-drained site of my garden for a number of years, and it has always returned faithfully.

A. millefolium: This species is known as common yarrow, but there is nothing common about some of the marvellously coloured cultivars and hybrids available. There's a veritable rainbow of shades from the soft peaches, pinks, and yellows of 'Summer Pastels Group' to the rich cherry of 'Cerise Queen' to the deep copper-orange of 'Terra Cotta.' Flowers generally fade in colour as they mature but remain attractive for weeks.

A. ptarmica: This species has some amusing common names, including goose tongue, brideflower, sneezewort (which is also a common name for *Helenium*), and my favourite, bastard pellitory. Foliage is lance-like with serrated edges, and the flower heads are white. 'The Pearl' is a popular variety with white, button-like double flowers. This variety can be dried and used in cut flower arrangements.

A. siberica: Siberian yarrow is more tolerant of moist soil than other species. Its foliage is different from the common yarrow, with strap-like, glossy green leaves arranged around the central stem. Flower heads are compact, with each floret larger than those of *A. millefolium* cultivars. Pink blossoms fade to nearly white as the season progresses.

A. tomentosa: Woolly yarrow is a low-growing species useful as a ground cover, with corymbs of small, yellow flowers and fuzzy, aromatic foliage.

Aconitum

wolfsbane, devil's helmet, blue aconite

Family: Ranunculaceae
Hardy to: zone 2
Bloom period: June–September
Growing requirements: damp soil, sun to partial shade
Height: 24–60 inches
Where best used: back of border, mixed borders

Propagation: division of tubers in early spring; seed
Problems: Occasional fungal diseases such as stem blight and powdery mildew.
Notes: Deer-resistant. All parts of monkshood plants are extremely toxic.

One of the oddities of common plant names is that you'll often see both a holy and a hellish common name attributed to a plant. So it is with *Aconitum*, which is variously known as monkshood or devil's helmet. These names stem from the fact that the flowers look something like the cowl of a friar's robe, and apparently also resemble a helmet favoured by old Beelzebub.

Belonging to the Ranunculaceae or buttercup family, monkshood is related to hellebore, trollius (globeflowers), clematis, delphinium, and larkspur, as well as the common buttercup. Gardeners in warmer climates who have difficulties growing the tall, stately delphinium find that the more heat-tolerant monkshood makes a very satisfactory substitute for back-of-border planting.

When we first moved to our property in Scots Bay, we had no idea what was planted in the few gardens around the yard, and were a bit puzzled when one of the first plants to emerge in spring showed bright green, lacy foliage. A trip down the road to an abandoned farmstead showed us hundreds of similar plants growing around the remains of the house foundation, along with the ever-familiar ditch lilies (*Hemerocallis fulva*), and it wasn't long before the plants had grown enough to make a positive identification. I've since seen patches of monkshood growing in ditches and meadows throughout the Annapolis Valley, and the drifts of deep blue or blue-and-white flowers are extremely attractive.

Monkshood does best in at least six hours of sun a day; plants growing in shady sites will require staking because they are inclined to sprawl and get leggy. They are very happy in our clay soil, which holds moisture—if your soil is lighter and drier, make sure to mulch to keep the plants happy, especially if they're in full sun. You may need to stake your plants if they're in an open site where wind can get at them, because they often grow so tall that their stems

'Stainless Steel'

topple in windy conditions. Another option is to shear the plants back by about one-third their height in mid-spring. This will cause them to produce fresh growth that is bushier, although they may also be slower in flowering.

Divide clumps in early spring before they have grown more than an inch or two in height, and don't be surprised if they don't bloom again for a couple of years after transplanting. Some species will self-seed but not prodigiously; you can easily weed out or transplant seedlings to another site, though it will also take several years of growing before they're mature enough to flower.

When the first round of blooms on your monkshood has finished (particularly if you didn't cut them back in the spring), don't let the plants go to seed. Instead, cut them back to about six inches tall: this will stimulate the plant to sprout new foliage and have a second set of flowers in late summer or early fall, providing a cool blue addition to the usual hot colours of the later growing season.

Like many of its Ranunculaceae relatives, monkshood is highly toxic in all its parts and should never be consumed. It's recommended that you wear gloves when handling the plants to prevent skin irritation or possible absorption of toxins through cuts. The good news is that fatal poisonings, although possible, are extremely rare, and more a facet of history or literature (Leopold Bloom's father died of aconite poisoning in James Joyce's *Ulysses*). The plants are also resistant to deer and other wildlife.

Recommended species and cultivars

Aconitum napellus: The most common species grown, with purple-blue or blue-and-white flowers.

A. x 'Stainless Steel': A striking cultivar with steely-blue and white flowers.

A. napellus 'Carneum': You may have to stretch your imagination to see this variety's flowers as red or pink (as the name suggests), but they are a reddish-cream colour and have done well in my garden.

A. carmichaelii: The fall-flowering monkshood, blooming from September into October. Don't bother to cut this variety back as it will not have time to rebloom before a killing frost.

A. lamarckii: Yellow monkshood blooms earlier (mid-June to July) but is not as tall or showy as *A. napellus* or *A. carmichaelii*.

What to do with tall perennials

The blooming of delphinium in my garden invariably coincides with at least one wind or rainstorm. Peonies, with their huge flower heads, are always candidates for being victimized by such weather, and since they bloom in my garden at the same time as the delphinium, it's a sure bet they too will be knocked down.

Other perennials that can be affected by wind and rain include coneflowers (*Echinacea*), monkshood (*Aconitum*), foxgloves (*Digitalis*), tall rudbeckia, sea hollies (*Eryngium*), tall phlox, tall bellflowers, and fall blooming asters. Some tall species have sturdy stems that will withstand normal rain and wind, but in Atlantic Canada we are often subject to the end of hurricanes in late summer and early autumn, and even the strongest plant will collapse under sustained gale-force winds.

We can try several things to protect our plants from weather ravages. With some species, cutting them back by one-third to one-half their height in mid- to late spring will cause them to grow up bushier and shorter in height. You can do this with asters, delphinium, phlox, aconitum, and other late-season perennials; they will likely bloom later, but their shorter stalks should also be better able to withstand the weather. Don't try this with digitalis, poppies, or sea holly, however, as they flower from basal rosettes of leaves, and cutting off the flowering stalk may mean no blooms at all.

Another option is to stake your plants so they have some support to hold them upright. Ideally, you should set stakes before the plants get too tall. Stakes can be made of wood, plastic, bamboo, steel, or other metals, although if you need to stake a lot of plants it can be expensive to buy fancy metal or plastic-clad stakes. My own choice is to use bamboo stakes, which come in a variety of sizes and tend to be easy to work with.

Stakes should be about a foot taller than the perennial before being set into the ground. Set your stake so that it will be lower than the top of your plant. Avoid damaging the perennial's roots by setting stakes just beyond the diameter of the plant's foliage. Drive the stake straight down at least six inches, and then secure the plant to the stake using strips of pantyhose, plant tie, or other material that won't damage the plant's stem or foliage. A special self-sealing plant tie made of Velcro is especially useful; it holds to itself without needing to be tied to the stake and is reusable for several years.

For peonies, you may wish to buy specially designed peony rings to hold your plants and their heavy flowers off the ground. I've also bought long (18–30 inch), inexpensive bungee cords, which I carefully wrap around the plant and hook onto a sturdy plant stake. You need to use long cords, especially if you have large peonies, because too short a cord will bunch the plant up too much, crowding the foliage and buds and setting up conditions for fungal disease such as botrytis.

Actaea

snakeroot, cohosh, bugbane

Family: Ranunculaceae

Hardy to: zone 4

Bloom period: late summer–early autumn

Growing requirements: moist soil, sun to partial shade

Height: 3–6 feet, including flower spike

Where best used: mixed borders, foliage plant, late-bloomer

Propagation: seed (division not recommended)

Problems: No serious pests or diseases.

Notes: Keep well mulched in drier soils and full sun.

It's daunting enough for most of us to wrap our tongues around the botanical name of a particular plant, especially if that name is nothing like the common name. Roses, for example, are easy to deal with, as their genus is *Rosa;* so we only need to learn the various species names, such as *R. rugosa, R. virginiana, R. hugonis*, and so on. But then there are plants with far more cumbersome botanical names, such as the ostrich or fiddlehead fern—now known as *Matteucia struthiopteris.* I say, "now known" because this plant's botanical name was formerly *Pteris pennysylvanica.* Plants get renamed when taxonomists and other researchers determine that a plant's characteristics align it more closely with one family than with another, a task made easier today by DNA typing.

flowers on 'Black Negligee'

So it is with *Actaea*, a handsome plant genus with several ornamental species, and known by a variety of common names, including snakeroot, cohosh, baneberry, and bugbane. This genus was formerly known as *Cimicifuga*, and you will still see references to that name in many books, on plant labels, and on websites. Only the horto-snobs will chastise you for using *Cimicifuga* rather than *Actaea*. I certainly won't.

Whatever you want to call it, bugbane is a beautiful plant in bloom or out. Its lacy, fern-like foliage seems oblivious to depredation by deer, slugs, or other pests, and the purple-leafed varieties are especially handsome. Bugbanes are slow-growing and seldom need to be divided; if you want more plants the best way to get them is to sow seeds of non-sterile varieties. I have divided mine successfully early in the spring and by replanting in very moist soil, but they do tend to sulk for the rest of that growing season.

Red (*A. rubra*) and white (*A. alba*) baneberries grow wild in parts of Atlantic Canada, including Nova Scotia and New Brunswick. While these are beautiful plants, their fruit is not edible and all parts of the plant can cause gastrointestinal upset if consumed. Additionally, the plants can cause skin irritations in some people, so wear gloves when handling any *Actaea* species.

foliage of 'Black Negligee'

Actaea flowers in late summer, which is another reason to incorporate this long-lived perennial into your plantings. Beginning in mid- to late August, they produce tall spikes composed of many white or pink florets. Some cultivars have deep purple stems and flower spikes, providing even more contrast to the fragrant, bee-attracting flowers. Some species will produce berries, which are harmless to birds but toxic to humans and other mammals.

Although most books and plant tags will note that actaea can be grown in sunny or shady spots, note that if the site is too deeply shaded, your plant won't flower as profusely. Actaea does well in clay provided it doesn't dry out, but no matter what sort of soil you have, make sure you mulch

baldfaced wasp on 'Pink Spike'

around your plants. If they get too dry, they will develop brown edges to their foliage.

With cultivars, you will find one or two with green foliage, but the popular cultivars include a variety of purple- to nearly black-foliaged choices, each claiming to be the darkest in colour. Of the selections I grow, 'Black Negligee' appears to have the deepest colour; the foliage *is* almost black. Others to look for include 'Atropurpurea,' 'Hillside Black Beauty,' 'Pink Spike,' 'Brunette,' and the compact, bronze-leafed 'James Compton.'

Alchemilla

lady's mantle, nine hook, lion's paw

Family: Rosaceae

Hardy to: zone 3

Bloom period: May–July

Growing requirements: full sun to partial shade; average, moist, but well-drained soil

Height: 12–15 inches; spread 24 inches

Where best used: border edging, mixed plantings

Propagation: division of clumps every few years; mild self-seeder

Problems: No serious pests or diseases.

Notes: Deer-resistant. Deadhead to promote rebloom and to prevent seedlings if unwanted.

No one would ever call lady's mantle spectacular when describing its tiny, chartreuse-green flowers, at least as far as size is concerned. And it's hard to believe that this is a member of the rose family, given those tiny flowers. But this perennial has two particularly charming traits that make it one I recommend to most gardeners. Although the flowers individually are small and almost insignificant, taken as a mass of bloom they look like yellow-green lace frothing

flowers of lady's mantle

along the edge of a perennial border. Equally delightful is the appearance of the leaves when dew or raindrops land on them: tiny hairs hold the moisture droplets on the leaves so that they look like they are spangled in crystals, creating a magical effect on summer mornings or after a brief shower.

There's something aesthetically pleasing about a perennial or mixed garden bed that is edged at least partially in lady's mantle. When in bloom, the froth of tiny chartreuse flowers lends a distinctively soothing, airy look to a border's design; and the leaves, even when not bespangled with dew, are striking with their unusual bear-paw shape.

If you like the colour chartreuse—and I do, very much, at least in the garden—you'll find that the flowers of lady's mantle, which will start to open any time after mid- to late May, combines beautifully with other colours, either offering a striking contrast or providing colour harmony. As the flowers mature, they turn a light brown colour. Some gardeners cut and dry sprays of the flowers for use in arrangements, but if this doesn't appeal to you and you don't like the colour of the flowers as they age, simply deadhead your plants. This will prevent self-seeding, of course, and may also prompt the plants to rebloom.

I have lady's mantle planted in a number of locations around our property, from partially shaded to full sun. The secret to success in all cases is to provide moist soil that drains fairly well—this plant doesn't like full sun if the soil tends to dry out quickly. Mulching around your plants will help to retain soil moisture, as well as preventing self-seeding, although I've never found that lady's mantle self-seeds very much, especially compared to some other perennials.

Those gardeners troubled by deer will be happy to learn that lady's mantle is rarely browsed by the pesky animals. I've also never seen slugs do any damage to the plants, probably because of the downy hairs covering the leaves. No serious pests or diseases trouble the species, although you should divide plants every few years to regenerate vigour and to prevent the crowns from developing rot.

Lady's mantle has long been used in herbal remedies, being listed in *Culpeper's Complete Herbal* (originally published in 1652 as *The English Physician*) as useful against "bleeding,

lady's mantle works well at the front of a border

vomiting and the flux" as well as an aid to conception. It does have astringent and styptic properties, and is used in more modern applications as a component of cosmetics, healing salves, and as an infusion or tea taken to relieve excessive menstrual flow. However, if you're tempted to use this or any herb, please consult a professional herbalist or other medical practitioner first.

Amsonia

bluestar

Family: Apocyanaceae
Hardy to: zone 3 or 4
Bloom period: late spring to early summer
Growing requirements: full sun to partial shade
Height: 2–3 feet

Where best used: Front to mid-border. Large drifts make especially appealing displays.
Propagation: division in fall; stem cuttings; seed
Problems: No serious pests or diseases.
Notes: Good fall colour in foliage.

When I saw a photo of bluestar in a book of perennials more than a decade ago, I immediately decided that I needed to have it in my garden. My delight had far more to do with the delicate, soft blue flowers than with the fact that its common name shares the name of a beer brewed in my birth province, Newfoundland and Labrador. This delight is shared by any gardener who has a love for blue-flowered plants, as true blue is the most seldom-seen colour in blossoms.

Amsonia is a member of the Apocyanaceae, the periwinkle or dogbane family, which includes many exotic tropical species such as *Plumeria* (frangipani) and *Carissa* (Natal plum). *Apocynum androsaemifolium*, the spreading dogbane, is a low-growing shrub often seen spreading along roadsides, with fragrant flowers and milky sap in leaves and stems. The most common garden ornamental from this family is *Vinca*, commonly known as vinca, myrtle, or periwinkle, a woody sub-shrub grown as a ground cover that is loved by some and loathed by others.

Like vinca and related species, amsonia has five-petalled, star-shaped flowers. The blooms of bluestar are soft Wedgwood blue, and while each individual flower is only about 1/4 to 1/2 inch wide, the flower cluster contains many individual

hybrid 'Blue Ice'

blossoms and is visually appealing. Of the two most commonly available species, *A. tabernaemontana* has willow-like foliage, while *A. hubrichtii*'s foliage is much more needle-like. Both can produce beautiful fall colour, provided that wind doesn't defoliate the plants before the colour display begins.

common bluestar species A. tabernaemontana

Any literature I've ever read on amsonia says that this perennial will self-seed. However, my plants have apparently never read the literature, because I've yet to find seedlings in a decade of growing bluestar in my garden. It may be that seedlings are shaded out where I have the plant located. If you want more bluestar plants, you can divide the perennial in early autumn, but be aware that you'll need a sharp pruning saw or knife to cut through the tough, fibrous crown of the plant.

Amsonia produces a milky sap when its leaves or stems are broken, and this may be why deer don't find the plant palatable. While there are cultivars of bluestar available that have larger or darker blue flowers, these aren't commonly available in much of Atlantic Canada except through a good mail-order or seed catalogue. The only cultivar I've found occasionally at nurseries is one called 'Blue Ice,' which is shorter in height than the species but has showier blue flowers.

Anemone

windflower, thimbleweed, anemone

Family: Ranunculaceae
Hardy to: varies with species
Bloom period: spring or late summer
Growing requirements: full sun to partial shade, well-drained, fertile, but moist soil
Height: 6 inches to 5 feet

Where best used: perennial borders, spring or fall colour
Propagation: division or root cuttings
Problems: No serious pests or diseases.
Notes: Rabbit-resistant. Several species spread rapidly.

Although anemones belong to the buttercup family, on first glance some can look like poppies, which is probably why they appeal to me so much. There are two main seasons of bloom: the petite-flowered types flower in spring or early summer, while the tall, larger-flowered species are stars of the late summer or early autumn garden. Look at a clump of them in bloom and you can see where they get the common name windflower, as the stems sway in the lightest of breezes.

One of the first plants I tucked into the shade garden I developed was a sweet little white-flowered anemone, *A. canadensis*, which I bought at a local nursery. The species spreads enthusiastically, so that by the time it blooms in mid- to late June and presents a sea of snow-white flowers, I forget how I dug up many of its runners in early spring.

Not all anemones are overachievers, but they are all very beautiful. As with many of the plants discussed here, a number of species can be used in the home garden, with different species having different bloom periods. You will sometimes find the spring-flowering pasque flower (*Pulsatilla*) and the rare but lovely hepatica or liverwort (*Hepatica*) included in the *Anemone* genus, depending on who is making the classifications.

The fall-blooming anemones are one of those plants that you probably pass by in the garden centre because they're not in bloom. They can be slow to establish, and they like good drainage, especially through winter. I have only tried these plants a couple of times, and when they didn't overwinter I

blue form of A. nemorosa

A. multifida *'Rubra'*

didn't think to try them again until I saw a magnificent clump of them in a friend's garden near Annapolis Royal. I'm now patiently nurturing a couple of plants in a section of garden where I don't mind if they take off: the fall-bloomers also tend to be vigorous once established in conditions they like.

Although you'll often see fall-flowering anemones blooming in full sun, they do best in light shade—like astilbes, they'll tolerate full sun as long as they have adequate moisture through the summer. But they also need good drainage, and you should mulch them over winter, especially while they are establishing themselves.

A. huphensis *'September Charm'*

Recommended species and cultivars

Anemone canadensis: As noted above, this spring-flowering white-flowered species does spread by yellow-brown rhizomes, but is easier to control than, say, *Aegopodium* (goutweed). Zone 3.

A. nemorosa: European wood anemones can have white, pink, or blue flowers. This species includes one of my favourite spring flowers, the cultivar 'Vestal.' Lloyd Mapplebeck gave me a pot of this clump-forming perennial several years ago when it stopped me dead in my tracks. It has stunning white flowers with pompom-like, ruffled centres, and dark green foliage that sometimes has a wine-coloured cast to it. Highly recommended. Zone 4.

A. palmata 'Luteum': This lovely clump-forming species has a generous number of flowers that are the palest yellow shade; long blooming throughout June. Zone 4.

A. multifida 'Rubra': The so-called red windflower actually has small (nickel-sized) flowers in a deep fuchsia-pink. Zone 3.

A. hupehensis: The Chinese anemone is the beautiful tall anemone seen in late summer or early autumn. Flowers can be snow white, pink, or purple, and can be double, depending on cultivars. 'September Charm' is a popular cultivar with rose-pink blooms. *A.* x *hybrida* is a hybrid known as the Japanese anemone, a bit later blooming and with larger flowers. 'Honorine Jobert' is one of the most common cultivars, with pristine white blooms. Zone 5.

NO GARDEN BULLIES ALLOWED

When it comes to plants, one gardener's pest can be another gardener's pleasure. You see a plant offered at a yard sale or church bazaar, are charmed by its pretty foliage or flowers, and buy it for two dollars. In fact, you like it so much you buy several of it and plant it in different spots in your garden. In a year or so—or when a visiting gardener sees it and reacts in horror—you discover that you've bought a garden thug: one of those plants that wants to take over your garden and possibly, the universe.

The absolute bane of my gardening existence is goutweed (*Aegopodium podegraria*), also known as bishop's weed, snow-on-the-mountain, and ground elder. This relative of carrots and Queen Anne's lace spreads rapidly by underground rhizomes, from which new clusters of leaves will emerge, and new rhizome branches begin from various nodes of the original rhizomes, and on and on. To make matters worse, if you let its admittedly pretty white flowers go to seed, you'll have even more plants the following year.

Many people may never have a problem with the variegated form of goutweed, which is used often in shaded areas, such as around trees, without too much trouble. Problems arise, however, when the plant reverts to its all-green form. Variegated plants produce less chlorophyll so tend to be less vigorous, but the all-green form of goutweed has aspirations of world domination.

What's invasive in one part of the country—or even in one garden—isn't necessarily a problem elsewhere. One of the plants known to be problematic for some gardeners is a lovely perennial commonly called goose necked loosestrife. For some, it becomes very troublesome, spreading by rhizomes and crowding out other plants. In my garden, it died twice, unable to deal with my heavy clay soil. The Japanese lanterns that I intentionally planted in a raised bed beside the barn thrived for a few years then gave up the ghost. Plants that are problematic in other parts of Canada may well be controlled by our colder winter temperatures, so that perennial crowns die or seeds fail to overwinter and germinate in large numbers.

Sometimes you may want a particularly vigorous plant to protect a sloping area from erosion, or to fill a shady spot where nothing else will grow. I have grown some of the plants listed on page 106 because I wanted them for a specific spot, and the clay keeps them in check. The main thing to remember is that they can be a problem. The worst two offenders, or at least the ones I am most frequently asked about, are goutweed and creeping bellflower; these will always be with us, unless we can convince the deer to dine on them.

What do you do if you are having problems with a garden bully? There is no one easy answer, primarily because so many of these plants do spread by rhizomes, meaning they are hard to kill by either organic or chemical pesticide formulations. If you dig up the plants, you have to make sure to get all of the roots and rhizomes, or else they'll come back again. Cutting the plants off to the ground regularly is helpful: without stems and leaves to make chlorophyll to nourish the plant, the underground parts will eventually die out. Likewise, covering an area with black or clear plastic to smother and bake the weedy plants can be effective, but you need to leave that down for at least six months, perhaps even longer, and it doesn't work well if you have other perennials growing in amongst the thug.

Planting garden thugs inside of root barriers can produce mixed success—you have to put the barrier down so far in order to contain the plants, and this is a real challenge if you're working in heavy or rocky soil.

If there are certain plants you really like but want to contain, you can plant them in containers. I do this with mint, after having overrun my father's vegetable garden many years ago by planting mint as the start of a herb garden. I like the look and taste of some of the more interesting mints (chocolate, pineapple) but don't want to be dealing with a mint invasion. I once saw ribbon grass (*Phalaris*) planted in a site surrounded by a concrete sidewalk that contained it, and that was also effective.

For those plants that produce copious amounts of seed, you have several options. Mulching heavily around the plants will reduce the likelihood of seed germination, although it probably will let a few seedlings slip through. Deadheading before the plants go to seed is also an option. I grow biennial teasels because I like their winter architecture— their seedheads and stems can withstand just about any weather—and they are a good pollinator and bird plant. They're also highly deer-resistant, being extremely prickly. They produce many seedlings in spring, but since it takes two years for the plants to grow to flowering size, I leave a few seedlings each year, but dig the rest out and compost them. Occasionally one pops up in an unusual place, but they have never become a problem.

When choosing new plants, pay attention to what literature or even the supplier's labels say about it. Phrases like "easy to grow," "ground cover," or "good beginner plant" can indicate that you should check with others before adding the plant to your borders.

Unless otherwise noted, the plants listed on the next page spread by rhizomes or underground stems.

Plants to avoid (or at least plant with extreme caution)

Aegopodium podegraria: a.k.a. goutweed, bishop's weed, snow-on-the-mountain

Ajuga: Bugleweed makes a good ground cover, but can get out of control if it moves into the lawn.

Anemone canadensis: windflower, Canada anemone

Artemesia 'Limelight': Spreads quickly in light soil (died off in wet clay in my garden).

Campanula rapunculoides and *Campanula takesimana*: creeping and Korean bellflowers

Dipsacus: Teasel is an amazing plant, but does sell seed heavily.

Elymus arenarius: blue Lyme grass

Houttuynia cordata: Chameleon plant doesn't appear to be a problem in my garden, but in lighter soil and warmer parts of the country it can spread quickly.

Lamiastrum: Yellow archangel. Cultivar 'Herman's Pride' is a clumper that doesn't spread.

Lysimachia clethroides: goosenecked loosestrife

Lysimachia nummularia: Creeping Jenny/Charlie, particularly the all-green variety

Lysimachia verticillata: yellow loosestrife, particularly 'Firecracker,' the purple-leafed cultivar

Macleaya: Plume poppy is an elegant and unusual plant, reaching great heights and producing thick runners from which spring more plants.

Mentha: mints of all cultivars

Oenothera biennis: evening primrose, sundrops

Phalaris arundinacea: gardener's garters, variegated ribbon grass

Physalis alkekengi: Chinese/Japanese lanterns

Physostegia: Obedient plant. The variegated forms are less rambunctious.

Sedum acre: Yellow stonecrop shouldn't be planted in an alpine garden or trough.

Veronica repens: Some of the creeping forms of Veronica can spread, but can usually be dug out before they get too out of hand.

Viola 'Freckles': This particular violet self-seeds quite profusely, although I find it easy to remove when it pops up somewhere unplanned.

the evil goutweed

Armeria maritime

seathrift, sea pink

Family: Plumbaginaceae

Hardy to: zone 4–8

Bloom period: Late spring until late summer. Deadheading will produce reblooming.

Growing requirements: full sun, good drainage

Height: 6–12 inches, including bloom

Where best used: front of border, alpine or scree gardens, troughs

Propagation: division

Problems: No serious pests or diseases.

Notes: Very drought- and salt-tolerant. Good pollinator plant.

Some garden perennials get all the glory, with their show-stopping displays of colourful blooms, distinctive foliage, and dramatic height and form. Others are quiet little workhorses, maybe not even noticed by visitors to the garden. These are the backbones of a border, blooming for weeks on end without any special care.

Armeria, or seathrift, is one of those perennials. I can't remember where I first saw this dainty but robust little plant, or even when I planted it myself. But I do know that for years several clumps of seathrift have been producing large numbers of small, bright pink or red flowers, popping up out of densely mounding, grasslike foliage in my garden.

I also remember my complete astonishment at discovering small clumps of seathrift clinging tenaciously to what little soil exists in the Tablelands of Gros Morne National Park in Newfoundland and Labrador. The rocks of the Tablelands are composed of peridotite, which is high in magnesium and low in calcium, making it less than ideal for many types of plant life. Yet here was a common garden perennial, growing in an area that looks more like the badlands of the southwestern United States than part of the Atlantic provinces. My delight in armeria rose boundlessly that day, and whenever I look at it in my garden I see a testament to the tenacity of plants.

In the wonderful book *Wildflowers of Newfoundland and Labrador*, Peter Scott writes informative entries to accompany the watercolour paintings of artist Dorothy Black. Under the entry for armeria, Scott writes, "This plant is used in Iceland as greens: cleaned of soil and dead leaves, it is boiled in milk and served with butter." I've never tried seathrift greens

'Joystick'

as a potherb, primarily because there are plenty other choices for greens, but also because my long-suffering spouse would rebel at eating something that so resembles grass.

Scott also notes that the flower stalks of seathrift are hollow, which makes them strong enough to withstand the winds so often found in maritime climates. As their botanical name suggests in both genus and species, the plants are commonly found in coastal areas. Highly salt-tolerant, they work well in seaside gardens and are useful when planted bordering walkways and other areas that are affected by the use of de-icing salt in winter.

'Joystick'

Seathrift does best when planted in full sun in soil that isn't overly rich, so you don't need to worry about adding fertilizer around plants. The low-growing perennial works nicely in scree gardens or in alpine trough displays, providing the planting areas have good drainage. While the most commonly seen varieties of seathrift have bright pink flowers, there are also vibrant red-pink and pure white forms. Flowers are born in rounded heads composed of numerous florets, each one surrounded by a papery bract that remains behind when the blossoms have faded. Deadheading your thrifts will prompt them to keep flowering, although later flushes of blossoms will not be as profuse as the first bloom period. In particularly windy areas, you may want to provide a loose mulch as a protective cover for the winter months, as thrift foliage tends to remain evergreen but can brown in cold and windy conditions.

Recommended species and cultivars

Armeria juniperfolia: For the alpine enthusiast, this tiny thrift looks like a pincushion of grassy, short needles that grow a scant two inches tall and produce button-like flowers in white, rose, or lilac, depending on the cultivar ('Alba,' 'Bevan's Variety,' or 'Rosa Stultz,' respectively).

A. maritima 'Joystick' series: These include several cultivars named with 'Joystick' and their respective flower colours—white, red, and lilac—that were developed for the cut-flower trade, with longer stems than the standard species.

A. maritima 'Nifty Thrifty': Bicolour green and white foliage with hot-pink flowers.

ROCK GARDENING

Rock gardening, also referred to as alpine gardening, typically involves small, compact plants, poor soil with good drainage, southern exposure—and rocks. Unlike, say, a lush perennial border, plants are spaced as individual specimens, tied together visually with stones or rocks. This helps to avert the competition they hate, provides good aeration, and allows for appreciation of each plant's diminutive form.

Because so many alpine species are small and often slow-growing, many varieties can share a small space. For city dwellers with only a balcony or rooftop, or for those with limited mobility, many alpines do very well in trough or container gardens.

With alpines, the secret is location and what rock-gardening enthusiast Bernard Jackson calls "a frugal existence." Think about where such plants appear in nature: in alpine conditions, which are open, windswept, and sunny—although subject to harsh wind and other weather conditions. A south-facing slope with plenty of sunlight is an ideal place to start an alpine planting, where the drainage will be excellent. Too

An attractive rock garden with many different types of plants.

heavy a soil (such as one with clay) or too moist a location will prove fatal to many alpines.

I remember how astonished I and my friends in the Nova Scotia Rock Gardening Club were by a presentation from Swedish alpine enthusiast Peter Korn. He simply dumps piles of sand on top of grassy areas where he wants to start a site, adds the plants and whatever rocks he wants as accents and structural interest, and then mulches with pea gravel. Most of us are probably reluctant to try that, so a good soil mixture for alpines is one-third sharp sand (not beach sand), one-third garden soil, and one-third leaf mould or shredded peat moss. Alpines don't like fertilizer and will gain what nutrients they require from the leaf mould and garden soil.

Although literally thousands of species are used in alpine gardening, some of them are hard to find locally unless you belong to a rock gardening club, which often hold an annual plant sale and swap. The following easily grown alpines are available at many nurseries. (Avoid overly vigorous creeping plants such as bugleweed (*Ajuga*), snow-in-summer (*Cerastium*), and golddust sedum (*Sedum acre*), which can easily overwhelm less vigorous plants.)

Arabis: Rock cress is a creeping spring bloomer with flowers in white or shades of pink or purple.

Armeria: (See profile page 107) Seathrift thrives in the harshest of conditions, and has grass-like foliage and clusters of red, pink, or white flowers on leafless stems.

Campanula: (See profile page 124) Creeping bellflowers have blue, purple, or white flowers.

Delosperma: Perennial ice plants have succulent foliage and bright magenta or yellow flowers.

Dwarf conifers: These add a striking contrast of texture and height to an alpine planting.

Gentiana

Dianthus: (See profile page 135) Many pinks are tiny, ground-hugging clumps of foliage with brilliant red, pink, or white flowers.

Gentiana: Best known for their cobalt-blue flowers, gentians are ideally suited for rock gardens.

Penstemon: Spikes of brilliant-coloured flowers, with a variety of species and forms.

Phlox: (See profile page 204) The creeping phloxes, such as moss phlox (*P. subulata*), work brilliantly in alpines.

an alpine Campanula

Sedum: (See profile page 224) Hundreds of creeping varieties of sedums are used effectively in alpine gardens.

Sempervivum: Commonly called houseleeks or hen-and-chicks, these beloved succulents are easy to grow and come in a number of different foliage colours and forms.

Thymus: Low-growing herbs with fragrant foliage and masses of tiny flowers, thymes are often used in walkways and between stepping-stones.

Aruncus

goatsbeard, bride's feathers

Family: Rosaceae
Hardy to: zone 2
Bloom period: early to midsummer
Growing requirements: rich, moist soil
Height: 3–6 feet; dwarf form less than 2 feet
Where best used: moist, shady areas; pollinator plantings; back of border

Propagation: by seed; mature plants almost impossible to divide or move
Problems: No serious pests or diseases.
Notes: Deer- and slug-resistant. Pollinators love the flowers.

I sometimes wonder if goatsbeard would be more popular if it had a different common name. Somehow, the image of a goat's flowing beard, coupled with the thought of the unpleasant scent of the animal, doesn't exactly inspire the average gardener. This is a great pity because aruncus is a magnificent and easy-to-care-for plant, creating a spectacular show that lasts for a long time. Perhaps it would be more popular if marketed under the less-common but delightful name of bride's feathers!

Visitors to a garden with the common goatsbeard could easily mistake a well-grown plant for a shrub; the species can reach six feet in height and breadth so it's not a plant for a small garden. When it flowers, it produces stately plumes of white, astilbe-like flowers that are a magnet for pollinators such as bees and beetles.

Aruncus is a large perennial, preferring moist, partially shaded sites.

Since the commonly available species *A. dioicus* is a large perennial, and since it's virtually impossible to divide or move once it matures, aruncus needs to be sited in exactly the right spot. It needs moist soil, preferably well amended with plenty of organic matter, and with that one requirement filled, it will be happy in full sun to partial shade in our climate. Think of aruncus as an astilbe on steroids, needing soil moisture but otherwise tolerant of a range of light conditions. (Astilbes are sometimes called false goatsbeard.)

Aruncus dioicus is native to North America, although Allan Armitage notes that some authors in Europe claim it's native to Europe or Asia. As the species name suggests, this goatsbeard has both male and female plants, so you need both in order to have seed production. Some people like to cut the flower heads off after blooming; I prefer to leave them on, because the seed heads do last well into winter. The cultivar 'Kneiffii' has finely cut foliage and grows a little shorter than the standard species, usually to about 3 feet tall.

For those with smaller gardens who want to try something unique and charming, look for the tiny dwarf goatsbeard, *Aruncus aesthusifolius*. It can easily be mistaken for a miniature astilbe, with its finely cut foliage and creamy plumes of flowers. Unlike *A. dioicus*, dwarf goatsbeard grows to about a foot tall with a tidy mounding habit. In full sun, the foliage will often take on a reddish cast in autumn; since mine is situated in a moist shade garden, I've never seen this for myself. As with its larger cousin, this plant needs moist, rich soil and is quite happy in sun or shade given that requirement.

Aruncus species and cultivars are quite slug- and deer-resistant, making them appealing for the gardener who is troubled by these garden nuisances.

Asclepias

milkweed, butterfly weed

Family: Asclepiadaceae
Hardy to: zone 3 or 4
Bloom period: mid- to late summer
Growing requirements: Best in full sun, but will tolerate light shade.
Height: 1–5 feet
Where best used: pollinator gardens, mid- to back of border

Propagation: Best done by seed. Resentful of transplanting or dividing and may sulk for several years before blooming again.
Problems: Aphids are often plentiful on the plants; some rusts and leaf spots possible.
Notes: Milkweeds produce a white, milky sap that can be irritating to those with sensitive skin, so it's recommended that you wear gloves when handling the plants.

One creature's noxious weed is another's essential tool for survival. Take the milkweeds, *Asclepias* genus. In many parts of the United States and Canada (including the Maritime provinces), common milkweed (*A. syriaca*) is listed as a noxious weed. This means it has a tendency to spread profusely and to be harmful in some way to crops or livestock.

However, without milkweeds, there would be no monarch butterflies, and the clearing out of stands of milkweeds throughout the northern hemisphere has been a contributing factor to the decline

butterfly weed

in monarch populations. Monarchs must lay their eggs on milkweed plants: the eggs hatch, the young feed on leaves and flowers, growing through their various instar stages, until they pupate and turn into butterflies. Milkweeds are toxic, yet the caterpillars can ingest the toxins with no problems, and the adult butterflies are thus toxic to birds, which tend to avoid them.

Although common milkweed is listed as noxious, other species and cultivars are regularly sold as garden plants and are monarch-friendly, so if you're concerned about monarch populations but also don't want to spread a possibly weedy species, opt for one of these other easily found milkweed species, which are often sold as butterfly weed (not to be confused with butterfly bush, *Buddleia*).

milkweed, butterfly weed

seeds of swamp milkweed

The key to growing asclepias in your garden is patience. In the spring, the plant is quite late to emerge from the soil, so you might want to mark where your plants are so you don't inadvertently dig them up. Once they've started growing, however, they shoot up quickly. Butterfly weed varieties tend to be lower growing, between 1–3 feet at maturity, while swamp milkweed can easily reach 5 feet tall. Flowers appear in midsummer in terminal clusters, and can be white, rose, yellow, orange, or red, depending on species and cultivar.

yellow form of butterfly weed

When planting milkweeds, either from seedlings or from purchased plants, make sure you situate them where you want them. Asclepias resent transplanting or dividing, and tend to sit sulkily without flowering for several years after transplanting. Sow seeds into peat pots that you can plant without disturbing the young roots of your milkweeds, and you'll find that they establish well as compared to seedlings moved out of plastic flats.

As noted above, Monarch caterpillars must have milkweeds in order to reproduce, and they will obviously chew the leaves and flowers of your plants. If plants with holey leaves are a problem for you, avoid plants that are hosts for butterflies, including the milkweeds. Other insects also dine on the leaves of asclepias, but bear in mind that if you spray for any insect pest anywhere in your garden, you are unlikely to attract monarchs. (See page 88).

Recommended species

Asclepias incarnata: In my heavy clay soil, swamp milkweed has been a terrific success but hasn't been invasive. Its rosy pink flowers turn to wonderful seed pods bursting with silk-tasselled brown seeds in autumn. A white form is also available. Hardy to zone 3.

A. tuberosa: Butterfly weed prefers an average, well-drained soil, tends to sulk in heavy clay, and often dies due to winter wet. Flowers may be yellow, orange, or red. Hardy to zone 4.

Aster

Michaelmas daisy, aster

Family: Asteraceae
Hardy to: zone 2
Bloom period: spring to fall
Growing requirements: full sun to light shade, average soil with good drainage
Height: 8 inches (alpine forms) to 6 feet (tall autumn asters)

Where best used: alpine species in rockeries; others for late summer or autumn colour
Propagation: division of clumps
Problems: fungal diseases on foliage, aster yellows (see page 117)
Notes: Many species are native. All are excellent pollinator plants.

Asters can be a real pain when it comes to positively identifying them in the wild. *Roland's Flora* reports that there are 175 species and most are native to North America. Nearly 20 of those grow wild in Nova Scotia, with similar numbers of wild species—many of the same ones—throughout the rest of Atlantic Canada. These plants hybridize quite readily, which makes them ideal for plant breeders but not quite so delightful for the home gardener trying to decide whether those are purchased hybrids or wild species growing in the garden.

'Jenny' New York aster

I've dug many a purchased variety of aster out of our garden beds during spring cleanup sessions, mistaking them for the wild asters that grow happily all around our property. At the same time, I've left wild asters growing in beds, thinking they were the cultivated varieties I purchased and tucked into borders. My mistake has become obvious as summer winds on and the plants start to bloom, and the blue- or white-flowered plants are nothing like the hot-pink variety I thought were there. My solution now is to carefully mark where the cultivars are, but also to practice aster laissez-faire. If it's an aster and it's in the garden, it stays there, because asters are great plants for pollinators.

purple New England (tall) variety

Taller aster species and hybrids are prone to flopping over, particularly if grown in rich soil that stimulates them to grow quickly and vigorously. Some gardeners stake these taller varieties, but another option is to shear the plants off by about half their size in early to mid-June. This encourages the plants to grow into a more compact and bushy form, but may delay flowering by a week or two.

Asters come in a range of flower colours, from white and off-white to shades of blue, pink, purple, and almost red. While most asters are flowers of the late summer and

When is an aster not an aster?

Plant taxonomists are busy people. Not content to leave plants as they were classified by Carl Linnaeus, they've used tools, including DNA typing, to determine relationships between various types of plants, sometimes renaming a genus or species, sometimes moving plants to a different, or an entirely new, family and genus. The asters belong to a family formerly known as Compositeae but now known as Asteraceae. Both names refer to the complicated or composite form of flowers found in this family, which includes sunflowers, echinaceas, centaureas, and rudbeckias, among many others.

Asters are sometimes listed in the genus *Symphytotrichum*—that's because taxonomists have divided the asters up into almost a dozen different genera. To make matters more complicated, most of the species found in Europe have been left as asters while those found in North America have been reclassified. So you'll see alpine asters, natives of Europe, listed under *A. alpinus*, while you may find calico, New York, and New England asters listed as *Symphytotrichum lateriflorus*, *S. novi-belgii*, and *S. novae-angliae*, respectively. (No one will scold you if you still refer to all of them as asters, however.)

Some aster relatives also use the word in their common names, but aren't actually in the *Aster* genus. The annual flower Chinese aster (*Callistephus*) is one, but so is the perennial Stokes aster, *Stokesia laevis*, which features raggedly fluffy flowers in white, blue, violet, or, less commonly, yellow. Although listed as hardy to zone 5, the Stokes aster requires good drainage and should be mulched for winter protection.

Another related garden perennial is *Boltonia asteroides*, which—as its botanical name suggests—is known as Bolton's aster or even false aster. It's a lovely addition for late-summer gardens and can reach up to 7 feet in height. Unlike the "true" asters, boltonia will grow nicely in wetter soils such as along pond and stream edges. It's hardy to zone 4.

'Lady in Black'

autumn garden, there are also alpine asters (*Aster alpinus*), which flower in May and June. Alpine asters are very compact and particularly demanding of good drainage, making them ideal for a scree or gravel garden.

The asters may be troubled by a variety of fungal diseases, such as powdery mildew and leaf spot, which are usually not fatal but can be unsightly. Good air circulation around the plants will help to reduce fungal infections. While asters require good drainage, they will show signs of stress in drought conditions by dropping their leaves. You can protect your plants from drought stress by mulching around the crowns, but you may need to add supplemental water during particularly dry spells.

Aster yellows disease

One disease that often shows up in asters and its relatives is called "aster yellows," although it seems to be a bigger problem in warmer climates and in plants brought in from other parts of Canada and the U.S. The disease isn't restricted to members of the aster family; you may see it in a variety of vegetables, including tomatoes, lettuce, celery, onions, and carrots, as well as in numerous ornamental plants, grasses, and grains, and even weeds such as plantain and pineapple weed.

The disease is caused by a phytoplasma, a parasitic organism related to bacteria that requires an insect vector to spread it from plant to plant. Sap-sucking insects called leafhoppers spread the phytoplasma that causes aster yellows. Plants affected with aster yellows may have stunted growth and curled and yellowed leaves, although the leaf veins will remain green. Plants may display deformed flowers that look like leaves or smaller flower heads growing out of the centres. They can also show a witch's broom appearance, with masses of shoots growing from a single point on a stem.

This disease has no cure, so infected plants must be removed and burned to prevent further spread. Do not compost infected plants. In home gardening situations, the disease is more an annoyance than a serious problem, and attempting to control leafhopper populations as a means of stemming the disease is not generally worth the effort. Aster yellows tends to be more prevalent when summers are cool and wet. Controlling weeds by mechanical removal or use of organic products such as horticultural vinegar or corn gluten meal can help to curb the spread of the disease.

Astilbe

Family: Saxifragaceae

Hardy to: zone 3

Bloom period: late spring to late summer (depending on cultivar)

Growing requirements: Moist, compost-rich soil is essential. Can take shade to full sun with moist soil.

Height: 1–5 feet

Where best used: shady sites with moist soil, woodland gardens, beside ponds

Propagation: crown division

Problems: No serious pests or diseases.

Notes: Deer- and slug-resistant; many have bronze, wine, gold, or red tints in stems and leaves.

I was a little slow climbing onto the bandwagon when it came to astilbes. I think it was because I saw them languishing in pots in a nursery during midsummer, with crisped foliage and flowers long spent. It wasn't until I went to a garden with numerous different astilbes, sporting various colours of plumed flowers and growing in shady sites alongside hostas. Then, the finely textured foliage juxtaposed with the wide leaves of the hostas stole my heart.

elegant flowers on an astilbe

Until I started researching astilbes for this book, I wasn't aware that they are a member of the Saxifrage family, and thus are related to such diverse plants as coral bells (*Heuchera*), foamflowers (*Tiarella*), Indian rhubarb (*Darmera*), and saxifrages (*Saxifraga*). If these plant genera have anything in common with one another, it's in the huge variety of leaf sizes and shapes. You'd never know, from looking at the umbrella-like leaf of a darmera, that it's related to the cut-leaf astilbe. The foliage of an astilbe resembles a delicate fern, but that laciness doesn't mean the plants are fragile. Give them what they want, and growing astilbes will be trouble-free for many years to come.

Astilbes will grow happily in medium shade, brightening up a low-sun area with their colourful flowers and rich foliage. They'll also grow in a sunny site, provided that their soil is kept moist by watering or mulching. Without adequate moisture astilbe foliage will get brown edges and even die back or go dormant.

When they are happy, most astilbes grow quite vigorously, and may require dividing every three or four years. You'll need a sharp knife or spade in order to cut through the tough rhizomes, or underground stems, from which the plants send up new growth. In some cases it's easiest to dig up the entire plant, divide it into a number of sections, and then replant the smaller sections, rather than to try to divide the plant while it's still in the ground.

'Color Flash Lime'

While some gardeners remove the flower stems of astilbes once the bloom is past, I leave them on the plants until the following spring, because I like the look of the drying seed heads as they go into autumn and winter. Likewise, it's a good idea to leave the foliage intact until spring, rather than cutting it down in the autumn; the leaves can help to protect the crowns of the plants throughout the winter months.

Plant breeders love hybridizing astilbes, and as a result, there are many wonderful varieties, with flowers in cream, white, or shades of rose, red, magenta, purple, lavender, and peach. Some varieties have a bronze or wine tint to their leaves, and deep purple or near-black stems. If there is any aggravation about these plants, it's that some of them are sold merely by colour as opposed to having a cultivar name. This makes it frustrating when you purchase an astilbe based on cultivar name, and take it home only to realize you already have it. I don't think one can ever really have too many astilbes, though.

Along with being great plants for moist and shady sites, astilbes have few problems with pests or diseases. Occasionally they will develop wilt from a fungal disease, in which case the infected plant should be removed and destroyed if you choose not to use pesticides. Astilbes are resistant to slugs and deer, although there are reports that Japanese beetles will chew the foliage. However, Japanese beetles have not yet been reported in much of Atlantic Canada.

Recommended cultivars

'**Peach Blossom**': peachy pink flowers, sweet fragrance
'**Fanal**': deep red blooms
'**Amethyst**': lavender-purple blossoms
'**Pumila**': lilac blue, late season flowering
'**Vision in Red**': fragrant, red-purple blooms with red stems; bronze foliage
'**Color Flash Lime**': brilliant chartreuse foliage with pink flowers

Astrantia

masterwort

Family: Apiaceae

Hardy to: zone 4

Bloom period: June–September

Growing requirements: moist soil is preferred; sun to partial shade

Height: 15–24 inches; spread about 18 inches

Where best used: pollinator plantings, shade gardens, front to mid-border

Propagation: Very difficult from packaged seed, but will self-seed if happy. Division of crowns works well.

Problems: No serious pests or diseases.

Notes: The blossoms dry well for use in everlasting arrangements.

There ought to be a whole lot more love shown for masterwort, because it's a beautiful, carefree perennial, beloved by pollinators, and good in sun or shade. Its genus name, *Astrantia*, comes from the Latin words for star and flower, although in England one of the plant's common names is Hattie's pincushion.

Masterwort is a member of the Apiaceae family (long known as the Umbelliferae family), meaning it is related to Queen Anne's lace, parsley, carrots, dill, and fennel, and features flowers comprised of tiny florets in an umbel (umbrella-shaped bloom). Like these relatives, it's a great plant for attracting and nurturing pollinating insects.

'Ruby Wedding'

My first encounter with masterwort was in the pages of a magazine, where a fine macro photograph showed me the complexities of its lovely flowers. In the course of getting to know the plant better, I read that it has blossoms resembling those of clover, but that doesn't begin to do them justice. They look more like flowery fireworks or, as that common name from England suggests, botanical pincushions, though each individual "bloom" isn't huge. Tiny flowers are tightly clustered together in a bouquet surrounded by a ring of colourful bracts (usually greenish-white, pink, or wine-red) that hold their colour for a long time, making these flowers beloved by floral designers. Astrantia flowers invite you to study them a little more closely and remember exactly what you love about gardening.

This perennial is a great choice for soils that stay cool and moist, and provided it has such soil, it will do well in full sun to partial shade. If you plant it in a drier site, be prepared to mulch around the plant's base to cool its roots and help the soil retain moisture. I have several different cultivars located around my garden, including three in a damp shade garden under a group of native spruce trees, and these do better than the plants growing in a sunnier, drier location. Masterwort works well in a mixed border towards the front of a planting, so that you can enjoy the profuse clusters of flowers up close. Deadheading will often prolong the bloom season until autumn.

Astrantia maxima: 'Largest masterwort,' as its name suggests, has the largest of flower heads, several inches across, usually light pink.

A. major: Great masterwort is the species from which most of the cultivars are developed, including these:

> **'Sunningdale Variegated'**: golden- or green-variegated foliage and white flowers
>
> **'Hadspen Blood,' 'Moulin Rouge,' 'Rubra,' and 'Ruby Wedding'**: Cultivars with flowers that range from deep pink to burgundy.
>
> **'Star of Heaven'**: White flowers have bracts tipped with green; rosy tint to florets.
>
> **'Lola'**: Light green foliage and masses of medium pink flowers.

Astrantia has no real problem with pests or diseases, although slugs will occasionally chew the foliage. I have noticed that my clumps have been slow-growing enough that I've yet to need to divide any of them.

When I first went looking for masterwort, I had problems locating it at nurseries, but it's now more commonly stocked as more gardeners learn about this versatile, carefree perennial.

'Star of Heaven'

'Sunningdale Variegated'

Baptisia

blue false indigo

Family: Fabaceae

Hardy to: zone 3

Bloom period: early summer (June–July)

Growing requirements: full sun, good drainage; drought-tolerant once established

Height: 3–4 feet

Where best used: mixed borders, butterfly gardens

Propagation: by seed; division of clump not recommended

Problems: No serious pests or diseases.

Notes: Deer-resistant. Does not like transplanting except as a very young plant.

Every year, the Perennial Plant Association declares a perennial of the year. Some years the choices are less than exciting because they're very common and even overused in gardens. However, in 2010, the association selected blue false indigo, an excellent and often underutilized perennial. A member of the Fabaceae, or pea, family (formerly Legumoseae), baptisia is related to lupines, sweet peas, and the similar-looking yellow false lupine, *Thermopsis*.

Impatient gardeners need not apply when it comes to growing baptisia. This

Baptisia australis

mounding, shrub-like perennial takes a few years to establish itself, and as long as five years from planting to blooming. In the fourth year after I planted my first clump of baptisia, I went out in the spring and left a shovel near the plants, dropping the broad hint that if it didn't flower that year, it was going to be moved to the compost heap. I don't know if that impressed it, but that was its first year flowering, and it's steadily grown and bloomed ever since.

The good news about baptisia is that it grows slowly and steadily into a handsome clump between 3 and 4 feet in height and width, and unlike other perennials doesn't need to be divided every few years. In fact, make sure you're satisfied with your site selection before planting baptisia, as the perennial puts down a long, central taproot as it grows. Blue false indigo prefers a well-drained soil and a site where it will get full sun, otherwise you'll find that you need to stake or otherwise support the plant to keep its stems from flopping. Once established, the perennial is very drought-tolerant.

Baptisia is one of those plants that deer tend to avoid. Like other members of the Fabaceae, it contains several bitter-tasting compounds that make it less desirable to marauding deer.

As with other taprooted species (poppies, hollyhocks), baptisia resents being dug up and moved, although young seedlings can be transplanted with minimal fuss. If you must transplant your plant for some reason, make sure to dig deeply around the plant so that you'll be able to save as much of the taproot as possible. As with the initial planting, it will normally take several years before your baptisia will flower again.

Baptisia flowers are very attractive to bees and butterflies, and normally last up to a month. As the summer progresses, seed pods will form and turn a deep brown to black colour when they are mature.

'Twilite Prairieblues'

Floral designers often use these seed heads in dried flower arrangements. If you want to leave them on the plant to provide winter interest, they will last for quite a while until heavy snowfalls or ice break them off.

While there are numerous species of baptisia listed in reference books and some gardening sites, Atlantic Canadians have traditionally had only a couple of choices easily available for planting. The easiest to locate is the straight *B. australis*, blue false indigo; however, during the summer of 2010 I did notice several hybrids and cultivars for sale at local nurseries, no doubt because of the promotion of the plant as perennial of the year. 'Purple Smoke' has violet purple flowers on black stems and is hardy to zone 4.

'Twilite Prairieblues' was developed at the Chicago Botanic Garden and is a hybrid between *B. australis* and *B. sphaerocarpa*. Its flowers are almost burgundy in colour and accented with yellow. A related hybrid, 'Starlite Prairieblues,' has softer blue flowers, also accented with yellow.

Campanula

Family: Campanulaceae
Hardy to: varies with species
Bloom period: late spring to early fall
Growing requirements: full sun to light shade; well drained but moist, compost-rich soil
Height: 2 inches to 4 feet

Where best used: low-growers ideal for front of border, walls, rockeries; taller species mid- to back of border
Propagation: seed, division, seedlings
Problems: No serious pests or diseases.
Notes: All attract hummingbirds and bees.

Most gardeners have favourite plants—although those favourites may vary from time to time depending on new varieties, or difficult winters, or merely changes in tastes. However, I recommend bellflowers in every perennial garden unless it's located in a complete swamp. My own garden has at least a dozen species and cultivars, and they are essential for those who love the carefree look of a cottage garden.

Bellflowers are among the most beautiful perennials, and arguably among the most varied as well as the easiest to grow. There are creeping species with tiny leaves and stems that smother themselves in dainty blue, purple, or white flowers, and there are tall, stately species that bloom for weeks on end without pause. Some species are particularly tolerant of harsh conditions, as witnessed by their growing in the wild in less than congenial circumstances.

As noted above, campanulas grow in a range of soils and conditions as long as the site has good drainage. After that, you're free to experiment according to your hardiness zone.

C. lactiflora *'Loddon Anna'*

C. glomerata, *the clustered bellflower*

Campanula carpatica Carpathian bellflower: One of the most popular low-growing bellflowers, ideal for front of borders or walls. The 'Clips' series includes forms in white and various shades of blue and purple. Zone 2.

C. cochleariifolia 'Elizabeth Oliver': Known as 'fairy thimbles,' this one has dainty double blooms on spreading roots, good for walls. Zone 3 with winter protection.

C. garganica 'Dickson's Gold': A low-growing specimen noted for its gold foliage (more of a lime-green in shade) and pale blue flowers. Easily crowded out by more aggressive species, so plant it where it has a place to shine, such as on a wall or in an alpine bed. Zone 4.

C. glomerata Clustered bellflower: As the name suggests, this species holds its flowers together in clusters at the top of its foliage. Zone 2.

C. lactiflora milky bellflower: One of the few bellflowers with a cultivar ('Loddon Anna') boasting soft pink blooms, a long bloom period from early August to October. Zone 4.

C. medium: Canterbury bells or cup-and-saucer bellflowers are biennial, taking two years to grow from seed and flower. Plant transplants or seeds every year for several years and they should self-seed to provide an ongoing display. Zone 2.

C. persicifolia: Peach-leafed bellflower is one of my favourites for the large white or blue bells on tall spikes, and its long period of bloom. Produces a few seedling plants but not overwhelming. Look for 'Chettle Charm,' which has white flowers tipped in sky blue. Zone 2.

C. poscharskyana: Serbian bellflower is a low-grower with starry, open "bells." Good for front of borders; it does spread but not invasively so. Requires very good drainage. Zone 3.

C. punctata: 'Cherry Bells': Bright pink flowers with speckled interiors, very appealing to hummingbirds. Reblooms. Can be aggressive in some gardens and abruptly die out in others, but worth trying for its gorgeous flowers. Zone 4.

C. rotundifolia: The scotch harebell or Bells-of-Scotland is a tough, tough plant. I've variously found it clinging to the side of cliffs at Cape Split near where I live, on beach edges in Digby and Yarmouth counties, and growing on the inhospitable terrain of the Tablelands in Gros Morne, Newfoundland and Labrador. Zone 2.

Campanula rapunculoides: Creeping bellflower is the scourge of many Atlantic gardeners. While the flowers are pretty, the plant travels by rhizomes, which are very difficult to remove completely from a garden.

C. takesimana Korean bellflower: Although this species is quite enthusiastic in its growth habit and should be avoided in small gardens, there are cultivars bred from it that are very attractive, including the pink-flowered 'Elizabeth.'

Centaurea

Family: Asteraceae

Hardy to: zone 3

Bloom period: mid-spring until autumn; some rebloom

Growing requirements: light shade to full sun

Height: 1–4 feet

Where best used: sunny, moist, but well-drained site; pollinator gardens

Propagation: Division every 3–4 years. Some knapweeds self-seed easily.

Problems: Aphids, mildews, rots can be present but not usually fatal.

Notes: Very good sources of nectar for pollinators, especially bees and butterflies.

There are literally hundreds of species of *Centaurea* in the world, including weedy species that live in Atlantic Canada, although they were introduced from Europe and are not native here. The weedy knapweed, *C. nigra*, is sometimes mistakenly referred to as a thistle: although in the same family as thistles (the Asteraceae family), our wild knapweed and ornamental varieties do not have spines like thistles (*Cirsium*). The bachelor button, or cornflower, *C. cyanus*, is a beloved annual flower grown by many gardeners.

Persian cornflower

Of the perennial species, four are commonly grown in gardens. These include the pink-flowered species, *C. hypoleuca* and *C. dealbata*, also known as the Persian cornflowers; the spectacular yellow-blooming basketflower, *C. macrocephala*; and the blue or purple-flowered *C. montana*, also known as mountain bluet. I grow all of them, and each centaurea brings a little something different to the garden. The purple-blue mountain bluets are tough, long-blooming perennials that self-seed and create a misty sea of blue flowers that cools down a planting filled with brighter, hotter-coloured flowers. The hot-pink species are very eye-catching with their rich colours and are butterfly magnets, although all centaureas are prolific nectar producers beloved by pollinators. For that reason alone, I recommend centaurea species to other gardeners interested in supporting pollinators.

It's the fluffy, large yellow flowers of *C. macrocephala*, however, that will cause visitors to my garden to stop in their tracks and exclaim, "What is that and where can we get it?" Taller than the other species at around 4 feet, the plant looks nondescript with its strappy, bright green leaves—that is, until the flower heads start to form and open. Bees flock to the bright yellow blooms, and as the flowers dwindle, they leave behind handsome seed heads that last well into winter.

C. macrocephala

Each of these ornamental species has similar characteristics: they are all clump-forming perennials that grow best in full sun, although they will grow in light shade with only a little reduction in flower numbers. They do well in average soil that is moist but well drained, and once established can be quite drought-tolerant. You may wish to stake or otherwise support your taller centaurea species as they can be prone to flopping or being knocked over in windy conditions.

Of the various centaureas I grow, only the mountain bluet is a particularly enthusiastic self-seeder. It's not overwhelming in its seedling production, and I either dig out new plants and put them somewhere else or give them to friends looking for new plants. Deadheading mountain bluet will prevent a lot of seedling production and will also prompt the plant to produce more flowers. The yellow

mountain bluet cultivar 'Amethyst in Snow'

centaurea doesn't rebloom, but it does produce a few seedlings, all of which are eagerly snapped up by other gardeners each spring.

If you're looking for something a little different, several cultivars of mountain bluet have gold foliage, including 'Gold Bullion.' There is a white form of the species (*C. montana* 'Alba') and a very attractive variety named 'Amethyst in Snow,' which is a white form with a rich purple centre.

Chelone

turtlehead

Family: Scrophulariaceae

Hardy to: zone 3

Bloom period: midsummer to mid-autumn

Growing requirements: moist soil, partial shade to sun

Height: 2–4 feet

Where best used: edges of ponds or streams, other wet areas

Propagation: seed (may self-sow) or division

Problems: No serious pests or diseases.

Notes: Native to eastern North America. Seed heads provide winter interest.

*C*helone (rhymes with "baloney," as Allan Armitage helpfully mentions) is the Greek word for tortoise, and you can certainly see how the plant received its name, as its flowers do resemble the head of a turtle.

This relative of snapdragons is appealing as a garden plant for a number of reasons. The foliage is deep green and very glossy, making turtlehead handsome even when not in bloom. The white- or rose-coloured flowers appear from mid-August onwards in my garden, but other gardeners and wildflower watchers report flowers in wild plants as

pink-flowered form of turtlehead

early as late June. Chelone remains in bloom for a long time, as its flowers begin to open at the bottom of a spike of many blossoms, and continue until the top blossoms have opened, over a period of weeks. When flowering is complete, the seed heads remain on plants throughout the winter, making a handsome display for winter interest. If you're a fan of butterflies, you may find caterpillars of the checkerspot butterfly genus dining on the plants.

The nomenclature of the few turtlehead species is a bit confusing; you'll variously see the genus classified as a member of the Scrophulariaceae or the Plantaginaceae. The species native to Atlantic Canada is *C. glabra*, which has white or pinkish flowers, while the species most commonly found on sale is the rose turtlehead, *C. obliqua*, which is a star performer in my late-summer shade garden. It thrives in the wet winter and spring soil, so much so that I've been able to divide it and plant it in other moist sites on my property. Adequate moisture is the key to success with chelone; if your soil is dry, you'll need to water as you do for astilbe and other moisture-loving plants. If the leaves of your turtleheads start to brown, the plant is stressed for moisture: mulching around its base helps to retain soil moisture and keep the roots cool.

Cornus canadensis

bunchberry, crackerberry

Family: Cornaceae

Hardy to: zone 2

Bloom period: late May to mid-June; occasional reflowering later in the season

Growing requirements: partial sun to shade, moist woodland soil rich in humus

Height: 4–6 inches

Where best used: shade and woodland gardens, bird gardens

Propagation: divide in early spring; seeds by winter sowing or cold frame

Problems: No significant pests or diseases. Slow to form colonies.

Notes: Edible berries. Too-deep shade will reduce flowering.

My father was an airline pilot, so our family was transferred fairly often until I was in my mid-teens. During one particular stint in St. John's, Newfoundland, our house was built against the side of Mount Scio, a couple of miles from what is now the Memorial University Botanical Garden, so I had an entire wooded hillside as my backyard. It was in this wooded area that I learned to identify a number of plants that continue to be favourites today: balsam fir, paper birch, witherod, Canada lily of the valley, clintonia, partridgeberry, and the snow-white flowers and scarlet fruit of what Newfoundlanders refer

to as crackerberry, but which more people know as bunchberry, *Cornus canadensis*. To this day it remains a favourite plant in my botanical lexicon.

Some taxonomists put bunchberry into an entirely different genus from *Cornus* and name it *Chamaepericlymenum canadense*. There still seems to be some debate over where to classify bunchberry, so I turned to one of the horticultural gurus, Allan Armitage, who continues to name the plant under the genus *Cornus*—good enough for me. Whatever you wish to call it, bunchberry is native to North America and found throughout the Atlantic provinces.

Cornus canadensis

Some references call bunchberry a herbaceous sub-shrub, because the plant is slightly woody at the base of its stems, but others refer to the plant simply as a perennial. As with their woody relatives, the flowering dogwoods, the flowers themselves are tiny but surrounded by pristine white or pinkish bracts, which most of us think are petals but are in fact modified leaves. Bunchberry spreads slowly by underground runners, so patience is required in developing a showy display of the plants.

berries of bunchberry are edible but bland

On Battle Harbour Island, off the coast of Labrador, we saw large, gorgeous expanses of *C. canadensis*, as well as its relative, *Cornus suecica*, the Eurasian bunchberry, which is quite similar in growth habit and initial appearance. However, the flowers of *C. suecica* are blue-purple and even showier against the white bracts, and the leaves grow in opposite pairs rather than in a whorl around the stem. The two species cross-pollinate and produce hybrids, but I don't know of any commercial sources for these.

The best place to plant bunchberry is under shrubs or deciduous trees where they'll receive some sunlight but also shade—the most important growing requirement is adequate moisture or else they will dwindle away. Bunchberry doesn't like being disturbed, so you might want to plant some spring-flowering bulbs first, then add *Cornus canadensis*, and be assured of a nice display of colour right into autumn.

In her wonderful book *Wild Plants of Eastern Canada* (Nimbus, 2008), Marilyn Walker mentions that although bunchberry is a slow-grower, it is a speed demon when it comes to fertilization. When the flower opens, its four stamens rocket straight up from the flower centre, sending pollen in all directions. Scientists have measured this plant action at an acceleration of 99,000 feet (24,000 metres) per second, requiring an extremely high-speed camera to film the action. While this won't affect your growing of the plant, it's a fun tidbit to bring up at a dinner party with other plant addicts.

Corydalis

Family: Fumariaceae
Hardy to: varies with species
Bloom period: spring to frost
Growing requirements: rich, moist, but well-drained woodland soil; partial shade to sun
Height: 6–24 inches

Where best used: front of border, edging, specimen plant
Propagation: seedlings, division
Problems: Slugs can chew foliage; good winter drainage is essential.
Notes: Some species will go dormant after blooming.

When I was first building my garden here in Scots Bay, I read about corydalis in an introductory book (the name of which now escapes me) on easy garden perennials,. This particular book only talked about the small yellow corydalis, *C. lutea*, and how it is one of the longest-blooming perennials. Then I discovered the many other species, including several with blue flowers, and I was besotted. That spring saw me seeking out corydalis in nurseries, and I've never been without them since.

If you are at all interested in plant families, you will be interested to know that corydalis is related to bleeding-heart (*Dicentra*). These two genera were formerly in a subfamily of the poppy family, *Papaveraceae*, but have been reclassified to their own family along with a number of other, lesser-known genera. Corydalis has unusual, spurred flowers that have been described as minnow-like in shape; a number of them are found on each flower stalk. The foliage is often bluish-green in colour and quite lacy or fern-like in texture, making the plants appealing even when not in bloom.

Corydalis makes a good plant for a shade or woodland garden, provided your soil has good drainage. While they like moisture, species of this plant resent winter wet and soggy soils, so if you have clay soil, make sure that the site is well amended with compost and sand to improve drainage.

C. solida

C. elata

C. lutea

Some corydalis, especially spring-flowering species, go dormant after blooming, particularly if the summer is hot and dry. It's a good idea to make sure you label such plants and their location so that you don't inadvertently dig them up while weeding or planting something else.

How you propagate your corydalis depends very much on the species. Garden sages say not to divide *C. lutea*, but you can dig up seedlings in the spring and transplant them. I've never had a problem with this species over-seeding, but some have reported it being overzealous. I *have* divided *C. elata*, the gorgeous blue corydalis, with no difficulty when I wanted to share it with another gardener; this beautiful blue bloomer is slow to form clumps and I've never experienced it self-seeding.

I've had varying success with a number of corydalis species over the years, because I like to challenge my zones *and* my soil from time to time. Some have been in my garden for years; others were marginally hardy, succumbed to the wetter parts of my garden, or were just not the right plants for my site. Those that have done well continue to thrive year after year with minimal care.

Recommended species and cultivars

Corydalis lutea: The smallest of the yellow-flowered species, and one of the longest-blooming perennials: it will stop flowering with a hard frost or snowfall. Zone 3.

C. cheilanthifolia: Fern-leafed corydalis is another yellow species, with much larger foliage and flower heads. Does self-seed. Zone 3.

C. elata: The electric blue flowers of this upright-growing corydalis are show-stoppingly lovely and fragrant to boot. This is the superior blue-flowered species to grow in our region. Zone 4 with winter protection.

C. flexuosa: Another blue-flowered species, which has a number of cultivars, including the well-named 'Purple Leaf.' Although some literature says this is hardy to zone 5, I'd give it winter protection and make sure your soil drains well.

C. solida: Low-growing species, with rose-pink flowers. Zone 4.

C. 'Blackberry Wine': This hybrid grows to 10 inches in height and has fragrant flowers that are mauve tipped in wine. Cut it back after blooming to promote a second flush later in the season. Zone 5.

C. 'Chocolate Stars': You may see this advertised under species *C. quantmeyeriana*, or *C. temulifolia*. It's appealing for its chocolate-coloured foliage in spring, which fades as summer progresses, and its pale pink blooms. More drought-tolerant than some of its relatives, but also less tolerant of any drainage issues. Zone 5.

Delphinium

delphinium, larkspur

Family: Ranunculaceae

Hardy to: zone 3

Bloom period: June–July

Growing requirements: full sun to light shade; compost-rich soil, good drainage but adequate moisture

Height: 2–6 feet

Where best used: back of border (tall species); front of border for Chinese cultivars

Propagation: division, cuttings, seed

Problems: Aphids, slugs, spider mites, mildew, and rots. Taller cultivars usually require staking.

Notes: All parts of plant are toxic. May rebloom after deadheading. Flower stalks can be dried for indoor arrangements

The blooming of delphinium in my garden generally coincides with what we not-so-fondly call the annual "delphinium-peony monsoons"—heavy rains, accompanied by a warm but exuberant wind, that tend to topple too-heavy peony and delphinium that weren't staked early in the season because the gardener was too busy. Despite that meteorological annoyance, I wouldn't be without delphinium in my garden: to me, they are one of the essentials of a flower-filled cottage garden.

Delphinium is often listed as a challenging perennial. The tall varieties really ought to be staked or otherwise supported, lest they tip over during a weather event like mine have done. They're susceptible to a variety of insect pests and diseases, although I think that tends to be more in the warmer areas of their growth range than here in Atlantic Canada. They don't like too much heat, which is why gardeners in hotter areas of North America look covetously at our plantings of handsome blue, white, purple, and rose-flowered delphinium. Butterflies and hummingbirds love these plants, and they are gloriously beautiful in

a deep blue delphinium with contrasting white "bee" or centre

bloom. Enough of them have blue flowers to warrant putting up with their diva-esque personalities, if you're as besotted by blue as I am.

Chinese dwarf delphinium 'Blue Butterfly'

old-fashioned tall bicolour delphinium

Delphinium is happiest in sunny gardens with rich but well-drained soil. You can avoid problems with mildew and crown rot by keeping plants well spaced and dividing them if they get too crowded.

Even with the best of care, delphinium can often become exhausted and fail to return after a couple of years, so you may want to add additional plants or divide yours yearly to maintain vigour. That said, I've had a large clump of white and another of sky-blue delphinium growing in my garden for many years without them dying out, perhaps because they are old and vigorous varieties.

How best to stake delphinium is a subject open to debate. Bamboo stakes and plant ties are probably the least expensive option, but you'll have to stake each individual stem in order to have the plants look their best. Grow-through supports are also available from specialty garden companies, some with adjustable rings that you slide up the stake as the plant grows, but these can be quite pricey, especially if you have numerous clumps of delphinium around your garden. (See sidebar on staking, page 95.)

Once your plants are finished their big flush of bloom, cut them back to side shoots or to the top of leafy growth. Side shoots will produce smaller spikes of flowers, and if conditions are good, the plant may enjoy a second, though smaller, blooming later in the season.

The tall, stately delphinium that put on such a show in midsummer are known as the elatum hybrids, and regularly reach 6 feet or more if not knocked over by wind. The most common are the Pacific Giant hybrid series, which includes the "Knights" (Galahad, Percival, Black Knight, King Arthur). The "Magic Fountains" series have shorter, sturdy stems that don't require staking and are named according to their flower colour; they have a contrasting centre, or "bee," so you'll find names like 'White with Dark Bee,' which is descriptive but not imaginative. A New Zealand breeder named Terry Dowdeswell has developed a series called the "New Millennium" delphinium, which are more vigorous, disease resistant, and gaining in popularity across Canada.

For front of border display, consider planting the Chinese delphinium (*D. grandiflorum*). It rarely grows taller than 24 inches and has finely cut leaves like a Japanese maple and flowers that may be white or various shades of blue depending on the cultivar.

Related to delphinium but grown as annuals are the true larkspurs, *Consolida ambigua*. These self-seed for some gardeners and also make good dried flowers.

Dianthus

pink, sweet William, carnation

Family: Caryophyllaceae
Hardy to: zone 3
Bloom period: spring to late summer
Growing requirements: Sun to light shade, slightly alkaline soil. Good drainage is essential.
Height: 3–24 inches

Where best used: rock gardens, mixed borders, trough plantings
Propagation: seed or division
Problems: root rot if soil too wet; assortment of insect pests, none usually serious
Notes: Deer-resistant. Attracts butterflies. Drought- and salt-tolerant.

I'll confess that I regularly get confused between some of the species of pinks commonly grown in the garden. The two I know best are the beloved sweet William (*Dianthus barbatus*) and the sea-urchin-like *D. caesius* 'Tiny Rubies' that I grow in a concrete trough. Ask me about maiden, china, cottage pinks, though, and I'll probably go cross-eyed and change the subject. I do grow a number of them, but some of my plants have come from other gardeners, who in turn weren't sure which species or hybrid they had, so we agreed to refer to them as dianthus and leave it at that. Happily, many growers also simply list the genus and the cultivar of dianthus.

There's a good reason for this confusion: there are around three hundred species in the dianthus family, from my cherished 'Tiny Rubies' to the much-larger florist's carnation. The flowers get the common name "pinks" because they look like they were given a good trim with pinking shears.

a pink showing grassy foliage

'Coconut Punch'

Flowers are usually red, white, or some shade of pink, with numerous bicoloured forms, especially in the sweet Williams; many are extremely fragrant, although some of the newer

sweet William

cultivars are less scented than their older counterparts. Some pinks have evergreen foliage, which can range in colour from steel blue to brilliant green to darker green flushed with red. Many of the dianthus aren't long-lived, so remember to divide yours regularly to ensure that you have plenty of these charming blooms every year.

If you have ordinary soil with good drainage, neutral to slightly alkaline in pH, pinks ought to do well. In my garden, they've performed best either in troughs or in areas where the soil has the least amount of clay, because overwintering sogginess will kill many species. I've found sweet William to be the most tolerant of clay and wet, although older varieties tend to be biennial, germinating one year and flowering the next, then fading away.

Besides being fragrant and wonderful for front of border, dianthus attracts many butterflies, bees, and other pollinators, while being resistant to deer. If you keep deadheading your dianthus varieties faithfully, they'll often keep blooming for weeks on end.

Recommended species and cultivars

There are dozens of species and cultivars to choose from, many simply referred to by *Dianthus* and cultivar name.

Dianthus alpinus: Alpine pinks form very low-growing mats of grey-green foliage, resembling sea urchins. Excellent for rock or trough gardening.

D. barbatus: Sweet William. Perhaps the most striking is 'Sooty,' a deep wine variety that looks almost black in some lights, and which is effective planted near a gold-foliaged plant to set off its dark flowers. Sweet William often reseeds in the garden for many years, making it a favourite of cottage gardeners.

D. chinensis: China pink has a more upright growth habit than some of its relatives. Often grown as an annual or biennial, but may return for years.

D. caesius (sometimes called *gratianopolitanus*): Cheddar pinks form tidy mats with blue-green, grass-like foliage, ideal for front of border or ground cover. They are quite salt-tolerant, and also lightly drought-tolerant. 'Firewitch' was the Perennial Plant of the Year in 2006, and is brilliant magenta with a white eye.

D. deltoides: Maiden pink forms mat-like mounds of dark green foliage and produce dozens of petite, brilliant flowers. One of the most popular cultivars is 'Flashing Lights,' with neon scarlet-pink flowers.

THE SALT-SPRINKLED GARDEN

Those of us who live near the ocean are faced with a particular set of challenges. Not only do we get more than our share of fog and wind, there's the whole issue of salt damage on our trees, shrubs, and perennials. If you live very close to the ocean, perhaps on a bank overlooking the water, you may get direct hits from particularly large waves during storms as well as overrun during the exceptionally high tides that can occur several times a year. Flooding from ice jams can also be a problem in some winters, but for the most part, salt spray from wind or from waves hitting the shoreline are the most common causes of salt problems in the oceanside garden.

The other source of salt damage to plants is from the application of winter salt to roads, driveways, and walkways. You'll often see brown needles on white pines and other salt-sensitive evergreens growing along highways, the result of salt spray thrown to the roadside by passing vehicles.

High concentrations of salt in soil can cause numerous problems with plants, including stunted growth, wilt, leaf scorch, poor seed germination, and even death. Happily, areas that enjoy significant rainfall each year are less apt to have a lot of salt in their soils because the precipitation reduces salt concentration. Wind, fog, and temperature fluctuations are more of a problem to many seaside gardeners than salt in their soils.

Excessive salt spray on foliage can also be a problem, resulting in leaf scorch or burn. However, if you take a walk on a beach and look at the plants that grow there, you'll notice that their foliage may have one of several features protecting them from salt accumulation. Some species have downy or fuzzy hairs on their leaves, often giving the plants a white, silver, or greyish cast to their leaves. These hairy structures capture salt spray and prevent it from accumulating on the plants themselves. Other plants may have thick, glossy foliage that repeals moisture from sticking, while still others have waxy coverings protecting their fruits.

For a list of salt-tolerant plants, please see Appendix C, page 243.

Dicentra

bleeding-heart, Dutchman's breeches, squirrel corn

Family: Fumariaceae

Hardy to: zone 2

Growing requirements: moist, rich soil; partial shade to full sun

Height: 10–20 inches for *D. eximia*; 2–4 feet for *D. spectabilis*

Where best used: shade garden, ground cover (creeping species), mixed border

Propagation: division or seedlings

Problems: No serious pests or diseases.

Notes: Deer-resistant. May go dormant in hot weather. The plant's sap can cause skin irritation in some people.

My first encounter with Dicentra was with the species *D. cucullaria*, the quaintly named Dutchman's breeches. This spring-flowering ephemeral is native to milder parts of Atlantic Canada, and grows in great profusion on the Cape Split peninsula near my home. Another interesting native plant is *D. canadensis*, or squirrel corn, which has white flowers tipped in yellow and is occasionally sold for shade gardens.

D. spectabilis, *old-fashioned bleeding-heart*

For most of us, however, the most familiar *Dicentra* species is what some refer to as the old-fashioned bleeding-heart (*Dicentra spectabilis*), a lush, shrub-like perennial that can grow to 4 feet tall and wide in the right conditions. In mid-spring, delicate heart-shaped flowers of pink or white dangle like pendants from arching green stems. These flowers last for at least a month for most gardeners, but there's no need to deadhead the plant, as it will not rebloom.

Dicentra spectabilis will often go dormant in hot weather. My foggy garden doesn't usually get a lot of consistent sunny, hot weather until early August, but for many Atlantic gardeners, especially those inland, consistently hot summer weather will begin in late June or early July. Don't be alarmed if your plant's foliage turns yellow and the plant starts to look tattered; it's simply responding to the temperature and heading into a protective dormancy. You can cut the foliage down to the ground if you wish. As the weather cools down in late summer or early fall, your plant will probably start to grow new foliage again, and may even produce a few blooms, but it will be back to its vigorous self next spring.

An equally attractive, although very different, member of the *Dicentra* species is the fringed bleeding-heart, *D. eximia*. This is a much lower-growing plant, usually between

10–18 inches tall, and has a creeping, mounding growth habit. It's a lovely selection for a ground cover under trees in a shade garden and if grown in moist, rich, but well-drained soil, it will produce white, pink, or red flowers throughout the gardening season. Even when not blooming, its lacy foliage is fern-like and attractive.

Dicentra eximia doesn't go dormant in my garden, although it will if conditions are hot and dry. The western bleeding heart, *D. formosa,* has a similar growth habit and is more drought-tolerant, but I've also found it to be less tolerant of clay soil and winter wet.

Most literature recommends leaving old-fashioned bleeding heart undivided, suggesting that you dig up seedlings in early spring if you want to share your plant or to transplant it elsewhere. Because I have one plant in the front garden that I refer to as "the bleeding-heart that ate Scots Bay" (it has reached nearly 5 feet tall and remained blooming until August in some years), I have actually dug the crown up in the spring, split it, and replanted it in several locations, with all the divisions surviving nicely. The fringed bleeding-hearts can be divided without difficulty in early spring, though the new divisions will probably sulk for a season before they grow in earnest.

Plant breeders have been experimenting with creating new forms of both the old-fashioned and the fringed bleeding heart. There is a gold-foliaged form of *D. spectabilis,* 'Gold Heart,' which is very attractive and seems more heat-tolerant than some.

D. eximia, *fringed bleeding-heart*

white form of old-fashioned bleeding-heart

Dictamnus albus

gas plant, burning bush, dittany

Family: Rutaceae

Hardy to: zone 3

Bloom period: spring to late summer

Growing requirements: full sun to light shade; rich, well-drained soil

Height: 2–4 feet

Where best used: mixed borders, pollinator gardens

Propagation: Seed. Do not divide.

Problems: Slugs and snails on young plants.

Notes: Deer-resistant. The plant's volatile oil can cause a rash on skin exposed to sunlight.

I read about dittany, the gas plant, long before I ever got my plant greedy hands on one, and was intrigued because it was described as being exquisitely fragrant. I was also bemused to read that the plant exudes a volatile gas at night that can be lit with a match on calm summer evenings. Despite the fact that such a parlour trick isn't supposed to harm the plant, I've never attempted it, because this perennial was too hard to find, and took several years to establish.

Dittany is a gorgeous plant, so be sure to situate it where you can admire its flowers and fragrance, because it has a long taproot that resents being moved. Dictamnus likes a rich soil that drains well and is a little on the alkaline side. I always side-dress around ours with mushroom compost, which tends to be somewhat alkaline, and the plant has been thriving splendidly.

Patience is required while dittany establishes itself; it may take as many as four years to turn into much of a plant in your garden. It tends to be slow to emerge in my garden in the spring, but I mark its location well and avoid doing anything in its vicinity until it's up and growing. Dittany will self-seed, but seedlings may also take several years to establish and up to five years to bloom, so you are apt to mistake them for weed seedlings when they are tiny.

There are two main forms of dittany, one with pristine

rose flowered form

white-flowered form

white flowers, one with purple-pink marked blossoms (*D. albus* var. *purpureus*). Both seem to be equally fragrant, as the oils that give dittany its fragrance infuse the leaves as well as the flowers, probably the reason why the species is not bothered by foraging deer. Don't deadhead your gas plant when the flowers are spent— it will produce handsome, star-shaped seed heads that will last in the garden long after the blooms are past, and can be used in dried flower arrangements.

Despite the need for patience when growing dittany, it's a pretty easy plant to deal with once established. Since you don't have to divide or move it, you can pretty much just enjoy the deep green leaves and the stunning flowers.

plant dittany where you want it as it resents transplanting

seedheads of dittany

Digitalis

foxglove, fairy thimbles, witches' gloves, dead men's fingers

Family: Scrophulariaceae or Plantaginaceae

Hardy to: 3 or 4 to 8

Bloom period: early summer (June–July)

Growing requirements: full sun to partial shade; acidic, well-drained soil

Height: 18–60 inches

Where best used: mixed borders, pollinator plants, mid- to back of borders

Propagation: division, seed

Problems: slugs

Notes: Hummingbirds and bees love them. All parts of plant are toxic.

I remember reading about foxgloves as a child and thinking that the author was genuinely referring to gloves worn by foxes. It wasn't until much later that I learned two things: one, that "foxglove" was a flower, the genus name of which, *Digitalis*, refers to fingers; and two, "fox" was a variation of "folks," meaning fairies. So the gloves were not worn by foxes but rather by fairy folk.

The common foxglove (*D. purpurea*) is a native of Europe and is another showy perennial that works well in a cottage garden or in any site where it can spread and put on a brilliant display. It's also a biennial, producing rosettes of furry leaves the first year, and then in the second year putting up spectacular spikes of flowers in cream, pink, or deep rose, often spotted with crimson, chocolate, or wine freckles inside the bells. I've been letting mine go to seed for a number of years now, so there are always a few seedlings among the flowering plants. If you cut your plants back instead of letting them go to seed, they'll produce young plants, or offsets, around their crowns, which you can then divide off the main plant and replant elsewhere.

common foxglove flowers

Other types of foxgloves are more perennial in nature, returning year after year, and also dispensing a few seeds for seedlings. In our garden, we have four different species as well as several striking hybrids.

Perhaps the most notable thing about foxgloves is that the plant is the source of the drug digitalin, used in treating heart conditions. For obvious reasons, the entire plant is toxic and should be handled with gloves. The Nova Scotia Museum's Poison Plant Patch website advises that "Children should not be permitted to suck the nectar from these 'bells' nor drink the rainwater collected within. Nor should adults indulge in herbal preparations containing digitalis without informed supervision."

Foxglove's toxicity also means that while it's attractive to bees and hummingbirds, it is quite resistant to deer, rabbits, and squirrels. The plant's toxicity, coupled with its medicinal properties, has also led to the diversity of common names by which it has been referred to in folk and herbal lore across the ages.

Foxgloves love moist but well-drained soil, a little acidic, and generously amended with compost. They will take full sun in our climate but also partial shade, though they won't flower as profusely in partial shade.

Digitalis parviflora *'Milk Chocolate'*

Recommended species and cultivars

Digitalis purpurea: The common foxglove, tallest of the species recommended here, and biennial in nature. Blossoms generally grow on one side of the stalk, whereas some species have flowers in whorls all the way around the flower stem. Zone 4.

D. grandiflora: One of two yellow-flowered forms commonly grown in gardens, this is a short-lived perennial that grows 2–3 in height and produces pale yellow flowers speckled with brown dots. Reseeds in our garden. Zone 3.

D. lutea: The straw, or small yellow, foxglove is quite perennial in our garden, and more shade-tolerant than some other species. The flowers on their 2–3 foot stalks are not as large as the common and grandiflora foxgloves, but they are strikingly accented with red dots inside the bells. Will rebloom if deadheaded. Zone 3.

D. x mertonensis: The Merton or strawberry foxglove is a hybrid that is always described as having flowers the colour of crushed strawberries. Zone 4.

***D. parviflora* 'Milk Chocolate'**: For the chocolate-loving gardener, this is a true find; not as showy as other species, but strikingly unique with its tall spikes of petite, chocolate-coloured flowers. Don't eat it, however! From a distance the spikes of flowers look like beads or braids. The foliage is glossy green and the plant is quite perennial, occasionally producing seedlings. Zone 4.

Echinacea

echinacea, purple coneflower

Family: Asteraceae

Hardy to: zone 3

Bloom period: July-October (some rebloom if deadheaded)

Growing requirements: Sun to partial shade, good soil with good drainage. Drought-tolerant once established.

Height: 2–4 feet

Where best used: sunny borders, pollinator gardens

Propagation: seed (species), division (cultivars)

Problems: Some newer hybrids do not tolerate Atlantic winters very well.

Notes: Excellent perennial for bees and butterflies.

My long-suffering spouse became extremely exasperated with me one day years ago when I said something about a white purple coneflower in the garden.

"How can it be a white purple flower?" he demanded. "It's either white or purple." I had to explain to him that the species is purple coneflower (*Echinacea purpurea*) but that plant breeders had developed white-flowered forms of this beautiful summer-flowering perennial.

If you're a fan of echinaceas, you know that along with purple and white forms, there are now green, yellow, gold, orange, salmon, hot pink, and red varieties, as well as several double-flowered forms. Echinaceas are a plant-breeder's delight, and gardeners have become equally besotted with the newer flower colours. Echinaceas are one of my favourite perennials, and I've been testing out the newer colours for over five years.

A few different species of echinaceas are grown for ornamental use. *Echinacea purpurea*, that purple coneflower that so exasperated my spouse, has broad leaves and can grow up to 5 feet tall. *E. angustifolia* tends to grow only to about 2 feet tall, and features narrow leaves and downward-flexed petals on its flowers. *E. paradoxa* is the yellow coneflower, and has been crossed with *E. purpurea* to produce many of the colourful new hybrids.

Coneflowers are stars of the midsummer garden, beginning to flower in early July for some gardeners. The first of mine don't generally begin to flower until the latter part of July,

'Sundown'

'Green Envy'

'Hot Papaya' double-flowered echinacea

'Hope'

but then several of the cultivars keep up the performance until frost draws the curtain on the gardening year in late October. Even then, the bronze, copper, or brown central cones remain on the stiff stems, providing seeds for songbirds and textural interest for the gardener until well into winter.

When the new orange and yellow varieties first came on the market I didn't hesitate to purchase the then-pricey plants and add them to my garden. What I discovered (and what other gardeners have confirmed) is that some forms are more cold-tolerant than others. The "Meadowbrite" series developed at the Chicago Botanic Gardens may tolerate the cold winters of the Windy City, but they don't appreciate the erratic temperatures of Atlantic winters. Nor do they like excessively soggy soil; as with most drought-tolerant perennials, coneflowers may put up with dry conditions but they don't like wet feet. The original species tend to be more accepting of heavy clay, but give them good circulation to help prevent stem and crown rots.

Recommended cultivars

'Green Envy': Features a green central cone and green petals that gradually flush with purple.

'Coconut Lime': A double form with green central cones and white petals tipped with green.

'Pink Double Delight': As its name suggests, a pink form with a pompom-like central cone.

'Hope': This cultivar's breeder donates a portion of the sales from the pale pink coneflower to breast cancer research.

The "Big Sky" series was developed by Itsaul Plants of Georgia, and boasts a rainbow of new colours, some of them with bicolour petals, most with lovely fragrance. The series includes 'Sunrise' (pale yellow), 'Sundown' (orange fading to purple), 'Harvest Moon' (deep gold), and 'After Midnight' (deep magenta, red cone).

'Tiki Torch': Brilliant orange flowers.

'Tomato Soup': The reddest of the coneflowers to date, it really is the colour of tomato soup.

'Hot Papaya': The first double orange coneflower on the market.

'Mac n Cheese': A gold form that holds its colour and doesn't fade as the flowers mature.

Echinops

globe thistle

Family: Asteraceae

Hardy to: zone 3

Bloom period: midsummer to autumn

Growing requirements: sun to partial shade; average, well-drained soil

Height: 2–6 feet

Where best used: mixed borders, pollinator gardens

Propagation: Grows easily from seed. Dividing is difficult.

Problems: No serious pests or diseases.

Notes: Pollinators, including butterflies and hummingbirds, love them. Deer-resistant.

When I was living in Delhaven, not far from Blomidon, a local woman—a terrific perennial gardener—offered me a number of her extra perennials, including lambs' ears, Shasta daisies, and the tall, purple-blue species of globe thistle. Those plants followed me when I made the move to our current home, and I've shared their progeny with many other gardeners since that time.

Globe thistles are not for every garden because they are quite tall, and their underground root systems are thick, woody, and difficult to cut through. However, if you want a tough, dependable, long-blooming perennial with striking foliage as well as dramatic flowers, and you have the room for them, globe thistles are fabulous. Don't be worried by the common name: globe thistles are not invasive the way common wild thistles may be, although both are beloved by birds, bees, and other creatures.

The leaves and flower bracts of echinops are prickly but not as fierce as, say, a teasel (*Dipsacus*) or a barberry shrub. This prickliness may contribute to their usefulness as a deer-resistant perennial. The plants sometimes lose their lower leaves in the same way that tall asters and phlox do, but if they are planted behind lower-growing plants in a mixed border, no one will ever know except you.

hummingbirds love globe thistles

Most literature recommends planting globe thistles in well-draining soil, although I have some planted near a pond in heavy clay and they've done just fine. Once established, globe thistles are quite drought-tolerant; another group that seeded themselves are growing in little more than gravel on another site on our property. They do self-seed a little (it's never been a problem in our garden); these seedlings are easy to move and transplant elsewhere while they are still small.

Echinops are excellent in a drift at the back of the border.

Dividing a globe thistle clump requires patience, strength, and a very sharp shovel or knife; you may easily cut young offsets and roots from the perimeter of a clump. I once decided to dig up and move an entire clump, and it took most of the afternoon and some rather salty language.

If you enjoy bringing cut flowers into your home, globe thistles have a lovely fragrance. Each plant is quite floriferous, so it will happily spare a few stems without looking the worse for it. For those who enjoy longer-lasting arrangements, these are also easy flowers to dry: cut them when they're still immature and a little on the small side or they're apt to fall apart when dried.

The various species and cultivars of echinops can be confusing. Three species of globe thistle (of about 120 in the genus, none native to North America) are commonly offered by nurseries, along with a few different cultivars. Mislabelling sometimes happens, or you'll find that a nursery calls its offerings merely "Echinops" with no explanation of species or cultivar. You may also see cultivars labelled without species, in which case you may want to see the plant in flower to verify the colour.

Of the species sold in our region, the most frequently seen is *Echinops ritro*, which in my garden routinely grows to 5 feet and taller in height and has dozens of pale, purple-blue flowers. 'Taplow Blue' and 'Veitch's Blue' are two popular cultivars, each having more steel-blue flowers than the basic species.

Echinops bannaticus is a little shorter (generally between 2–4 feet in height) and has a very bushy foliage habit; cultivars 'Blue Glow' and 'Blue Ball' are both available at nurseries.

Finally, the tallest of the species is the great globe thistle, *E. sphaerocephalus*, which easily tops 7 feet in height. 'Arctic Glow' is an unusual, white-flowered cultivar of great globe thistle; I found it to be the least vigorous and most prone to succumbing to winter wet in my garden.

Epimedium

barrenwort, bishop's hat, mitrewort, fairywings

Family: Berberidaceae
Hardy to: zone 4 with winter protection
Bloom period: April to early May
Growing requirements: partial shade to full sun; humus-rich, evenly moist, well-drained soil
Height: 8–12 inches

Where best used: ground cover, woodland gardens
Propagation: division of clumps in early spring
Problems: No serious pests or diseases.
Notes: Deer- and rabbit-resistant. Some species and cultivars have evergreen foliage.

The epimedium will probably never win an award as the showiest spring perennial. Each individual flower—yellow, pink, red, or orange depending on the cultivar—is about the size of a pea, although there may be a dozen or more on each flowering spike. There is a wee drawback to them, too: while in containers, they flower even earlier than they do in the ground, so often that by the time a seasonally run nursery opens, the flowers are all but past. On April 8, 2010, I was poking around a friend's nursery that was not yet open for business and the epimedium plants were all coming into bloom. Granted, that was an unseasonably warm spring, but you get the point: often barrenwort gets left on the plant table because it's "only" leaves by mid-May.

'Sulphureum'

E. *x* rubrum

However, this is a wonderful plant for most gardeners. To start with, it's one of those species that nuisance wildlife like deer and rabbits shun in favour of other, tastier plants. Its new foliage is lovely: pale green, often flushed with rose-red highlights. The heart-shaped leaves put on a brilliant fall-colour display, and depending the species or hybrid, leaves will persist over winter. Barrenwort makes a great ground cover, but it does take a few years to establish itself.

In many books epimedium is recommended for dry shade, including for planting under hardwoods with their thick root systems and heavy canopies. I had a long talk about these plants several summers ago with Lloyd Mapplebeck, who teaches horticulture at the

Nova Scotia Agricultural College in Truro and also runs a small perennial nursery. He told me that in our climate, we can plant epimedium in full sun provided it has moist (but not soggy) soil; we don't get the heat of much of Canada and the United States, and the barrenwort is like astilbe in that it can handle sun so long as it has adequate moisture.

If you are planting barrenwort as a ground cover, be prepared to mulch well around your plant or plants to keep weeds under control while the perennial has a chance to establish and grow. Mulch of course has the added benefit of keeping plant roots cool and moist, a particular benefit if summers turn hot and dry.

If you want floral colour to go along with your barrenwort once their flowers have passed, try planting astilbes with them. The two very different foliage types also make for an appealing garden vignette. Other good companions include primulas, columbines, and geums.

'Lilafee'

foliage showing new spring colour

Recommended species and cultivars

Epimedium grandiflorum **'Rose Queen'**: This variety has large (for barrenwort) flowers that are deep pink with contrasting white spurs.

E. grandiflorum **'Lilafee' (also called Lilac Fairy)**: Large lavender flowers with bronze-tinted spring foliage that turns red in autumn.

E. **'Orange Queen'**: Also seen sold as 'Orangekönigin,' this cultivar has coppery orange flowers. Unique and attractive.

E. x *rubrum*: One of the most common, with reddish purple flowers and handsome foliage.

E. x *versicolor* **'Sulphureum'**: Flowers somewhat resemble miniature daffodils: yellow petals surrounded by white to pale yellow sepals.

E. x *youngianum* **'Niveum'**: Deep green foliage with sprays of pure white flowers.

Eryngium

sea holly

Family: Apiaceae

Hardy to: zone 3

Bloom period: July–October

Growing requirements: full sun, excellent drainage

Height: 2–6 feet

Where best used: gravel or alpine garden, mixed borders, pollinator gardens

Propagation: offsets or seedlings

Problems: No serious pests or diseases.

Notes: Deadhead to control self-seeding. Birds eat the seeds. Attractive to butterflies and bees.

How many of us fall in love with a plant based on a photo we saw in a book or magazine? That was certainly the case for me with sea holly. I was instantly smitten with their flower heads, which are composed of a cone of tiny florets surrounded by a ruffled, sometimes prickly, ring of bracts, usually in the same silver, blue, green, or purple colour as the flowers. It's these bracts that make sea hollies especially appealing, as they hold their colour for months on end, giving the plant a particularly long season of bloom. Sea hollies also make good cut flowers, and are popular with florists for use in long-lasting or permanent arrangements.

I remember being quite astonished when I discovered sea holly belongs to the Apiaceae family. Certainly sea hollies don't look like many of their relatives (think dill, Queen Anne's lace, and caraway, as well as *Astrantia*, profiled earlier), but like those relatives they attract many pollinators, especially bees.

Full sun and good drainage are the key to making eryngium happy in a garden, although I've found *E. planum*, the flat sea holly, and *E. yuccifolium*, the so-called rattlesnake master, to be tolerant of some sogginess. Eryngium don't need particularly fertile soil, which can actually make them floppy in growth habit and in need of staking. To add to their appeal, they are salt- and drought-

alpine sea holly

flat sea holly

tolerant, and many species are deer-resistant, although I have heard reports of deer damage in some gardens.

Sea hollies dislike being moved because they have taproots, but you can easily dig up and move seedlings early in spring. They will normally take two years to develop enough size to put up blooms.

I like the fact that many sea hollies self-seed, because some of them behave as biennials, growing rosettes of leaves the first year and then flowering, setting seed, and dying the second year. So I never deadhead mine, but several years ago during a gardening talk, I met a gardener who was highly indignant that her eryngium had scattered seedlings around her garden. Others at the talk promptly solved the problem by reassuring her they'd relieve her of her seedlings!

rattlesnake master

Eryngium alpinum: One of my favourites. Although it is not as hardy in my garden as other species, alpine sea holly has spectacular lacy bracts surrounding the central cone of blue flowers. Grows to about 3 feet in height.

E. amethystium: Even the flower stems of amethyst sea holly are a rich blue. This is a shorter species than some, usually growing no more than 2 feet high, with flower stalks reaching perhaps another foot taller.

E. giganteum 'Miss Wilmott's Ghost': This is one species that can grow quite tall (to 5 feet). It has green-grey flower heads surrounded by silvery bracts, all of which fade to a handsome tan by late autumn. The story behind the common name is that English plantswoman Miss Ellen Wilmott (1858–1934) used to drop seeds of this Eryngium into friends' gardens, where it would germinate and grow vegetatively the first year, then produce its spectacular, ghostly flowers in the second year.

E. planum: Perhaps the easiest and most perennial of sea hollies, in part because it produces numerous seedlings. Flat sea holly is extremely floriferous, sending up multiple stipes (flower stems) bearing metallic-blue flowers. A new cultivar, 'Jade Frost,' was released several years ago: while the flowers are the standard colour, the foliage is variegated green and creamy white, with tinges of pink in the new growth.

E. yuccifolium: I grow rattlesnake master in part for its name, which annoys my snake-hating spouse, but also because it's a dramatic and unusual plant. Its foliage is yucca-like, strappy, and has prickly leaves, from which a spike of flowers arises and towers 5 feet and more in height.

Eupatorium

Joe-Pye weed, boneset, snakeroot, wild ageratum

Family: Asteraceae

Hardy to: zone 3 or 4

Bloom period: late summer to fall

Growing requirements: full sun to partial shade; average to wet soil

Height: 2–7 feet

Where best used: massed plantings, butterfly gardens

Propagation: division of clumps in early spring

Problems: No serious pests or diseases. Resents drought conditions.

Notes: Tolerant of wet conditions. Very attractive to butterflies.

The eupatoriums include several species, most of which are largely the same to the average gardener. They are tall, clump-forming perennials that flower later in the summer, making them great "fallscaping" plants. They are also remarkable butterfly magnets, and if you've ever seen a swarm of monarchs, viceroys, and other butterflies flitting around them, you know that this is no exaggeration.

Despite the common name of Joe-Pye weed, these plants are not weedy at all in my experience. Native to North America, they often bloom along roadsides and ditches, beside streams, and in other wet or marshy

purple bush Eupatorium

areas. They actually have a host of rather confusing common names, including "snakeroot," which also refers to a related species, *Ageratina*, as well as to members of the *Actaea/Cimicifuga* genus. The common name "boneset" refers to the use of this plant in treating broken bones in traditional medicine; indeed, according to Marjorie Harris in *Botanica North America*, Joe Pye was a First Nations herbalist who sold various plant extracts and medicines to settlers in the New England states. One common name sometimes given to eupatorium is hardy or wild ageratum, which makes sense when you look at the fleecy, compact flowers that cover the tops of each stem of this perennial.

While some species of eupatorium are indeed benign (though their efficacy as herbal remedies may be questionable), one species, *E. rugosum,* is toxic in all its parts and best handled with caution. That species happens also to be the parent of cultivar 'Chocolate,' which is a very attractive garden perennial with fluffy white flowers and chocolate- to purple-tinted foliage. I have been unable to find warnings for 'Chocolate' eupatorium, but err on the side of caution and use gloves when handling it, and don't let pets or children try to eat it, despite its charming name.

Joe-Pye weed prefers full sun and an average soil, and will often require staking in soil that is overly fertile or in a partially shady situation. The plants need room and a site where they can show off their stately beauty, as most can easily reach 7 feet under ideal conditions.

If you have a damp or marshy area in your garden, this is the place to plant eupatorium: in fact, in dry summers you may have to water your plants if the leaves begin to wilt and turn brown. Mulching around the plant will help to keep its roots cool and keep moisture in the soil.

'Chocolate'

Eupatorium species are ideal for a butterfly garden and work well with other later-blooming perennials such as garden phlox, echinaceas, *Miscanthus* ornamental grasses, and the stately 'Herbstsonne' shining coneflower (*Rudbeckia nitida* 'Herbstsonne'). Deer and rabbits rarely bother eupatorium, and although some insects may chew its leaves, it has no significant diseases or pests. Several shorter varieties are available: 'Purple Bush' usually grows to 36 inches, while 'Phantom' stays under three feet tall.

Euphorbia

euphorbia, spurge

Family: Euphorbiaceae
Hardy to: varies with species
Bloom period: Late spring. Bracts hold colour and give appearance of being in bloom all season.
Growing requirements: full sun, average soil with good drainage
Height: 8 inches to 3 feet

Where best used: sunny locations, mixed borders
Propagation: division
Problems: No serious pests or diseases.
Notes: Deer-resistant. Many spurges exude a milky sap which can be caustic on skin or if splashed in eyes.

One of the things that delights me about plants is the way one genus can have so many different species (and cultivars, of course). The first euphorbia I remember growing was the houseplant *E. millii*, which is known to most of us as crown of thorns. Imagine my surprise when I learned while at college that this plant was related to an even more common plant known for its popularity as a Christmas plant: the poinsettia.

Here's a little botany for those who care about such things. The brightly coloured "petals" on poinsettias and other euphorbia relatives are actually modified leaves called *bracts*. The actual flowers are in the centre, quite small and not particularly showy, but they have their own charm. The bracts will remain colourful for many weeks, and as an added bonus, quite a few of the spurges have nice fall colour. Some will even produce a smaller, second set of blooms in late summer or early autumn.

Euphorbias tend to be pretty undemanding; give them good drainage, full sun, and that's about it. Divide them occasionally (those that are inclined to spread by rhizomes) or pot up seedlings from those that spread seed.

As mentioned in the notes above, many spurges have a white, milky sap in their leaves and stems, which you will notice if you break a stem while working around them. Be very careful not to splash this sap into your eyes, or you'll end

'Bonfire'

'Fireglow'

up in the emergency room of your local hospital, getting your eyes lavaged as I did a few years ago. I'm now extremely careful working with spurges, although I have a number of species and cultivars throughout my gardens.

Many euphorbias are good for xerophyte gardens, because they can handle dry conditions without being too bothered. We can't grow some of the tender or heat-loving types, but there are plenty of hardy choices to keep us entertained.

'Purpurea'

'Fens Ruby'

Recommended species and cultivars

Euphorbia amygdaloides 'Purpurea': Purple foliage offers fine contrast to yellow/green flowers. Zone 5 with winter protection.

E. cyparissias: One of the hardier varieties, with foliage that resembles pine needles. Tends to spread by rhizomes and seed but hasn't been problematic for my garden. 'Fens Ruby' has gorgeous reddish foliage, often reflowers in late summer. Zone 4

E. dulcis 'Chameleon': Another form with purple foliage and lime green/bright yellow flowers. Excellent autumn colour. Zone 4

E. griffithii 'Fireglow': One of my personal favourites because of the coppery orange flowers and bracts. However, 'Fireglow' does run, and isn't suitable for small gardens. New shoots resemble a reddish-orange asparagus. Zone 4

E. myrsinites: Donkeytail spurge has acid yellow flowers and blue-green foliage. This species seeds profusely for some, but it also requires good drainage in order to survive winters. Zone 5.

E. polychroma: So called "cushion spurge," a tidy clump-former with brilliant green bracts surrounding yellow flowers. Cultivars include 'Lacey,' which has variegated foliage, and 'Bonfire,' with deep purple foliage surrounding electric green and yellow flowers. Zone 3.

FERNS IN THE GARDEN

Ferns are receiving a different treatment from every other plant in this book for a number of reasons, most having to do with their morphology. Unlike other plants profiled here, ferns do not flower, but reproduce by spores, which depending on the species, are formed on separate stems or on the undersides of the fronds. We enjoy a number of species as ornamental plants both indoors and out.

Although every fern starts out as a tightly curled collection of fronds known as fiddleheads, not every fern is edible like the young ostrich fern, *Matteucia struthiopteris*, (a favourite spring vegetable in many Atlantic Canadian households). Some ferns are quite toxic—the common bracken fern *Pteridium aquilinum*, is carcinogenic to many types of livestock, and is under investigation as a possible reason for stomach cancer in Japan, where it is routinely eaten as a vegetable.

evergreen ferns near a pond

While we normally think of ferns as forest dwellers that require shade and moisture, the general key to success with these plants is adequate moisture and humus-rich soil with decent drainage; with those requirements filled, many ferns can take full sun. *Dryopteris* and *Polystichum* are most tolerant of a little dryness. Ferns are remarkably problem-free, untroubled by pests—including rabbits, voles, and deer—and seldom need dividing unless you want more plants for other parts of your garden.

Not every nursery carries ferns: they can be tricky to grow in containers because if they dry out on a hot summer's day, they die. I acquired several of the species of ferns now in my garden by digging them up on a woodlot (with the owner's permission) or on my own woodlands. Interest in ferns with colourful foliage (see *Athyrium* and *Dryopteris*) has meant a greater availability of these species.

Japanese painted fern

Good ferns for gardens

Athyrium: The athyriums include some highly attractive and popular species. Lady fern, *A. filix-femina*, was a particularly popular fern during the Victorian era, and continues to be used in sheltered shade gardens today. It is hardy to zone 3. Perhaps the most popular and easily recognized of the ornamental ferns is the Japanese painted fern, *A. nipponicum* var. *pictum*, which has silver and purple tints to its foliage and stems. Numerous cultivated forms are available, with various silver, red, and green colouring, including 'Burgundy Lace,' 'Silver Falls,' and 'Pictum-Applecourt,' the latter of which has uniquely multiple tips on each frond.

Dryopteris: Variously called the wood, shield, autumn, or male fern, *Dryopteris* is a medium-sized, clump-forming genus, sometimes with evergreen foliage. One of the most attractive is the autumn fern, *D. erythrosora* 'Brilliance,' with pink, orange, and gold new foliage and equally attractive fall colour. 'Brilliance' is hardy to zone 5 with winter mulch to protect it from freezing and thawing.

'Brilliance'

Matteucia struthiopteris: The ostrich fern is a stately, elegant fern that spreads by rhizomes, so you'll find a colony of plants after a few years. Normally found along streams and riverbanks, it adapts well as a shade ornamental under trees, along house foundations, and in mixed borders. Young, unfurled fiddleheads are covered with a brown, papery sheath, and spores are formed on separate cinnamon-brown fertile fronds that emerge from the centre of the crown. Native to Atlantic Canada and hardy to zone 1.

Polystichum: The holly, Christmas, or shield fern is common through much of the region, and is easily recognized by its evergreen fronds. *P. acrostichoides* is the Christmas fern (my personal favourite), and is hardy to zone 3.

Filipendula

meadowsweet, queen of the prairie

Family: Rosaceae
Hardy to: zone 3
Bloom period: late June to August
Growing requirements: sun to partial shade, moist soil, lots of room
Height: up to 8 feet

Where best used: moist, even soggy, garden sites (near ponds, wetlands, clay soil)
Propagation: seed or division
Problems: No serious pests or diseases. May spread in some gardens. Needs staking in windy sites.
Notes: Fragrant flowers. Great butterfly plant.

I don't know why I was slow to become a fan of filipendula, because it's a magnificent plant in the right setting, and attracts copious numbers of butterflies, bees, and other pollinators when it is in bloom.

It's hard to believe that filipendula species are part of the rose family, as each individual flower is a tiny thing, part of a larger plume composed of hundreds of the flowers. If you're not acquainted with this genus of statuesque plants, the quickest way to describe them is like astilbes on steroids. Like astilbes, filipendula need moist soil or their attractive, lacy foliage will turn brown and crispy. Like astilbes, they have plumes of tiny flowers, giving them an airy yet eye-catching appearance. Unlike astilbes, most of them tower in the garden, so they aren't ideal for a small backyard plot. If you have the space, however, filipendula is an excellent choice.

giant meadowsweet

The secret to growing filipendula well is to provide it a constantly moist soil, so not surprisingly it thrives in several of the soggier parts of my garden. If your garden is plagued by winds, you'll likely need to stake your plants so they aren't beaten down. Other than that, filipendula is an easy-to-care-for plant, troubled only by Japanese beetles (if they're present in your area) and occasionally mildew or rust.

Filipendula spreads by underground stems, and can create a dramatic effect in a perennial or mixed border. My plants have not spread significantly, perhaps because the heavy clay slows their increase, possibly because they haven't been planted all that long. They're also known to self-seed, but while I've been waiting for seedlings from mine, I've yet to have any success, possibly because I have mulched too heavily.

Golden foliage of F. ulmaria *'Aurea' contrasting with* Actaea *foliage*

Recommended species and cultivars

Filipendula rubra: This species is native to the prairies of the United States and rightly given the common name queen of the prairie. It's almost shrub-like in its vigour, easily reaching 7–8 feet in good growing conditions. The flowers, which appear in mid- to late summer, are a striking rose-pink, although in seedlings the colour can be more peachy than true pink. 'Venusta' is a variety that is usually easy to find at nurseries.

F. ulmaria: European meadowsweet flowers earlier than *F. rubra*, usually beginning in late June. Its flowers are white and have a lovely fragrance. This was one of the plants used in the Middle Ages as a herb scattered on floors of dwellings to reduce unpleasant odours, hence the name meadowsweet. It is also used in herbal medicine and is a source of salicylic acid, from which the anti-inflammatory and analgesic pain medication aspirin is derived.

F. ulmaria 'Aurea': The appeal of this shorter-growing (2–3 feet) cultivar isn't the flowers, which are relatively insignificant, but the luminous gold foliage. Give 'Aurea' some shade for at least part of the day so that sunlight won't burn its leaves.

F. ulmaria 'Variegata': As the name suggests, this cultivar has green foliage variegated with gold. It's also a shorter cultivar (2–3 feet).

F. purpurea: Japanese meadowsweet is a shorter variety, usually growing to 4 feet tall, with pink flowers.

Geranium

cranesbill, geranium

Family: Geraniaceae
Hardy to: varies with species
Bloom period: late spring to autumn
Growing requirements: partial to full sun, good drainage
Height: 6 inches to 4 feet

Where best used: wide range from groundcover to tall midborder plantings
Propagation: division or seed
Problems: No serious pests or diseases.
Notes: Deer-resistant. Some cranesbills have fragrant foliage; some are drought-tolerant.

When I discuss geraniums in this book, I'm referring to members of the *Geranium* genus, which includes a huge number of hardy, perennial, flowering plants. These aren't to be confused with zonal geraniums, which are annuals with brightly coloured flowers in shades of orange, red, pink, and fuchsia: those are members of the genus *Pelargonium*, and while they're great plants, they're annuals and so aren't part of this category. In the interest of clarity, I'll refer to the plants in this profile as cranesbills, which is a common name given to them because their seed heads resembled a crane's bill to some horticulturist in the mists of time.

'Okey Dokey'

I'm very fond of cranesbills for several reasons. They tend to have a long period of bloom, and some species and cultivars will rebloom if they are deadheaded or cut back after their first big flush of blooms. Even when not in flower, they have wonderful foliage, somewhat similar to maple leaves as the leaves are usually lobed and boast toothed edges. Several cultivars have deep purple or variegated green and yellow foliage, and some have fragrant leaves.

'Red Admiral'

For best success with cranesbills, provide them with full sun to light shade, and a soil that is rich in organic matter and moist but not soggy. Once established, many of the cranesbills are quite drought-tolerant; on the other hand, many of them are not at all forgiving of soggy soil over winter.

To keep cranesbills looking good, divide them every couple of years and don't be afraid to shear them back after they've bloomed. This is particularly true with the tall *G. pratense*, the meadow cranesbill, the foliage of which tends to sprawl after blooming. I cut mine down almost to the ground and I've been rewarded with a new flush of growth.

There is a dizzying number of cranesbill species and cultivars, including several that are native to North America. Of these, the spotted cranesbill, *G. maculatum*, seems to be the one of most interest as a garden plant. A cultivar of this species called 'Espresso' (zone 4) has rich coffee-coloured foliage, making it a lovely choice even when not in bloom. The main thing to check when selecting a cranesbill is to see how tall it grows and how much it spreads; some form tidy, low-growing clumps, and others are self-seeders or spreaders.

G. phaeum *'Summertime'*

Geranium cinereum 'Ballerina': One of the smaller, clumping cranesbills, with grey-green foliage, bright pink flowers veined with purple. Zone 3.

G. macrorrhizum: Good ground-covering qualities and oddly scented leaves that act as a deer deterrent, bright pink or white flowers. More tolerant of clay than some. Zone 2.

G. phaeum: A personal favourite, with nicely fragrant foliage and wine, almost black, flowers, which help explain its common name, "Mourning Widow." Self-seeds, so deadhead if you don't want extras. Cultivar 'Springtime' has gorgeous leaves splashed in white and gold. Zone 4.

G. pratense: Meadow cranesbill is among the taller species, easily reaching 3 feet when it blooms, with pale blue or white flowers, sometimes streaked or veined with contrasting blue. Tolerates all conditions in my garden. Tends to self-seed, so deadhead if you don't want extras. Zone 3.

G. 'Okey Dokey' and 'Hocus Pocus' are two low-growing cultivars developed from *G. pratense*, both with deep purple-green foliage and blue flowers. Zone 3.

G. renardii: A species planted mostly for its foliage, which is grey-green with a quilted appearance. Demands good drainage, as soggy soil will do it in. Zone 4.

G. sanguineum: The so-called "bloody" cranesbill is a handsome choice for front of borders. Delicate foliage is covered with deep magenta blooms in late spring. Often reblooms. Tolerates wet clay well. 'Max Frei' is a popular cultivar. Zone 3.

G. 'Johnson's Blue': Beautiful lavender-blue flowers in early summer. Divide to keep it vigorous, and cut it back after flowering to regenerate its growth. Zone 2.

G. psilostemon 'Red Admiral': A striking form, grows to 24 inches tall; covered in large, red-magenta flowers. Zone 4.

Geum

avens, geum

Family: Rosaceae

Hardy to: zone 3

Bloom period: late spring–early summer
Some will rebloom if deadheaded.

Growing requirements: evenly moist, compost-rich soil

Height: 6–24 inches

Where best used: ideal for sunny planting, usually near front of bed

Propagation: spring division of hybrids, seeds of non-hybrids

Problems: No serious pests or diseases.

Notes: Deer-resistant.

My first encounter with the geum was with one of the native species *Geum rivale*, the water or purple avens, which grows in the wetter areas of our lower pasture. This mistakenly led me to think that the various hybrids offered for sale at nurseries would do well in the wet areas of our garden. Not so much: they like moisture during the summer but they also want good drainage in winter or else they will simply fade away.

I further discovered that their fading away in my garden wasn't all my fault: some of the older geum varieties are notoriously short-lived and may act more like annuals than true perennials. However, plant breeders being what they are, they've been accepting the challenge of improving geum longevity, in part because they are such attractive plants when in bloom. Their foliage forms a bright green whorl of leaves from which the wispy stems emerge, each with numerous single- or double-blossomed flowers in brilliant shades of yellow, orange, and red. They tend to bloom in late spring to early summer, providing a

'Eos'

'Cooky'

'Mango Lassi'

Recommended species and cultivars

Geum chiloense 'Lady Stratheden': Beautiful bright yellow, double flowers. Definitely short-lived so divide it yearly or sow new plants so as to have a constant supply.

G. coccineum 'Cooky': Single, brilliant orange flowers like miniature roses, very floriferous. Deadheading will produce a lesser flush of flowers in late summer/early autumn. Will flower the first year when grown from seed.

G. rivale: Definitely suited to boggy areas and cooler temperatures, water avens is also sometimes known by the curious name of Indian chocolate. Not suited to most gardens, but good for those with wet sites near streams or ponds.

G. triflorum: Native to western North America, this delightful plant is known as prairie smoke. More tolerant of drought than some, its nodding flowers are not showy but its seed heads are feathery and rosy-pink in colour.

G. 'Mango Lassi': My favourite of the geums I grow, its double flowers are larger than some varieties and are yellow with apricot to red accents in veins and on petal edges. This has been a vigourous plant in my garden for three years, and I divide it to keep it doing well.

G. 'Eos': A colour breakthrough, the foliage of this cultivar is gold-green, a perfect foil for the brilliant orange flowers.

G. 'Blazing Sunset': A well-named cultivar with brilliant scarlet-red, double flowers. From a distance can be mistaken for a small poppy.

G. 'Mrs. Bradshaw': Another hot-coloured variety with scarlet orange flowers. Deadheading will increase the length of the bloom period.

burst of colour dramatically different from the blues and pastels of later-flowering bulbs, forget-me-nots, and other late-spring flowering plants.

Location is crucial to success with geums: in our climate, which can't be considered hot when compared to other regions, they are fine with full sun provided they receive regular moisture. Mulching around the plant will help to keep soil cool and moist in times of low rainfall. The site where I grow most of my geums is heavily amended with organic matter so that it drains better than it did a few years ago, and the plants have been doing fine.

For the gardener plagued by deer depredations, your geums will generally remain unscathed. I find them a good butterfly magnet because of their brilliant colours, and have seen hummingbirds swooping around ours in early summer. Provided they are situated properly, you'll find them pest-free for the most part. Occasionally spider mites can be a problem, but they can be controlled with regular misting from a hose.

Helenium

Family: Asteraceae
Hardy to: zone 3
Bloom period: August to mid-October
Growing requirements: moist soil, full sun is preferred
Height: 2–6 feet

Where best used: late summer/autumn colour, pollinator plantings
Propagation: division
Problems: No serious pests or diseases.
Notes: Butterflies and bees love helenium. Excellent plant for late-season colour.

In the past, helenium has been an underutilized perennial, which is a huge pity, because it's a lovely, trouble-free plant with several species native to North America. It attracts butterflies and bees, covers itself with small (2–3 inch), aster-like flowers, and best of all, is a late bloomer. This clump-forming plant brings a blaze of colour to the garden just as many perennials start to dwindle and deciduous foliage begins to show its autumn glory. The flowers of helenium come in shades of gold, bronze, copper, red, orange, and various combinations of these colours.

red-flowered Helenium

It may be that one of the common names for helenium, sneezewort or sneezeweed, has deterred many gardeners, who think it will exacerbate their allergies. That's not the case; the common name apparently came from the plant's former use by native Americans and others as a substitute for snuff, with the notion that inhaling the dried flower heads would cause sneezing, driving out colds, evil spirits, and other unpleasantries.

Helenium is a tough, easy-care perennial. I planted two yellow-flowered specimens (unnamed, merely labeled as *Helenium autumnale*, the regular species) about ten years ago in a soggy, partly shaded area of the garden. They have prospered and have been divided several times to share with others, but otherwise have been given no special treatment. The taller species and cultivars will sometimes become a little floppy if not in full sun, but you can rectify this by cutting the plants back in early summer. The result is a bushier, more compact plant less inclined to fall over in winds or heavy rains.

Heleniums should be planted in a spot with adequate moisture, or the lower foliage will turn brown and fall off. Mulching will help reduce this problem, or you can underplant with a lower-growing perennial or dwarf shrub that will mask the lower leaves. Helenium is reportedly sometimes prone to powdery mildew, which can also cause leaf drop, but I've never had this problem in any of my plants.

It should be noted that helenium is listed in some sources as being toxic and as causing skin irritation. I've never personally encountered this, but the only plants that have ever irritated me are *Urtica* (nettles) and *Euphorbia* (spurge). Still, to err on the side of caution, wear garden gloves when handling this plant.

The main species used in horticulture is *Helenium autumnale*, which has many lovely cultivars. You will sometimes, however, simply find plants labelled as Helen's flower and 'Autumn Shades' with no definitive colour listed, such as I did with my yellow-flowered plants. If you're cramped for space, look for one of the shorter-growing forms.

'Butterpat': A bright yellow form, about 3 feet in height.

'Bruno': Strong red flowers with coppery-bronze central cones. Height 3–4 feet.

'Moerheim Beauty': Dark bronze-red flowers, extremely eye-catching. One of the more commonly found cultivars.

'Mardi Gras': Medium-sized specimen (approximately 2.5–3 feet), crimson red flowers with striking brown eye.

'Indian Summer': Copper-coloured petals surround a yellow "eye," or central cone. Grows 3–5 feet tall.

'Ruby Tuesday': Relatively short for helenium at 2.5 feet.

'Autumn Shades' Helenium

Helleborus

hellebore, Lenten rose, Christmas rose

Family: Ranunculaceae
Hardy to: zone 4
Bloom period: late winter to mid-spring
Growing Requirements: partial shade to full sun; humus-rich, moist, but well-draining soil
Height: 1–3 feet

Where best used: moist but well-drained sites with light shade
Propagation: seed or self-sown seedlings
Problems: slugs and snails
Notes: Deer-resistant. Plants are toxic, so wear gloves when handling them.

Although hellebores have been a popular plant in Europe for many years, they have been slower to catch on in Atlantic Canada. It was about a decade ago that a garden magazine's cover photo of green-flowered hellebores stopped me in my tracks. I vowed to have these exotic-looking, fascinating plants in my garden one day.

Hellebores are another plant where the flower structures themselves are not showy; it's the brilliantly coloured sepals, a type of modified leaf that resembles a petal, that so command our attention. The foliage is typically semi-evergreen, meaning it stays green going into winter but by spring is looking very tired. New foliage begins to appear as the plants are flowering, and you may wish to carefully snip away old leaves so as to best display the blooms.

'Ivory Prince'

Numerous hellebore species are available, but most of the plants that do best in our climate are hybrids from *Helleborus orientalis*. Breeders have embraced these plants and created countless hybrids, so it's hard to recommend only a few. Where formerly most hellebores were white-, pink-, reddish-, or (in the case of species *H. foetidus*) green-flowered, newer cultivars can have a range of colour options formerly unseen, including yellow, deep wine to black, and metallic blue. Many double-flowered forms are available, and the latest introductions to the hellebore world boast water lily–like flowers. Naturally, newer types are more

Sunris

expensive, so although they're tempting, try out one of the more commonly available, and less expensive, hybrids before you venture into the exotic realms.

It took a few years and a few site locations to get the growing requirements right, but I now have a number of different hybrids of hellebores growing in my gardens. The biggest challenge for some of these plants is Atlantic Canada's winter conditions. Depending on the species or hybrid, hellebores start to form buds in late winter, and they don't appreciate freeze-thaw cycles and varying amounts of precipitation from rain to heavy snowfalls. One year a heavy cold snap in early April killed my plants off; another year, frost heaved the plant out of the ground and that did it in. But I'm nothing if not a determined gardener, and kept trying.

Finally, I found a site that drained well but also had good organic matter for summer moisture, and provided full sun in spring then dappled shade in summer. A fellow garden blogger, who actually sent me seedlings from her garden, suggested that I mulch my plants with evergreen boughs from about Christmas on, or as soon as we had a thaw in winter if the plants were buried by an early snowfall. Since I started handling my plants in this way, I've had no more casualties and have added other cultivars to the mixture.

Make sure you don't plant hellebores in a site that is too shady or prone to standing wet during winter and spring. Amend the soil with plenty of good organic matter, such as compost or well-rotted manure. If happy, hellebores often produce seedlings, which can easily be transplanted; mature plants can grow and prosper for many years without any attention.

Recommended cultivars

'Ivory Prince': The first hellebore to successfully overwinter in my garden, its flowers are cream flushed with rich pink.

'Pink Lady': Softly pink flowers with green centre.

'Onyx Odyssey': A real show-off with double flowers, nearly black in colour. Grow with a white-flowered species for a stunning combination.

'Kingston Cardinal': A handsome double bloom with rich raspberry-red colouring.

'Golden Sunrise': Sepals are bright yellow suffused with red speckles and red picotee edging, often fading to green as the plant goes to seed.

Hemerocallis

daylily

Family: Hemerocallidaceae

Hardy to: zone 3

Bloom period: June–September

Growing requirements: full sun to partial shade, good drainage

Height: 12–70 inches

Where best used: mixed borders, display gardens

Propagation: division (seed if hybridizing)

Problems: Slugs and snails on flowers. Deer like them all too well.

Notes: Some daylilies are rebloomers.

Let's get the bad news about daylilies out of the way to begin with: deer are very fond of them. The good news is, for those who aren't troubled by deer, there is a daylily for just about any garden situation. Many are extremely hardy, tolerant of all but the soggiest of soils, and will grow in shade as well as full sun, although they will have fewer blossoms in very shady conditions. Best of all is the almost endless choice in cultivars: daylilies are easy to hybridize, and there are more than sixty thousand named and registered cultivars.

The botanical name *Hemerocallis* means "beauty for a day," which is a good description for the flowers, each of which only bloom for one day before closing and fading away. The genus was formerly in the Liliaceae family, but has recently been reclassified into its own distinct family. The way to tell true lilies and daylilies apart is by their foliage. Daylilies are borne on leafless stems known as scapes, which grow from a clump of grass-like leaves. Lilies, on the other hand, have leaves growing all around a central stem that arises from a bulb in the ground, and the flowers appear at or near the top of the stem.

Most of us first became acquainted with daylilies because of the wild species *Hemerocallis fulva*, the tawny daylily, which also goes by the common name ditch lily or (mistakenly) tiger lily. This species is often found growing along roadsides, near abandoned

'Crazy Ivan'

'Pride of Canning'

'South Seas'   'Roses in Snow'   'Shango'

homesteads and other open spots, and spreads by runners coming from its thick, tough, bulbous roots. Cultivated daylilies tend to be clump-formers and while they multiply, they don't send out runners all over the place, making them much better choices for a garden.

Once planted, daylilies require very little care, although some gardeners prefer to remove spent blooms from the plant's scapes, just for appearances. They are minimally affected by disease, although some will get discoloured spots or streaks caused by fungus on their foliage. The best defense for this is to simply remove the affected leaves, but don't put them in your compost. Daylily rust has been reported in parts of Atlantic Canada, but as with the other diseases, it doesn't kill the plant, but instead makes its leaves cosmetically less appealing.

Daylily flowers come in a rainbow of colours, except for pure white and true blue. Many daylilies boast contrasting colours in the centre of their flowers (referred to as an eye if dark in colour and a watermark if light), and they can also have contrasting colours along petal edges. The flowers come in a variety of forms, including spiders, which have long, thin petals, and sizes, from tiny blossoms the size of a doll teacup to huge teapot-sized blossoms. What you grow depends on your tastes, but with more than fifty-five thousand named cultivars, you'll find that daylilies are much like potato chips: you can't have just one.

Recommended cultivars

'Destined to See': Pale peach blossoms edged in purple, purple eyezone and yellow throat.

'Roses in Snow': Exotic, rich, red flowers edged in white, green-yellow throat.

'Canadian Border Patrol': Cream with purple edge and eyezone.

'Night Beacon': Reddish-purple petals with blazing gold-green throat.

'Designer Jeans': Large flowers, mauve with lavender eyezone, green throat.

'South Seas': Unusual coral or pink flowers, highly fragrant.

'Wayside King Royal': Deep wine-purple with yellow throat, lovely fragrance.

'Pride of Canning': Developed by Canning Daylily Gardens not far from where I live, this soft yellow beauty is edged with gold ruffles.

Heuchera

coral bells, alumroot, heuchera

Family: Saxifragaceae

Hardy to: zone 3

Bloom period: midsummer

Growing requirements: full sun to partial shade, good drainage, slightly acid soil

Height: 8–24 inches

Where best used: front of border, edging, pollinator plantings

Propagation: division, seedlings

Problems: Mildew or stem rot can be occasional problems.

Notes: Hummingbirds and other pollinators love the flowers.

When I talk to garden clubs, I always remind people not to forget foliage when planning their gardens. A plant with handsome foliage, either because it has an interesting texture or a different colour from just plain green, looks attractive even when not in bloom. An excellent example of an all-star foliage plant is the heuchera. These plants normally have a rosette of leaves that look something like the foliage of a maple tree. Instead of being merely green, however, they can be any of a host of different shades.

a variety of heucheras in a display bed

Heucheras put up sprays of tiny, almost bell-like flowers that are beloved of hummingbirds, but some people clip off their flower stalks, preferring to focus only on the foliage. I don't do that because I like their airy appearance, with delicate pink, white, or rose flowers, often with contrasting stem colours. If you enjoy bringing flowers into the house, stems of heuchera blossoms work nicely in a cut flower arrangement.

Although there are many different species of heucheras, we mostly refer to them all simply by the genus name rather than the specific name. Heucheras are very rewarding to plant breeders, who have been unveiling new cultivars with new foliage colours at an amazing rate over the past few years. Where formerly most heucheras had green, red, or purple leaves, perhaps accented with a contrasting colour, cultivars are now available with gold, salmon, lime-green, near-black, peach, and amber leaves. My experience has been that some of the newer cultivars, particularly those with gold- or peach-coloured foliage, have been less tolerant of our winters than some of the darker-coloured forms.

Often heucheras will develop an odd appearance, with elongated, woody stems and

In an effort to bring us still more interesting plants for the garden, plant breeders have been successfully crossing the coral-bells, *Heuchera*, with foamflower, *Tiarella*. Most tiarella cultivars tend to be moisture- and shade-loving ground covers that bloom in mid-spring with sprays of delicate pink or white flowers that resemble miniature astilbes.

The hybrids between tiarella and heuchera are called foamy bells, and have the hybrid botanical name x *Heucherella*. They have been bred to have beautiful coloured foliage like heucheras while displaying taller, showier spikes of flowers like the tiarellas. Generally they prefer a moist but well-draining soil—winter wet will kill them off—and partial sun to fairly deep shade. Heucherellas are hardy to zone 4.

Recommended cultivars

'Hollywood': One of the newer reblooming varieties with larger, thicker stems of red flowers over glossy, deep wine foliage.

'Mint Julep/Mint Frost': One of my favourites although it is an old faithful. Rich green leaves with silvery overlay between the veins, and ivory flowers.

'Obsidian': Like its name suggests, this one is almost black.

'Frosted Violet': Another favourite, with pink-violet foliage that appears chocolate in shade, with pink, pearl-like flowers.

'CanCan': Silvery purple with a contrasting veining, purple underside, and quite lacy foliage.

'Frosty': Unusual for the heucheras, this one has green- and white-splashed leaves, holding stems of striking deep pink flowers. Particularly appealing to hummingbirds.

'Lime Rickey': Several heucheras have brilliant, acid green foliage, but this one seems to be the most dependable for Atlantic Canada.

'Amber Waves': The first of the gold-leafed forms to be widely promoted, it is still for sale, where other less-hardy forms have become more scarce.

foliage appearing only at the very top. If this happens, dig up the plant and then replant it so that the foliage crown is at soil level. You may have to do this every couple of years, either in the spring or early fall. Replanting is also a good time to divide off any additional rosettes that have formed around the main crown. Plants may also push out of the ground during winters when there are a lot of freeze/thaw days; if yours frost heave, do *not* simply push them back down into the ground, which will break roots. Mound up mulch around the crown and roots to prevent them from freeze damage until spring, when you can replant them.

Every year, a few more new heucheras hit the nurseries, some of which look remarkably like other varieties. One nursery wholesaler in western Canada has ninety-two different cultivars on its plant lists! My suggestion is to make sure you label the ones you already have, or even make a page of photos of each one you own. That way, you won't be tempted to bring home a purple-leafed form with silver veining when you already have one.

Hosta

hosta, plantain lily

Family: Agavaceae (formerly Liliaceae)

Hardiness: zones 3–8

Bloom period: midsummer

Growing requirements: light shade, moist but well-drained soil

Height: miniatures under 6 inches to 3 feet or taller

Where best used: shade gardens, mixed borders, collections, containers (smaller varieties)

Propagation: division

Problems: slugs, snails, deer, Hosta Virus X

Notes: Many hostas have fragrant blossoms.

Hosta is another plant that gardeners seem to either adore or heartily dislike, with no in-between. I was slow to come to the cult of hosta adoration until I saw a fine collection of well-grown hostas at a garden not far from my home. I discovered that my previous ennui with these plants had to do with people growing the same few, easily found varieties, and not letting them attain their full size before dividing them. The miniatures do not enchant me, but they are wonderful for those with small gardens and are beautiful in container plantings.

varieties of hosta planted under trees and in other shady spots

Although we automatically think of hostas as the ideal shade plant, many cultivars can tolerate a great deal of sun. Some of the newer varieties, such as 'Stained Glass,' are actually touted for being particularly sun-tolerant. I grow hostas in a variety of locations from full sun to light shade under hardwood trees to heavier shade under spruce trees; the more shaded plants tend to be slower-growing, but otherwise they appear quite content wherever they are, provided the soil is not overly soggy.

I always remind gardeners not to

panic in the spring if they don't see hostas emerging right away. Hostas tend to be slow to emerge, which protects the tender shoots from possible late-season frosts. Some people cut the flower spikes off, but I can't understand that: hostas produce spikes of lavender or pure white, bell-shaped flowers, often highly fragrant, and beloved by hummingbirds.

Pests are a problem to many hosta growers. Slugs and snails chew holes in the foliage but can be controlled by handpicking or use of diatomaceous earth around the plants. Some varieties, particularly those with thick, waxy leaves—which includes some of the blue-green forms—are more slug-resistant. Deer, unfortunately, also find hostas utterly delectable, and as discussed, there are no easy cures for deer other than high fences or growing plants in containers where they can't be reached. A disease called Hosta Virus X can also be troublesome in certain cultivars (see page 174).

As with daylilies, there are hundreds of hosta cultivars, and unless you're a true zealot you might not see a large difference between one green-and-gold form and another. I am drawn to some of the more unusual, either because of colouration or because of the cultivar name, and so far I have yet to come home with a new one to find I already have it in my garden.

Recommended cultivars

'Paul's Glory': Highly variegated green and gold foliage, with colours changing as the plant's leaves mature.

'Sagae': One of the biggest, with large heart-shaped green leaves edged with cream-yellow.

'Spilled Milk': Slug-resistant blue-green leaves variegated with white that looks like spilled milk.

'Abiqua Drinking Gourd': Thick blue leaves are cupped and catch dew and rainfall. Slug-resistant.

'Blue Wedgwood': One of the smaller hostas, with Wedgwood-blue, dimpled leaves, and lavender-blue flowers.

'Guacamole': As its name suggests, the leaves are guacamole-green edged in a deeper green. Flowers are white and fragrant.

'Captain Kirk': Any Trekkie needs this one: large leaves, bright gold through centre with deep green edging. Goes well with 'Enterprise,' 'Starship,' and 'Vulcan,' for those of that persuasion.

'Dawn's Early Light': Dazzling all-gold leaves deepen to chartreuse as spring progresses. Sun-tolerant.

'Sagae' hosta is one of the largest hostas.

HOSTA VIRUS X

A few years ago, articles began popping up about a disease that was positioning itself to become a real problem in the hosta world. This disease is caused by a virus and isn't vectored by insects, but is spread by contaminated hands, gardening tools, or other items that come in contact with broken leaves or stems of the infected plant. Its symptoms can vary with the cultivar, but if you notice a plant with wrinkled, contorted, or otherwise deformed leaves, or with unusual colouration for that variety, you probably have a plant with Hosta Virus X (HVX). The unusual colouration may be mottling, blotchy and erratic streaks of colour, especially along the leaf veins; it may look like dark ink from a fountain pen has leaked along those very obvious veins, or like the colour had been bleached out of the foliage. Some cultivars may have ringspots of different colour, while others may have only small dimpling, called tissue collapse, in the leaves.

HVX has no cure. Infected plants must be destroyed as soon as they are discovered so that infection isn't spread to other plants by the gardener working with them, dividing the plants, removing damaged leaves, or cutting flower stems. Tools that have come in contact with the plant should be scrubbed thoroughly to remove soil and plant material, then disinfected with bleach. When you are working with other hostas, use a cleaning solution of 10 percent bleach to keep those tools free of any possible transmission of the virus from plants that aren't showing signs of HVX.

It is also imperative that nursery operators remain vigilant in looking for signs of HVX in their nursery stock. When the disease first made an appearance, it wasn't well known and there have been incidents of infected plants being propagated and shared or sold because the odd colouring seemed interesting.

No cultivars are immune to HVX, but it seems that some are more susceptible. This may be because some plants were propagated and sold with the disease before it was diagnosed. Some of the more commonly affected cultivars include 'Blue Cadet,' 'Gold Standard,' 'Striptease,' 'Sum and Substance,' 'Wide Brim,' 'Janet,' 'Grossa Regal,' and 'Patriot.' If you have any of these plants and they are showing unusual colouration or distortion in their leaves (unusual for their standard appearance) or have unnamed cultivars with odd colouration, you should destroy the plants to be on the safe side. It's better to lose a plant you spent a few dollars on than to lose all your hostas to this disease.

The American Hosta Society has a significant amount of information available on its website: www.americanhostasociety.org/hostavirusx.html

Inula helenium

inula, horseheal, elecampane

Family: Asteraceae
Hardy to: zone 3
Bloom period: July–August
Growing requirements: sun to partial shade, moist soil, lots of space
Height: 7 feet or more in full sun

Where best used: mixed plants, back of borders, specimen plant
Propagation: seedlings, division
Problems: No serious pests or diseases.
Notes: Much used in homeopathic medicine.

Inula's bright yellow flowers are great for pollinators.

If you have space and like plants that make a dramatic statement with their size, consider adding inula, or elecampane, to your perennial border. The first time I saw elecampane, it was growing in a potager at the Annapolis Royal Historic Gardens, towering above other herbs and vegetables in the representation of an Acadian kitchen garden. Although not native to Canada, it was brought here by settlers, including Acadians, who used it as a medicinal herb to treat various ailments in humans, horses, and mules. Elecampane is a source of the polysaccharide inulin, which has many uses, including as a source of dietary fibre.

The common name elecampane is a mangling of the original Latin name *Inula campana*, which means "inula of the fields." According to medieval herbalist John Gerard in his 1597 *Great Herbal*, the species name *helenium* is a tribute to Helen of Troy, who was reputedly collecting elecampane when she was stolen away by Paris.

While elecampane is still used in herbal and homeopathic medicine, its value to most of us is as a dramatic perennial for larger borders. I can't stress enough the amount of space needed to grow this plant, as even in my windy, cool garden it reaches 6 feet tall and 4 feet in width. The lower leaves can be the size of one of the larger hostas, so I consider it a living mulch wherever it's planted—it effectively shades out anything that might try to grow underneath it.

In midsummer, elecampane produces stalks of yellow, aster-like flowers with darker gold central discs that deepen to a rich brown as the flower matures. They are often used in flower arrangements, but I leave my plant with its flowers intact so they can provide a source of food for songbirds in autumn and early winter. While a few seedlings germinate around the base of my parent plant each spring, I've never found the plant invasive—and anyone who has seen it in its full flowering glory has been quite keen to take a seedling or two for their own garden.

Iris

iris, flag

Family: Iridaceae

Hardy to: zone 3

Bloom period: early spring to midsummer; some rebloom

Growing requirements: Full sun, moist soil, good drainage. Japanese irises are most tolerant of wet soil.

Height: 6 inches to 4 feet

Propagation: division of rhizomes

Problems: iris borer, aphids, slugs, leaf spot, soft rot

Notes: Some irises are highly fragrant.

I am not a huge fan of irises, and so didn't think I would include them in this book. But then my long-suffering spouse pointed out that I do have a number of irises in my gardens, from the tiny spring-flowering *Iris reticulata*, to the tall Siberian iris in the back garden, to a couple of dwarf and average-sized bearded irises. That said, I'm definitely not a fancier, as many people collect irises with as much ardour as others collect alpines, daylilies, roses, or hostas.

yellow-bronze bearded iris

There are dozens of iris species, some of which grow from bulbs, like my spring-flowering miniatures, rather than from swollen, bulbous roots called rhizomes (some of which have "beards").

Irises are dramatic plants when in bloom, because their handsome flowers can come in a variety of colours, especially in the bearded varieties. Some cultivars are mottled, stippled, or accented with a contrasting colour, and blossoms come in almost every conceivable shade except true blue. However, irises only tend to bloom for a couple of weeks, after which we're left with their leafy, sword-like foliage. I don't find this foliage particularly attractive unless it's on one of the bicolour forms. Some bearded iris do rebloom, and some are incredibly, dramatically fragrant.

These plants do well in most well-drained soils, particularly in an area that is sloped, or in a raised bed. Don't plant irises too deeply; set the plants so that the tops of their rhizomes are showing above the soil surface. Planted too deeply, irises are inclined to produce fewer flowers, and to be even more susceptible to disease.

Irises do need regular dividing, and you'll know that it's time to do this when the plant begins producing fewer flowers and a clump of them dies out in the centre. They can be divided in spring or in early autumn, but if you divide later in the year, cut the foliage back by about one-half to make your task easier. Use a sharp knife to make divisions, and disinfect any tools you use to prevent the possible spread of disease.

Iris ensata: Japanese iris will live nicely in wet, boggy areas during spring and summer, but must have good drainage during winter.

I. pallida: Resembles a bearded iris, though grown for cultivars with variegated foliage. 'Variegata' has white-striped foliage; 'Aureovariegata' has gold-and-green foliage.

I. pseudacorus: Yellow flag is native to Europe and also tolerant of wet conditions. It may be invasive in some sites, although this doesn't appear to be problematic in eastern Canada.

I. siberica: The Siberian iris has grassy foliage and produces mauve, purple, yellow, or white blooms on tall stems.

I. versicolor: Blue flag iris grows wild throughout eastern Canada, and can be encouraged to grow alongside ponds or in other wet areas.

Although bearded irises are the most popular types for their rainbow of colourful cultivars, there is a real problem with growing them: The iris borer is the larva of a night-flying moth that chews into the rhizomes and along the edges of leaves; new growth may be stunted and rotten at the rhizome edge. It's difficult to find and control the iris borer, although some researchers are recommending beneficial nematodes, a type of predatory worm, as a means of keeping beds free of the pest. Controlling borer damage will also reduce the risk of soft rot in your irises, as the bacteria enter rhizomes through spots where the borers have chewed.

There are far, far too many unique bearded iris cultivars to mention, but dozens are on offer from various catalogues and nurseries. A few species of non-bearded irises make exceptionally fine plants for gardens.

Japanese iris by water

Lavendula

lavender

Family: Lamiaceae
Hardy to: zone 4–5 with winter protection
Bloom period: early summer to midsummer
Growing requirements: full sun, excellent drainage, average soil
Height: 10–18 inches

Where best used: edging plant, rock gardens, butterfly and bee plant, fragrance garden
Propagation: seed or cuttings
Problems: No serious pests or diseases, but excessive winter moisture can be fatal.
Notes: Short-lived but worth growing. Deer-resistant, attracts pollinators.

"As rosemary is to the spirit, so lavender is to the soul." Whatever wise sage (pun intended) penned these words knew well the power of fragrance in our lives. Rosemary, clean and pungent and vital, gladdens the spirit, especially when it's used for cooking. But lavender, pure and wholesome and soothing, quells the

Lavender is excellent at the front of a border, in a herb bed, or in containers.

turmoil of our souls at all kinds of levels. According to herbalists, the plant's essential oils are useful for treating burns, headache, insomnia, and depression, for repelling insects, and as a general-purpose antiseptic. Many recipes exist for making home-care products, and the flavour of lavender is considered delightful in teas, ices, seasonings for meats, and even jellies and chocolates.

Technically, lavender is a woody sub-shrub, but I decided to include it in the perennial section because it isn't very large and can be very short-lived. Although you'll see it referred to as "English" lavender, it's actually native to regions of the Mediterranean, where it basks in the warm sun and dry, ordinary soils. As much as I love it, lavender isn't a plant for those living in colder parts of Atlantic Canada. Full sun and good drainage, along with some protection from wind, are important to this plant's survival; if your soil tends to be heavy with clay, add sand and organic matter to improve drainage. If the soil is acidic, add a little lime to bring it closer to neutral or even alkaline pH. Space your plants well so that there is good air circulation around them, as they also resent too much humidity. Don't over-fertilize lavenders, as this will actually detract from the amount of fragrance the plants produce.

In cooler climates like ours, lavender can be subject to winter killing. Again, excellent soil drainage will help to prevent plants dying from waterlogged roots. The cold and blustery winds that frequently sweep our area can be hard on lavender plants, so I recommend mulching them after a hard freeze in late fall or early winter. A light mulch such as hay, straw, or evergreen boughs helps protect the plant, allows good air circulation, and prevents snow from compacting down too hard and breaking the woody plant off at the roots.

Don't be in a hurry to cut back your lavender in the spring, even if it looks like a bunch of dead twigs. Pruning is important to prevent die-out in the centre of the shrub, but should be done in late spring, when you can see signs of new growth happening and can safely prune out dead parts. If you plan to shear the whole plant to keep it bushy, only remove the top one-third of the stems.

Be very careful when selecting plants from a garden centre or nursery. Reputable nurseries only sell hardy lavenders that are suited to our climate, but other species are sometimes offered at department and grocery stores that aren't hardy and can only be planted in containers or treated as annuals. *Lavendula angustifolia,* sometimes found sold as *L. officinalis,* has a number of cultivars that do reasonably well in Atlantic Canada, including 'Lady' lavender (zone 5), 'Hidcote' (zone 4), 'Munstead' (zone 4), and 'Twickle Purple' (zone 5).

Lavandins, or so-called "French" lavenders (*L.* x *intermedia*), are sterile hybrids that were developed as a result of disease problems in the commercial lavender industry. The lavandins tend to produce longer, larger spikes of flowers, have a more pungent fragrance than *L. angustifolia,* and are commonly used in production of lavender-scented candles, soaps, and other cosmetic and domestic products. 'Grosso' is a popular cultivar grown commercially and is hardy to zone 5. 'Hidcote White' has pure white flowers.

Liatris

blazingstar, gayfeather

Family: Asteraceae
Hardy to: zone 3
Bloom period: midsummer to early autumn
Growing requirements: full sun to light shade, average but well-drained soil
Height: 2–4 feet

Where best used: sunny borders, cut flower or butterfly garden
Propagation: division or seed
Problems: Crown or stem rot may be a problem. Voles like the roots.
Notes: Deer- and drought-resistant. Very good butterfly plant.

Let's set the record straight right now: although the most common form of Liatris (*L. spicata*) looks *somewhat* like the highly invasive purple loosestrife (*Lythrum salicaria*), it is not a problem plant, but a highly valuable one to gardeners and ecosystems alike. To further the difference between the two spiky-flowered species, liatris is native to North America; purple loosestrife is not.

With that clarification out of the way, let me extol the many virtues of liatris. As noted, it is native to our continent, although not to Atlantic Canada. As a later-blooming perennial, it's a terrific addition of colour to gardens after the big push of perennial bloom; in my garden, it doesn't begin to flower until August, and will continue to do so throughout September and even into October. It grows in tidy clumps, never taking off like some plants do, and has grass-like foliage from which the spikes of pinkish-purple or white flowers appear. Interestingly, liatris begins flowering from the top of the spike and blooms downward, whereas many perennials bloom from the bottom of the stem upwards. And, importantly, it is a terrific pollinator plant, especially for butterflies and bees.

There is one caveat, which you'll find mentioned by other garden writers and perhaps have experienced yourself. The

white and purple forms of Liatris

newly emerging foliage of liatris can easily be confused for grass in the spring, so you should mark where your plants are, especially if they are still young and in small clumps, so that you don't accidentally weed them out. (Yes, I've done this in the past.)

Liatris *is an excellent perennial for late season*

Liatris is a plant of the prairies, like some of the coneflowers; it grows nicely in average soil that has good drainage. Too soggy a soil will set up conditions for crown or stem rot, plus the potential for the plants not surviving winter; too rich a soil results in lush growth that can require staking flower stems. If your garden conditions tend to be dry, liatris is a great choice, being quite drought-tolerant.

The most commonly available species is *L. spicata*, which as its name suggests, produces tall spikes of flowers. You may find the cultivar 'Kobold' ('Goblin'), which only grows to about 30 inches, including its bloom.

If you like to grow plants from seed, more options are available: Wildflower Farm in Ontario offers seeds of *L. ligulistylis*, the meadow blazingstar, which is a tall plant with button-like flowers on its spikes. *Liatris aspera*, the rough gayfeather, also has spikes of button-like flowers, which I admired growing in Missouri several years ago. It would be nice to see more of these species readily available, but nurseries have to have people asking for them before they're apt to try something new.

Ligularia

groundsel, ligularia, elephant ears

Family: Asteraceae

Hardy to: zone 3 or 4

Bloom period: mid- to late summer

Growing requirements: moist soil, full sun to partial shade

Height: 3–6 feet including flower spikes

Where best used: moist garden areas, at back of border

Propagation: division in spring

Problems: slugs and snails

Notes: Handsome, large-leafed foliage.

To be honest, I wouldn't care if any of my ligularia species ever flowered—the dramatic, interesting foliage is quite enough. The first form I ever bought, 'Desdemona,' was purely for its huge leaves, which are wine-purple on the undersides and deep green on top

Ligularia don't like too hot a garden environment, and they need plenty of moisture. Without adequate moisture in the soil, they will wilt around midday on hot summer days, looking like overgrown, unhappy lettuces. Add plenty of organic matter to your soil, even if it is consistently moist, and mulch heavily around your plants' roots to further help retain soil moisture.

In my research for this species, I read that ligularia can be troubled by slugs and snails, which like to chew the foliage. I hadn't ever noticed this, but then I rarely pay much attention to slug damage on any plants. I went out to my garden to have a look, and found that slugs do like the narrow-leafed ligularia the best. The big-leafed cultivars had a few chew marks, while Shavalski's ligularia showed no sign of damage, perhaps because the leaves are so much more finely cut, with less surface area to climb on. If slug damage does bother you, diatomaceous earth is a fairly effective control. Don't dust it on the plant, but apply it around the outer perimeter of

'Desdemona'

the plant's leaves; slugs and snails won't cross this organic control, which looks like powder but is composed of the sharp, silicon-rich shells of tiny organisms called diatoms.

Beyond the slug issue, ligularia are very low maintenance. I don't cut the flower stalks off because I like their appearance in autumn and winter. The only time I've divided any of mine is when a friend has pleaded for a piece of 'Desdemona,' a show-stopping plant in my back garden. The plants grow in polite, mounding clumps, don't spread by runners, and can go for many years without needing any division.

'The Rocket'

Recommended species and cultivars

Ligularia has several different species, each with fairly large leaves but different types of flowers. The bigleaf ligularia, *L. dentata*, has yellow-orange, daisy-like flowers in mid- to late summer. It includes two cultivars that are quite similar, 'Othello' and 'Desdemona.' Both have purple-coloured undersides to their large leaves. My personal favourite is the maroon-leafed 'Britt-Marie Crawford,' which is a stunning plant in my chocolate- and wine-themed garden, especially set against the backdrop of gold-foliaged plants like Filipendula 'Aurea.' Zone 3.

Narrow-spiked ligularia (*L. stenocephala*): Plant has greener, somewhat smaller leaves with serrated edges and tall, slender spikes of yellow flowers. Zone 4.

For a species with unusual foliage, look for Shavalski's ligularia, *L. przewalskii*; it has deeply cut palmate leaves, somewhat like a delphinium, and deep purple-black stems holding tall spikes of yellow flowers. Later in the season, the foliage also takes on tints of purple, adding to its interest. Zone 4.

Lobelia

lobelia, cardinal flower

Family: Campanulaceae

Hardy to: zone 2 or 3

Bloom period: midsummer to early autumn

Growing requirements: moist soil, partial shade to full sun

Height: 2–5 feet

Where best used: woodland garden, water gardens, boggy areas

Propagation: spring or autumn division

Problems: Some species are short-lived.

Notes: Attractive to hummingbirds and butterflies.

Mention the name lobelia and most of us think of the attractive and commonly used trailing annual found in container plantings during the summer months. That particular plant is from South Africa, is not hardy here, and is somewhat of a pain to grow well, especially in the summer. Perennial garden lobelias, on the other hand, are native to North America, and are less challenging to grow. Their spikes of red, white, or blue flowers are magnets for hummingbirds, too, so even though they are often short-lived perennials, they're well worth growing if you have the proper site for them.

That proper site can be in full sun to partial shade provided the plants have an adequate supply of moisture. They're not suited to a dry soil unless it is enhanced with plenty of compost and the plants are watered during dry summer spells. Otherwise, growth can be stunted, and disease can set in due to the plants being stressed. Beyond that, lobelias are low-maintenance. They are easy to divide in spring and will often self-seed, although not to the point of being overwhelming.

Lobelia cardinalis is the cardinal flower, and aptly named; its spikes of rich red flowers are eye-catching, especially against the pure green

cardinal flower

foliage. I wish this were native to Atlantic Canada, because I would rather enjoy seeing it blooming in woodlands and along streambeds, but its natural range extends only as far east as Quebec.

My favourite—perhaps because it has settled in so well and reliably self-seeds just a little—is the great blue lobelia, *L. siphilitica*. Apparently, the species name refers to the story, possibly an urban myth, that this plant was used by American Indians to treat syphilis. I have never been able to figure out if I managed to acquire two cultivars, or if the blue one I have occasionally throws white sports. It's a striking plant for late-summer gardens, providing a shot of cool blue (or white) at a time when many other perennials boast yellow, orange, rust, or bronze flower colours.

Some nursery websites offer a number of named cultivars of perennial lobelias, but I was unsuccessful in finding any cultivars other than the white form of great blue lobelia at local nurseries in my region. The short-lived habit of lobelias may deter nurseries from growing too many of them, which is a great pity as they are a handsome and useful garden plant.

water lobelia showing blue form with bees

water lobelia, white form

Lupinus

lupin, lupine

Family: Fabaceae

Hardy to: zone 3

Bloom period: late spring to early summer

Growing requirements: full sun to light shade, good drainage, rich soil

Height: 2–4 feet

Where best used: mass plantings, mixed borders

Propagation: Seed is best option.

Problems: aphids, mildew

Notes: Deer-resistant. May rebloom in early autumn.

Lupins are a quintessential part of a Maritime summer. (If you've ever seen the massed colonies of lupins blooming wild along roadsides, and in medians and other open, sunny sites, you know exactly what I mean.) I've been fond of these plants since I was a child, as they were one of my maternal grandmother's favourite plants. I used to pick them as wildflowers, although my father claimed he was allergic to them and my mother didn't appreciate the masses of aphids that often clung to the flower spikes.

Like their relatives, false indigo, false thermopsis, and perennial sweet peas, lupins don't like to be disturbed, so plant them where you want them, and don't try to transplant them, as you'll find they shock easily. Part of the reason these plants do so well in our late spring climate is that they don't like hot weather; they will meltdown in midsummer when temperatures start to get really hot, and often become infested with powdery mildew. So, unless you like the seed heads of lupins, consider cutting them way back once they have finished blooming. Lupins will often produce a fresh flush of growth, and may even bloom again when temperatures start to cool down in early September.

Lupins are a double-edged sword: they are toxic to livestock, so take care not to let seedlings get into pastures on or near your property—even though reported livestock poisonings are extremely rare in our region. You should also make sure that children do not eat the seed heads of these plants—like beach peas and other ornamental members of the pea and bean family, these plants are toxic, which often surprises people who grow and enjoy peas and beans. On the other

wild form showing variety of colouring

hand, lupins are also deer- and rabbit-resistant, so you shouldn't have any problems with them being destroyed in your garden.

As noted, aphids are attracted to lupin flowers, but can be managed with use of an insecticidal soap if you're adamant about controlling them, or a simple blasting of water from a hose if you'd rather avoid treatments, organic or otherwise. I tend to only wash off those that I want to use as cut flowers, especially in dry years when I would rather use my well to water newly planted shrubs and perennials.

Typically the most commonly available plants are seedlings, usually of the Russell hybrids that were developed in England. Sometimes specific colours will be available, such as yellow or "red" (really a very deep pink), but it often will take two seasons for lupins to flower. They also tend to dwindle out over a few years, so if yours are seeding around the mother plant, don't weed them out—they'll be your replacement lupins, though they will probably also revert to the original purple and blue shades. I let mine self-seed where they will, but also add a few new plants every year so that I get yellow lupins (my favourite) as well as a medley of other colours. Yellow false lupin, *Thermopsis*, is a much longer-lived relative, a clump former with spikes of lupin-like flowers in late spring. If you like yellow and can find it, it's well worth adding to your border.

red hybrid

*false lupin (*Thermopsis*), a reliable perennial alternative*

Lychnis

Maltese cross, catchfly, campion

Family: Caryophyllaceae
Hardy to: zone 3
Bloom period: spring to early summer,
Growing requirements: full sun, moist but well-drained soil
Height: 1–4 feet

Where best used: mixed borders, butterfly gardens
Propagation: division in spring
Problems: Can look messy after flowering.
Notes: Deer-resistant.

The pink family, Caryophyllaceae, is an interesting one, containing several annoying weedy species such as mouse-eared and common chickweeds (*Cerastium* and *Stellaria* species). These weeds, though annoying, also tend to have tiny flowers that are not showy, though very prolific.

However, there is nothing shy and retiring about the campions, another genus in the pink family; from the blazing red of Maltese cross to the flamboyant magenta of rose campion, these plants put on a dazzling performance in the summer garden, attracting pollinators of all sorts as well as satisfying the gardener's need for hot, drenching colours.

'Dusty Salmon' Maltese cross

The first time I spied rose campion in bloom, it stopped me in my tracks, literally; I pulled my car into a stranger's driveway and asked the homeowner what this plant was. She didn't know, but allowed me to dig one up. That plant wound up dying, since it was high summer and not a good time to transplant, but I was able to identify the plant and get potted ones from a nursery for my garden. Now I share with others, as this particular species tends to be hard to find in nurseries.

L. arkwrightii

'Molten Lava'

In recent years some botanical flora collections have put *Lychnis* into the genus *Silene*, but plants are still found bearing the *Lychnis* label in nurseries around the region. The lychnis and silene species tend to be short-lived perennials; however, many of them also tend to self-seed nicely without becoming overwhelming.

white form of Maltese cross

Recommended species and cultivars

***Lychnis* x *arkwrightii*:** This is a lovely hybrid Maltese cross with larger, individual flowers rather than the clusters of small flowers seen on Maltese cross. Flowers are blazing orange; one cultivar, 'Vesuvius,' has wine-tinged leaves and stems and is a real showstopper. A related hybrid, *Lychnis* x *haageana*, includes several cultivars with brilliant red-orange flowers and wine tints in foliage: 'Lumina Dark-Leaved Red' and 'Molten Lava' are fairly similar, both with large flowers that are hummingbird magnets.

***L. calcedonica*:** Along with the commonly seen red-flowered form of Maltese cross, there are white- and salmon-flowered varieties too. I find the white-flowered variety to be inclined to flop, so I shear it back hard after flowering. The salmon-coloured variety is named, not surprisingly, 'Dusky Salmon,' and has not seeded true, although it has formed a strong, handsome clump over the years.

***L. coronaria*, sometimes seen as *Silene coronaria*:** Rose campion has velvety silver leaves that form rosettes the first year, then produce flowers the following year. The most common flower colour is some variation of brilliant magenta, although there is also a white variety and 'Oculata,' an unusual variety that is white with a rosy pink eye.

***L. flos-cuculi*:** Although native to Europe, ragged-robin is common and naturalized in parts of Atlantic Canada, often seen growing in damp pastures and meadows. It works well in a pollinator garden and is quite content in cool, moist growing habits. 'Jenny' is a double-flowered cultivar.

Monarda

beebalm, Oswego tea, bergamot

Family: Lamiaceae
Hardy to: zone 3
Bloom period: mid- to late summer
Growing requirements: full sun to partial shade
Height: 2–5 feet

Where best used: pollinator plantings, mixed borders
Propagation: division, cuttings
Problems: Powdery mildew in some cultivars. Some tend to spread vigorously.
Notes: Adored by pollinators, but not by deer.

Monarda is among my most-recommended perennials for encouraging pollinators such as hummingbirds and bees. I do stress that while I adore it, beebalm is not a perfect perennial. If you have a small garden, you will need to be diligent in controlling beebalm, because it does spread—in some cultivars more prodigiously than others. There's also the problem of powdery mildew, although this seems to be more of a problem in some cultivars than others. But the flowers are glorious, the foliage and blossoms are both pleasantly scented with a lemony-mint fragrance, and there's no denying the joy of watching hummingbirds diving into the blossoms. Leaves and flowers of beebalm are edible, and can make an attractive addition to salads as well as being useful in creating a tea somewhat similar to Earl Grey (which is flavoured with true bergamot, a type of citrus).

In my garden, which has mostly damp clay soil and at least light shade in most spots, monardas bloom for six weeks or more. They don't all come into flower at precisely the same time, but they produce a fine show because I do let them spread pretty much unchecked, with one exception, noted below.

What to do about the powdery mildew situation? Some cultivars are promoted as being more mildew-resistant than others, and at least in my garden, I've had no problems with it in 'Raspberry Wine.' I gave a generous clump of this

'Raspberry Wine'

variety to plantsman Lloyd Mapplebeck in the spring of 2010 to see how he'd fare with it in Truro, as he'd expressed much exasperation over mildew in some cultivars. Mostly, mildew is aesthetically annoying but rarely fatal. Aside from choosing mildew-resistant cultivars, practice good sanitation: to limit the spread of the fungus, burn infected leaves rather than compost them, and disinfect any tools you use with a bleach solution. Some gardeners choose to shear infected plants to the ground. They then grow back, usually free of mildew, and simply bloom later in the season. Planting monarda in full sun with good air circulation and adequate soil moisture helps to reduce mildew problems.

If disease hasn't been a problem, leave your beebalm plants standing even after the blooms have disappeared. Birds enjoy the seed heads, and the plants will often stand quite nicely throughout all but the heaviest of snowfalls and winter winds.

Monarda didyma: This is the species from which most cultivars are developed, including:

'Blaustrumpf'/'Blue Stocking': It would take a great imagination to see this as blue-flowered—it's more of a violet shade, and the most mildew-prone of the varieties I have, despite being touted as mildew-resistant. Others find it quite heat- and drought-tolerant, neither of which is a concern here.

'Cambridge Scarlet': One of several red-flowered varieties.

'Jacob Cline': A popular red-flowered variety, which has shown little sign of mildew in my garden.

'Marshall's Delight': Bright pink flowers adorn this variety, which was bred in Canada and is mildew-resistant.

'Raspberry Wine': My personal favourite, although it is a vigorous spreader. Deep pink, almost wine-coloured, flowers and the tallest-growing of my varieties, reaching 6 feet in one particularly sunny spot.

'Sioux': There are few white cultivars, but this is one of them, often lightly tinged with pink.

M. fistulosa: Wild bergamot is native to the U.S. and parts of Canada, although not in our region. It's a clump-former but does spread by rhizomes, and has lilac-pink flowers. Allan Armitage notes that it appears to be less susceptible to mildew than *M. didyma.*

'Cambridge Scarlet'

wild bergamot and 'Jacob Cline' beebalm

Nepeta

catmint, catnip

Family: Lamiaceae

Hardy to: zone 3

Bloom period: early summer to autumn

Growing requirements: full sun to partial shade, average soil

Height: up to 30 inches

Where best used: edging, mass plantings, with deciduous flowering shrubs (e.g. roses)

Propagation: seedlings from non-sterile hybrids or species; otherwise division

Problems: No serious pests or diseases.

Notes: Deer- and rodent-resistant. Catnip makes felines delirious happy. All nepetas are good pollinator plants.

Garden and plant organizations sometimes make choices that cause gardeners to wonder what they're thinking. However, when the Perennial Plant Association named 'Walker's Low' catmint as their perennial of the year for 2007, those of us who grew the plant nodded in satisfaction, knowing it to be an attractive, long-blooming, and carefree perennial.

The names catmint and catnip are sometimes used interchangeably, although there are several different ornamental species of nepeta. *Nepeta cataria* is true catnip, used more for its herbal properties than as an ornamental, and so beloved by some of our cats that I can only grow it in hanging containers well out of their reach. A handful of nepeta hybrids, often labelled as *N.* x *faassenii*, are the popular ornamental varieties that work so well in perennial or mixed borders. The most hardcore of our catnip-addicted felines will chew on these plants too, particularly in winter when they go after the dried flower heads.

Catmint is a delightfully low-care perennial, seldom bothered by pests, happy with most growing conditions, and providing a long period of bloom. It will definitely flop over in

'Six Hills Giant'

too rich a soil or in too much shade, so give it a site with a few hours of sunlight and don't over-fertilize it. The smaller-leaved forms are excellent for front of border planting, as they cascade into sprawling froths of light purple-blue flowers and grey-green foliage, but they also work well as underplantings for roses, lilacs, and other shrubs. Bees and butterflies flock to catmints, which will often keep flowering until fall if you shear back spent blooms regularly. Although cats may find various catmints quite delightful, deer, rodents, and other pests do not.

The most challenging thing about catmints is figuring out their species and cultivar names. Often they are labelled only as *Nepeta,* with a hybrid name such as 'Six Hills Giant' or 'Walker's Low' tacked on the end. Authorities acknowledge that species and cultivars are often mixed up, so it can be difficult to know whether you've got a variety that will self-seed or one that is sterile. (Although if you find seedlings popping up around the plant then you know it's not sterile!)

Recommended cultivars

***Nepeta* 'Six Hills Giant':** Supposed to grow up to 4 feet tall, but I've never seen it that height in any garden or garden centre.

***N.* 'Walker's Low':** As the name suggests, this is the ideal choice for front of border plantings.

***N. subsessilis* 'Sweet Dreams':** More tolerant of moisture than others, this is a polite clump-former with a distinctly upright growth habit, bright green foliage, and pink flowers set into wine-coloured bracts. It may be a little more difficult to find than others, but is worth growing because it's very attractive and does not self-seed.

'Sweet Dreams'

'Walker's Low'

Oenothera

evening primrose, sundrop

Family: Onagraceae
Hardy to: zone 3
Bloom period: June–August
Growing requirements: full sun to light shade, average soil with good drainage
Height: 8–24 inches

Where best used: front of border mixed plantings, hilly areas as ground cover
Propagation: division in spring or fall
Problems: No serious pests or diseases.
Notes: Drought- and salt-tolerant. Source of evening primrose oil.

If you're like me, your first encounter with evening primrose was with the wild biennial species (*Oenothera biennis*) that grows throughout Atlantic Canada. That variety can be quite an opportunistic plant, growing anywhere ground has been disturbed and becoming quite weedy in nature. Some years ago, this species was discovered to be a source of a rare, essential fatty acid, and today evening primrose oil is used in a variety of medicinal and cosmetic applications. For gardeners, however, the more showy species of evening primrose—with their silken, poppy-like flowers—are the ones we enjoy throughout the summer months.

sundrops

Interestingly, evening primrose is kind of a double misnomer; the plants are not related to primroses (*Primula* species) and while some are evening-bloomers, others put on a spectacular show during the day. Each flower lasts only about a day, but the plants are such prolific bloomers that the floral display begins in June and with some species lasts until frost.

I like evening primroses because they do provide long-lasting colour and are quite easy to care for, providing you select the right species. They'll tolerate a range of growing conditions, although they are happiest in full sun to light shade. They aren't fussy about soil fertility, although they do usually prefer good drainage. Once established, they tend to be quite drought-tolerant and are also salt-tolerant, making them good choices for seaside homes or cottages. I've found the common sundrop to be very useful as a ground cover and weed suppressant; it tends to smother out weed growth in the sites where I've planted it.

Missouri sundrop

Recommended species

Oenothera fruticosa: The common sundrop begins the season with purple to reddish-green foliage that turns a deep green as the season progresses. It has an upright growth habit to about 18 inches and produces brilliant yellow flowers for at least a month. It spreads by runners but is easy to dig up and transplant elsewhere. I have found it very tolerant of moist soil and useful in a sloped area of the garden to hold the soil in place. Zone 3.

O. missouriensis: Missouri primrose, or Ozark sundrop, is gorgeous, with huge (5–6 inch) yellow flowers and a more sprawling growth habit than common sundrop. This species may also be labelled as *O. macrocarpa*. Zone 4.

O. speciosa: Showy evening primrose blooms during the day and has pink or white flowers. Sometimes found to be an aggressive spreader, although it died in my garden several times, probably because it requires better drainage than I gave it. Zone 5.

Paeonia

peony

Family: Paeoniaceae

Hardy to: zone 2

Bloom period: late spring to midsummer

Growing requirements: full sun to light shade; compost-rich, moist, but well-drained soil

Height: to 4 feet in bloom

Where best used: mixed beds, pollinator gardens, and sites where staking can be hidden by other plants

Propagation: division of herbaceous varieties, cuttings of tree species

Problems: Botrytis blight on foliage and flowers.

Notes: Some cultivars show very good autumn foliage colour. Don't worry about ants on flower buds.

I cannot imagine having a garden without peonies, even though they may only bloom for a couple of weeks, and often are knocked down by too-heavy flower heads. As I mentioned in the delphinium profile, the blooming of peonies in my garden heralds the annual "delphinium/peony wind and rainstorm"—invariably, we have at least one big storm while those perennials are in bloom.

Gardeners are sometimes nervous about peonies, because they've heard that the plants should only be divided at certain times of year, can be sulky about flowering, and can be prone to pest problems. But if peonies are provided the growing conditions they need, they'll be with you for many years.

'Primavera'

These growing conditions include a sunny site and well-drained soil. Like many plants, peonies resent cold, wet soil, and will do well in clay only if it's well amended with organic matter or sand to improve drainage. They can take some light shade, but flowering may be reduced and the plants will stretch toward the light if they have too much shade. Amend the soil with some well-rotted manure or compost before planting. Once established, peonies benefit from a yearly application of organic matter around the edge of the plant, and mulching helps keep soil moist and reduces weed infestations.

While it's true that peonies are best divided and moved in the autumn (although they don't require regular dividing, unlike many other perennials), container-grown peonies from a nursery can be planted before then. The main thing to remember is not to plant the crown too deeply, or the plant will not flower. Set the plant into the soil at the same level as it was in its container. If you've purchased bare-root plants, plant the crown so that the topmost bud is two inches below the surface. This will protect the crown and buds from winter or cultivation damage.

'Coral Charm'

Sometimes peonies are attacked by botrytis, a type of fungus that produces grey mould on buds, killing them off. Cut off and destroy infected foliage and flower buds immediately if you see signs of the disease (do not compost them), and the next spring, dust with organic sulphur fungicide to help prevent an outbreak of the problem.

Gardeners often wonder about the ants that they see milling around on peony buds. These ants are completely harmless: they seem to be attracted to nectar produced by the plants, but contrary to the folk myth, you don't need ants on peonies for the buds to open. Once the buds have opened, the ants usually disappear back into their regular business, but if you're concerned about bringing unwanted guests into the house when you cut blooms, just shake the flowers after you cut them to dislodge any ants that might be lingering.

For most gardeners, their favourite peonies are the common herbaceous hybrids, which may be labelled as either *Paeonia officinalis* or *P. lactiflora,* and include many

old-fashioned, unnamed variety

For the true peony aficionado, one of the must-haves is the tree peony, *Paeonia suffruticosa*. Tree peonies differ from herbaceous peonies in that they don't die back completely to the ground every fall, but have woody branches; they are usually grafted onto the roots of common herbaceous peonies to give them hardiness for North American gardens.

yellow-flowered tree peony

Unlike herbaceous peonies, tree peonies need to be planted a little deeper in the soil so that the bud graft is protected from cold winds. Tree peonies drop their leaves in autumn, but the woody stem of the plant remains standing through winter. For the first year or two after planting a tree peony, once the weather turns cold and the tree peony has dropped its foliage in late autumn, upend a large clay pot or bucket over the plant and leave it for the winter. This protects the plant until its roots are well established, a process that may take several years in Atlantic Canadian gardens.

The Itoh peonies (named for the Japanese hybridizer who developed them) are intersectional crosses between yellow tree peonies and regular herbaceous peonies, resulting in compact, deciduous plants with gloriously coloured flowers in shades including yellow, rose, and copper. Itoh peonies are more expensive than many hybrids and species because they are still quite uncommon, but if you've ever seen one in bloom, you can't help but fall under their spell.

different cultivars with flowers in white, shades of pink, red, and peach. But there are many other interesting species if you can source the plants and if you have deep pockets—peonies can be expensive. *Paeonia tenuifolia*, the fern-leaf peony, is a low-growing species with thread-like foliage and deep-red single or double blooms. Perhaps the most intriguing is *P. mlokosewitschii*, more commonly known as "Molly-the-witch," which has single, buttercup-like blooms of pale yellow and beautiful blue-green leaves with purple overtones.

Papaver

poppy

Family: Papaveraceae

Hardy to: zone 3

Bloom period: late spring to midsummer

Growing requirements: full sun, compost-rich soil with good drainage

Height: 1–3 feet

Where best used: mixed borders, pollinator gardens

Propagation: seed or division

Problems: Aphids, mildew can be present.

Notes: Plant with other perennials that can hide fading foliage.

Poppies are one of my favourite garden plants, whether annual, biennial, or perennial. The blowsy, old-fashioned orange Oriental poppies are imprinted in my memory, along with lupins and Johnny-jump-ups, as my maternal grandmother's favourite plants. Not surprisingly, Oriental poppies were also one of the first perennials I planted in my current gardens, and years later they continue to produce dazzling flowers in shades of scarlet, rose, and salmon.

Poppies of all kinds do best in full sun, and prefer a well-draining soil with compost worked into it. All the perennial types grown in Atlantic Canada tend to be quite drought-tolerant once established. That said, my seed-grown Oriental poppies have been extremely tolerant of less-than-ideal drainage in one of my garden beds. Poppies put down a taproot and resent being transplanted once they are beyond seedling size, and if you wish to divide them for some reason, do it while they are dormant in mid- to late summer. You can also dig them up with the intent of thinning them out, only to find that they regenerate from bits of roots left behind. I've never found this to be a problem, as I can never have enough poppies of any sort.

One drawback to Oriental poppies is that their hairy, lobed foliage does die back once the plants are finished blooming. The plants will put up new growth in autumn, but if you have a large planting of Oriental poppies they will leave a noticeable space in your midsummer garden. Make sure to incorporate other plants in the garden

Icelandic poppy

Icelandic poppy, 'Champagne Bubbles' varieties

'Patty's Plum'

that will bloom later, either perennials such as rudbeckias and asters, or annuals such as cosmos or nicotiana.

Breeders have developed several exotic shades, including 'Patty's Plum,' a smoky purple blossom, and 'Raspberry Queen,' a vibrant pink with intense black markings around its centre. If you're interested in growing Oriental poppies from seed, try the compact variety called 'Pizzacato.' I have found these to produce the largest and showiest blossoms, some of them the size of dinner plates.

Less dramatic than their Oriental cousins but no less lovely are the Iceland and alpine poppies, *P. nudicaule* and *P. alpinum*. They look quite similar except that the alpine poppy is much smaller, with delicate tiny flowers only slightly more than an inch in diameter. Both of these behave more like short-lived perennials, or even biennials, although if not deadheaded they produce many seedlings, providing you with a nice collection of these poppies every year. They are particularly intolerant of wet conditions, especially over winter, and don't like too-warm temperatures in summer, so they are well suited for most of Atlantic Canada. When they are happy, Iceland and alpine poppies have a long season of bloom, beginning to flower in my garden—and even in the walkway where seeds fell—in mid- to late May, and with deadheading continue flowering right through to a hard frost in autumn. They come in a variety of shades, including white, salmon, orange, yellow, pink, and cream.

None of these poppies have particularly striking seed heads—that privilege belongs to the opium or breadseed poppy, *P. somniferum*, which is an annual in Atlantic Canada. Oriental poppies have fairly large seed heads but they don't dry beautifully the way the opium poppy does, while alpine and Iceland poppies have small seed heads that aren't showy at all.

Oriental poppies

It should be noted that that epitome of exotic perennials, the Himalayan blue poppy, is not a member of the *Papaver* genus, but rather *Meconopsis*. This exquisite but diva-esque perennial is not for most gardens, and is difficult to acquire.

Perennial grasses

various genera

Family: Poaceae, Cyperaceae, Juncaceae
Hardy to: various
Bloom period: early summer to autumn
Growing requirements: full sun to light shade; other requirements as by species
Height: 6 inches to 10 feet

Where best used: collections, mixed plantings, specimen or edging
Propagation: division or seed
Problems: Generally no serious pests or diseases.
Notes: Do not over-fertilize. Excellent fall and winter interest.

I faced a bit of a quandary choosing the plants for this book. I couldn't leave out the ornamental perennial grasses, which are remarkable plants that have been gaining in popularity over the past number of years. The main problem was that there are at least a dozen genera that are popular with gardeners. So I decided the best option was to lump them all together, as I did with ferns. I encourage gardeners to embrace grasses: as with other types of plants, you'll find you can't have just one.

When we discuss grasses, we're actually referring to a number of families. True grasses are members of the Poaceae (formerly Gramineae) family. The sedges (Cyperaceae) and reed (Juncaceae) families both include some ornamental species and are usually suited for moist conditions. But they can be lumped together and called grasses for simplicity's sake.

There are grasses for pretty much every spot in the garden, from edging a border to commanding attention as specimen plants. Some are drought-tolerant, while

Pennisetum *'Hameln'*

mixture of grasses

others work well in moist, even wet, soils. Most are very well behaved, although there are several exceptions. Many grasses don't begin flowering until later in the summer, when some summer-blooming perennials are fading. For those of us looking to have four-season interest in our gardens, grasses keep their flower heads through the fall and well into winter, and are especially appealing if lightly dusted in frost, snow, or ice. In the spring, they can be divided if they're getting large, but all they require is that last year's stems are trimmed back so that the new year's can spring up anew.

There are two caveats to be aware of when choosing grasses. First, make sure that the variety you choose forms clumps and does not spread by runners. The grassy equivalent of goutweed is the so-called ribbon grass or gardener's garters (*Phalaris arundinacea*), which can be quite invasive; avoid purchasing *Miscanthus sacchariflorus*, which spreads by tough runners and is hard to control. Secondly, be very careful about hardiness zones when it comes to grasses: sometimes you'll find species for sale that are not hardy in Atlantic Canada. These are commonly sold as annuals—some of the *Pennisetum* varieties (fountain grasses, ornamental millets) are examples—but occasionally garden centres will sell them as perennials and not inform the customer.

a grass garden containing many species

Calamagrostis: Feather reed grasses have a tall, upright growth habit (up to 7 feet in height), are very adaptable to most growing conditions, and are hardy to zone 3. 'Karl Foerster' is one of the most popular varieties; 'Overdam' and 'Avalanche' both have green- and white-striped foliage.

Carex: The sedges are normally low-growing (under 24 inches) and hardy to zone 3 or 4, although some newer cultivars are listed as zone 5. They prefer cool, moist growing conditions.

Festuca: Fescues have very fine, narrow foliage and work well as front of border plants in well-drained soil. Most are hardy to zones 3 or 4. 'Elijah Blue' is popular for its powder-blue foliage and silver-blue flower heads.

Hakonechloa: Japanese forest grasses are low growers ideal for the front of a border; they have a cascading, waterfall effect, and while they do spread, they are not invasive. They work well with hostas and have similar growing requirements; provide extra shade for 'All Gold,' which will burn in hot afternoon sun. Zone 5.

Japanese forest grass

Juncus: The reeds have round, stem-like leaves and look like green porcupines with their tidy, clump-forming habit. The most intriguing are the spiral rushes (*J. effuses* f. *spiralis* and related cultivars) with corkscrew new growth. Ideal plants for a water garden; usually hardy to zone 4.

Miscanthus: The maiden grasses are among the most popular and showy of the ornamental grasses, doing best in fertile, moist, but well-drained soil. They can reach 10 feet or more, depending on the species or cultivar, although there are several dwarf varieties good for smaller gardens. Var. *Purpurascens*, flame grass, has excellent fall colour; 'Strictus' has green foliage with yellow bands horizontally across the leaves and is also known as porcupine grass; 'Huron Sunrise' is a Canadian hybrid with a white midrib. Most hardy to zone 4 or 5.

Miscanthus flowers, winter

Panicum: Switchgrass or panicgrasses are mid-sized plants with fine fall colour. Native to the tall-grass prairies of North America, these plants are happiest in full sun and are drought-tolerant once established. Their flower heads are not very showy but present a nice airy texture, especially juxtaposed against more showily flowered species. 'Cheyenne Sky' is compact and displays deep wine foliage tips as summer progresses; 'Shenandoah' is similar but grows to 5 feet, with excellent red colour; 'Dallas Blues' has steely blue foliage. Most are hardy to zones 3 or 4 with good winter drainage.

Phlox

phlox

Family: Polemoniaceae

Hardy to: zone 2

Bloom period: mid spring to early autumn

Growing requirements: full sun to partial shade, good drainage

Height: 6 inches to 5 feet

Where best used: low species good groundcover for sunny spots; tall varieties ideal for mixed borders

Propagation: division or cuttings

Problems: Mildew can be an issue with older cultivars of tall phlox. Newer cultivars are resistant.

Notes: Bees and hummingbirds love phlox.

Depending on your garden conditions, you can have phlox blooming from mid spring until autumn. The season kicks off with the low-growing moss phlox, the dazzling jewel colours of which provide a welcome relief to the dreariness of winter. Creeping and woodland phloxes are shade-tolerant forms that bloom later in the spring, while the showy tall phlox provide a welcome anodyne to the lull in perennial blooms that many gardens experience in midsummer.

'Bright Eyes' tall phlox

While I love the brilliant colours and creeping habit of moss phlox, it's been a frustrating plant for me over the years. It has been slow to establish because it needs good drainage, and its low, tangled stems invite weeds to tangle in among them. I do much better with woodland and tall phlox, which I also prefer because they tend to have such glorious fragrances.

One problem with tall phlox is that some cultivars are prone to powdery mildew, especially if they are grown in humid conditions and are over-fertilized. Happily, many

moss phlox

'David' tall phlox

newer varieties are touted as mildew-resistant, and while I sometimes get mildew in some Monarda and pulmonaria cultivars, the phloxes I grow have never shown even a slight tendency to this.

Tall phloxes can be prone to flopping over in windy conditions and often require staking. One solution for this problem is to shear the plants back by about one-half their height in early summer; they'll grow in bushier and shorter, and will bloom a little later than if you'd left them alone, but you won't have to bother with stakes or other types of supports.

Phlox subulata: Moss phlox is one of the quintessential spring-flowering perennials, producing a carpet of brilliant blossoms with needle-like foliage. It looks especially attractive in mass plantings over a wall or slope, or in an alpine garden where it will have great drainage. Shear the plants after blooming to tidy them up, or simply mow over them if they are growing into the edge of your lawn. Flowers can be a range of purples, pinks, cream, magenta, and fuchsia, and there are even a few bicolours available. Zone 2.

P. divaricata: Woodland or wild blue phlox is a lovely plant for lightly shaded woodland conditions, with a mature height of about 12 inches. It's nicely fragrant and its pale blue to mauve flowers light up a shaded area. The plants spread a little but are not at all invasive. Look for cultivar 'May Breeze,' which is white with a subtle blue flush. Zone 3.

P. paniculata: Summer blooming or tall garden phlox are essential to a showy summer perennial border. Many different colours are available, including shining white ('David'), rich orange ('Orange Perfection'), bicolour pink with deeper pink centre ('Bright Eyes'), and deep purple ('Nicky'). Several cultivars have bicolour foliage, further adding to the appeal of the plant ('Gold Mine,' with hot pink flowers; 'Becky Towe,' with salmon blossoms). Zone 3.

'May Breeze' woodland phlox

Polemonium

Jacob's ladder, Greek valerian

Family: Polemoniaceae
Hardy to: zone 3
Bloom period: May–July. Some reblooming if deadheaded.
Growing requirements: full sun to partial shade; well-drained, compost-rich soil
Height: 1–3 feet

Where best used: front of border for lower cultivars with fancy foliage; mid-border for others
Propagation: division or seedlings
Problems: No serious pests or diseases. Occasional powdery mildew if overcrowded in hot summers.
Notes: Deer-resistant. Butterflies, bees, and other pollinators love it. Good foliage texture and colours.

Polemonium is another plant with a wonderful variety of names. It is most commonly referred to as Jacob's ladder, but is also sometimes known as Greek valerian, abscess root, and sweatroot. There's even a species with the common name of skypilot (*P. eximium*), although I've yet to see it offered for sale in our region. Although some species are native to North America's arctic and mountainous areas, none are found growing native in Atlantic Canada.

The leaves of Jacob's ladder feature a staggered arrangement of leaflets on each stem. In something of a ladder arrangement, so this particular name makes sense. The creeping polemonium, *P. reptans*, has been used in herbal medicine to treat a variety of conditions, which explains the common names of abscess root and sweatroot. Although it's rarely used today in herbalism, this species has several very attractive cultivars for the rock or woodland garden.

Jacob's ladder is a perennial I recommend to new gardeners because it's an amenable plant, able to tolerate a variety of growing conditions and soils. Its

white Jacob's ladder

preferred growing conditions are full sun to partial shade and rich soil with good drainage (especially for some of the newer cultivars). That being said, for the past five years I've had *Polemonium* 'Snow and Sapphires' growing in a bed that is very wet in spring from snow melt, and the plant has seemed unbothered by its surroundings. Polemonium is deer-resistant and a magnet for bees and butterflies. Because it's a larval plant for several species of butterflies, its leaves may be chewed upon at times, but in all the years I've been growing Jacob's ladder I've never noticed any damage.

As the common Jacob's ladder plants get older, they may produce fewer flowers and die out in the middle of the clump or crown, which means they need to be divided and replanted. Dig them up in the spring and use a sharp knife or spade to divide the crown into several sections, cutting away the portions where there is no new growth. Replant the healthy sections and you'll find the plants grow with renewed vigour. The species tend to produce seedlings, which are easy to transplant into other parts of your garden or share with friends.

***Polemonium pauciflorum*:** A little different from the usual Jacob's ladder, this species has trumpet-shaped yellow flowers washed in red highlights. Some consider it an annual, but it does return and reseed in my garden. Zone 3.

Yellow Jacob's ladder

***P. carneum* 'Apricot Delight':** A charming species with salmon-coloured flowers. Nice in cut flower arrangements. Zone 5.

***P. caeruleum* 'Brise d'Anjou':** One of the cultivars with green and white foliage, which shows up nicely in lightly shaded parts of the garden. Zone 3.

***P.* 'Snow and Sapphires':** Developed from 'Brise d'Anjou' and very cold hardy (zone 3). The reason for its development was to make it more heat-resistant for warmer parts of the continent, but that's not an issue in Atlantic Canada.

***P. reptans* 'Stairway to Heaven':** My favourite of the cultivars with variegated foliage, this low-growing variety has tints of pink in its new growth and china-blue flowers. Zone 3.

'Stairway to Heaven'

***P. yezoense* 'Purple Rain':** The foliage of 'Purple Rain' has bronze and wine-purple casts to its leaves, and violet-purple flowers. Of all the polemoniums, I found this one most susceptible to mildew, and also most fussy about overwintering. Zone 4 with protective mulch and good drainage.

Polygonatum

Solomon's seal

Family: Ruscaceae (formerly Liliaceae)
Hardy to: zone 3
Bloom period: mid-May to late June
Growing requirements: shade to full sun if soil is moist
Height: 3–4 feet

Where best used: woodland gardens, shade plantings
Propagation: division in spring
Problems: Slugs and snails. No serious diseases.
Notes: Native to North America, hummingbird magnets.

From about the middle of May until early September, my gardens are host to a lot of hummingbirds. We have several feeders strategically located so we can view them from the kitchen window, and we also have a number of perennials and shrubs planted in that area. One of the hummers' favourites is the graceful Solomon's seal, an easily recognized plant with green-tipped white flowers that dangle like small pendants from the undersides of its arching stems. Several species are native to North America, with one, the hairy Solomon's seal (*P. pubescens*), found wild throughout the Maritimes. You may also see a type of Solomon's seal (*P. biflorum* or *P. commutatum*) growing near old farms and other rural properties—escapees from former gardens.

The stems of Solomon's seal are graceful and sweeping.

Although Solomon's seal will form colonies over time, it is slow to do so, and not at all invasive. It's been more than ten years since I first dug up some rhizomes from an abandoned homestead and transplanted them to our hummingbird-viewing garden, and they've never attempted to take over that area. I've divided the colony several times and planted the divisions in other shady spots on our property, and those too have been slow to spread. If you're in a hurry and want to create an area with plenty of Solomon's seal, make sure to plant a number of them. The plants tend to sulk for at least the first year.

Solomon's seal plants often start to look tired and develop yellow foliage after they bloom, especially if the summer becomes hot and dry. Don't be afraid to cut them back to the ground to tidy them up, but you don't have to deadhead if you just want them to grow naturally. You may wish to water them occasionally if summer continues to be dry, especially when starting out with a new colony, although once established Solomon's seal is quite drought-tolerant.

I recently learned about a dwarf species of Solomon's seal (*Polygonatum humile,* less than a foot tall), but I had never seen it for sale or tried growing it. Not a week later I saw it at Bunchberry Nurseries in Upper Clements, Nova Scotia, so naturally I brought it home and added it to the shade garden. I still prefer the larger species, though, because part of the appeal for me are the graceful sweeps of arching foliage, usually reaching 3 feet in height or better. Great Solomon's seal, *Polygonatum biflorum* var. c*ommutatum,* is a showstopper that can reach 6 feet in height, but mostly you'll find the common variety (usually labelled as *P.* x *hybridum*), which won't grow taller than 3 feet. If you're looking for something different, try the variegated form (*P. odoratum* 'Variegatum'), which has white-striped foliage that looks lovely in a shaded setting.

The flowers of Solomon's seal are attractive to hummingbirds.

Potentilla

cinquefoil, potentilla

Family: Rosaceae
Hardy to: zone 3
Bloom period: late spring to midsummer; some are continuous bloomers
Growing requirements: full sun to light shade, good drainage
Height: up to 30 inches

Where best used: mixed borders, pollinator gardens, alpine plantings
Propagation: division
Problems: May develop crown rot in hot, humid conditions.
Notes: Deer-resistant. Excellent butterfly plants.

I have to admit that I long resisted cinquefoils for two reasons. I am not a fan of the shrub potentillas, many of which have buttercup-yellow flowers and are ubiquitous in commercial plantings around gas stations and offices. Also, numerous weedy species are found throughout Atlantic Canada, again usually with buttercup-like yellow flowers. The first time I saw a herbaceous potentilla, however, I thought it was a geum until I looked at its foliage and then its plant tag — it had marvellous double flowers that were shades of scarlet, red, and yellow all at once. I bought 'Arc en Ciel' immediately and became a convert to the perennials.

Some plant authorities distinguish the shrubby plants from the perennials by

'Ron Macbeath'

calling the latter by their common name of cinquefoil, and I have followed this convention. Although the common name "cinquefoil" means five-leaf, species may have fewer or more leaflets on each stem. These leaflets do always radiate out from a central point (palmate leaves). Some species have been moved to other genus classifications: the three-leafed cinquefoil, *P. tridentata*, which I saw growing on the Tablelands in Gros Morne National Park, is now classified as *Sibbaldiopsis tridentata*.

Some cinquefoils have evergreen foliage, but it is important to mark where they've been planted. These plants are in the rose family, as is the common strawberry, and quite often the foliage of cinquefoils resembles that of a strawberry. I wonder how many times I may have removed a plant thinking it was a wild strawberry seedling, while letting wild strawberries—or wild species of potentillas—stay in the garden.

Cinquefoils need to be situated in the right spot, with good drainage so that they don't rot off in soggy soil. Smaller varieties work nicely in alpine plantings, although many cultivars have a sprawling habit once they begin blooming, so they may need more space than their initial clump of spring foliage may indicate. I grow mine in among echinaceas, sea holly, and other strong-stemmed species so that the cinquefoil flower stems are given some support. Bees and butterflies love cinquefoils, while deer and rabbits tend to leave them alone. Some species and cultivars will rebloom, especially if you deadhead them or shear them back once the first flush of bloom is past.

Recommended species and cultivars

Potentilla nepalensis: This is a reblooming species with flowers that resemble those of strawberries. The most well known is 'Miss Wilmott,' which has deep coral-pink flowers with a contrasting crimson centre. 'Ron McBeath' has cherry-pink flowers with similar contrasting rose eye.

P. atrosanguinea: The Himalayan, or ruby, cinquefoil has three leaflets on each leaf and silvery undersides. 'Fireball' can produce red, orange, or yellow, double flowers, while 'Gibson's Scarlet' has brilliant red, single blossoms. 'William Rollison' boasts blazing orange double flowers with yellow edges.

P. 'Arc en Ciel': Double, crimson blooms accented with yellow and orange; long blooming period.

'Arc en Ciel'

Primula

primrose, primula, cowslip

Family: Primulaceae

Hardy to: zone 3 or 4

Bloom period: spring to early summer

Growing requirements: partial shade to full sun; moist but well-drained, humus-rich soil

Height: 3–30 inches

Where best used: shade gardens, containers, rock gardens, alongside ponds or streams

Propagation: division or seedlings

Problems: Aphids, spider mites, and rusts may be present.

Notes: Many different species, forms, and flower colours.

In his poem "Foresight," the great English poet William Wordsworth wrote of primulas, "Primroses, the spring may love them; Summer knows but little of them." They are, indeed, a flower of spring, and by the onset of summer I'm usually left mostly with seed heads and clumps of cool green foliage. These fascinating plants are harbingers of spring and include more than four hundred different species, with many more hundreds of varieties and named cultivars.

Primulas have an interesting spot in botanical history, as polyanthus and auricula forms of primroses composed two of eight categories of florist societies that formed in Europe during the seventeenth and eighteenth centuries. At that time, "florist" referred to a breeder of new plant varieties, rather than a flower arranger or decorator, and members of the auricula and polyanthus societies took pride in displaying their plants in special tiered shelves known as primula "theatres."

Many species of primulas will take full sun if you live in a cool part of the region. They flourish in my windswept, coastal garden, but will prefer partial shade in warmer locations. Some species go dormant if the summer is

'Pacific Giant' hybrids

too hot but will wake up again as cooler weather comes in the fall, and you may even get a little rebloom in the polyanthas.

While all species of primulas prefer a moist, humus-rich growing medium, most will sulk and die if the ground is waterlogged, so good drainage is essential. Two species are more tolerant of winter wet and boggy conditions: Japanese (*P. japonica*) and drumstick primulas (*P. denticulata*). However, most primulas need snow cover or a protective mulch to help them get through the winter, especially in sites prone to lack of snow cover along with January thaws.

Recommended species and hybrids

Although there are more than four hundred species of primulas, a handful of species and hybrids can be routinely found at garden centres. In order to find some of the more unusual species, you'll have to grow your own from seed or find a grower who specializes in primulas.

Primula x polyantha: The most commonly sold hybrids, which come in a huge array of flower colours. Some varieties have flowers borne on stems, while others bloom right above the leaves. You'll see "strains" of primulas, including Cowichans, Gold Lace, and Pacific Giants, and each of these strains may have a number of different flower colours.

P. denticulata: Drumstick primulas produce rounded balls of blossoms in white or shades of rose, lilac, or blue.

P. frondosa: Bird's-eye primrose is one of the dwarf varieties, with pink flowers the size of a shirt button on 2-inch stems above petite, green-grey leaves.

P. japonica: Japanese or candelabra primroses produce their blooms on stems with several concentric whorls of flowers. They will colonize over time if they are happy, preferring moist, even boggy conditions.

P. sieboldii: Flowers of Siebold primrose often have lacy, scalloped edges and come in an array of colours.

P. veris: Wild cowslip flowers are not as large or showy as some of their cousins, but do produce a fine array of bloom, usually yellow or, less often, red.

drumstick primula

P. x polyantha *primrose variety*

Pulmonaria

lungwort, lords-n-ladies, Bethlehem sage

Family: Boraginaceae
Hardy to: zone 3
Bloom period: mid-spring to early summer
Growing requirements: full sun to partial
shade, moist but well-drained soil
Height: 8–18 inches

Where best used: front of borders, pollinator
gardens, shade plantings
Propagation: division, seedlings
Problems: Occasional slugs and aphids;
powdery mildew.
Notes: Deer-resistant.

Long before I actually had any pulmonaria in my gardens, I fell in love with this genus
for two reasons. The flowers of many pulmonaria start out with pink buds but mature
into various shades of violet or true blue, two of my favourite flower colours. But even
more charmingly, many of the species and hybrids have deep green leaves that may be
spotted, spangled, or painted broadly in a paler green or silvery tint. This makes them show
up beautifully in a shade garden,
and to my mind also makes them
as desirable as any hosta—while
also, unlike hostas, being resistant to
damage from deer.

Pulmonaria was dubbed lungwort
because its botanical name is derived
from the Latin word *pulmonarius*,
having to do with the lungs, and
because its mottled leaves look like
diseased lungs. At one time, some
plants received their names for
resembling body parts and were
thought to have medicinal properties
related to these parts. *Hepatica*, the

Many pulmonaria start out with pink buds that flush to blue.

liverwort, has tri-lobed leaves, in the same way that the liver organ is lobed; *Sanguinaria*,
bloodwort, exudes a sap that is red like blood. (The word "wort" comes from the Old
English *wyrt*, which refers to root or plant.) Regardless of the genus, the plants aren't
efficacious in treating any related bodily ailments.

Where pulmonaria *is* efficacious, however, is in being a bright spot in the early spring
garden. They often challenge hepatica and hellebores as the first non-bulb perennials to

P. longifolia *seedling*

'Redstart'

bloom in my spring garden, in mid- to late April, and are often barely emerged from the ground before they begin to bloom. Bees are very glad to see the flowers open, as they are a rich source of nectar for pollinators, especially in early spring. One old-fashioned name for pulmonaria is bee-bread, which also can refer to borage, a related plant.

Pulmonaria grow best in lightly shaded sites, but also do well in sites that receive full sun provided they have adequate moisture. Full shade will prevent plants from blossoming freely, but I have them growing under spruce trees and never lack for blooms.

Keep your plants well mulched and the soil moist, but also provide good circulation by not planting them too closely. Such care will help prevent outbreaks of powdery mildew fungus on foliage during hot weather. If you do find mildew has infested your plants (usually in August), cut them back to the ground and let fresh new growth appear. Don't add the trimmed leaves to your compost pile; get rid of them by burning to destroy fungal spores that would otherwise re-infest new growth.

Pulmonaria can have several different leaf shapes. Some have broad leaves spotted with silver or pale green: these are hybrids of the species *P. saccharata* and *P. officinalis*. Others have much longer, narrower leaves, often nearly completely solid silver and white with minimal green edging: these are offspring of the species *P. rubra* (the only species having pink or red flowers) or *P. longifolia.*

As with hostas, heucheras, and echinaceas, plant breeders have been busy developing some stunningly beautiful varieties over the past number of years. Seedlings of pulmonaria plants may not resemble their parents, so it can be hard to decide which cultivar your young plants may be. One thing is certain: once other gardeners have seen pulmonaria growing in your garden, they'll be keen to try them too, so don't worry about finding homes for excess seedlings.

Recommended cultivars

'**Sissinghurst White**': White flowers from pale pink buds.
'**Moonshine**': Silvery leaves edged in dark green, pale blue-white flowers.
Pulmonaria longifolia ssp. *cevennensis*: Deep cobalt-blue flowers.
'**Raspberry Splash**': Dusky rose-red flowers, foliage generously marked with silver.
'**David Ward**': Red flowers, white-edged leaves; protect from full sun.
'**Samurai**': A personal favourite, with narrow, all-silver leaves and cobalt flowers.

Rodgersia

rodgersia

Family: Saxifragaceae
Hardy to: zone 4
Bloom period: midsummer
Growing requirements: moist to wet, humus-rich soil
Height: 3–5 feet

Where best used: specimen plant, butterfly garden, wet areas
Propagation: Division in spring. Can be difficult to divide mature plants due to root systems.
Problems: Slugs sometimes eat foliage.
Notes: Excellent leaf texture; deer-resistant.

The first time my long-suffering spouse saw rodgersia growing, he thought it was a germinating horse-chestnut. Indeed, there is a species called *R. aesculifolia* with foliage very similar to that of horse-chestnut (*Aesculus*, horse chestnut genus; *folia*, leaves), with large, palmate leaves. I many times think this plant would be more popular if it had a common name other

The handsome, textured foliage of Rodgersia

than its genus, which isn't the easiest to say or spell. Nevertheless, I certainly recommend rodgersia to gardeners who want a great-textured plant for a moist part of their gardens.

Rodgersia is another perennial that requires patience; it's slow to get going, both after being transplanted into the garden and when it wakes up every spring. I've marked where mine are so that I don't disturb the soil around them; if you've ever tried to divide or move a more mature rodgersia plant, you know the root system is impressive.

While the flowers of rodgersia are very attractive (astilbe-like plumes in cream, pink, or red), it's the foliage of this plant that really commands attention. The leaves are large, wrinkled, and highly textured, and may be bright green, bronze, or even a handsome chocolate-copper brown. A well-grown plant may easily be mistaken for a small shrub, as some species may reach 5 feet in height and width.

Like their relatives, the astilbes, rodgersias like consistently moist soil; provide this, and they'll tolerate a range of light conditions, from shade to full sun. If the soil dries out, leaf edges will begin to turn brown. Despite their textured appearance, the leaves don't appreciate too much wind, so sheltering them from the most prevailing of summer winds is a good idea. If you live in the colder range of rodgersia's winter tolerance, it's also a good idea to mulch the plants over winter for protection from cold, especially if snow cover is typically light or irregular. My rodgersia are routinely buried by drifts of snow and have

closeup of 'Chocolate Wings' foliage

never suffered. Likewise, they are quite pest-free: slugs may chew the foliage, but not significantly, and rodgersia is quite deer-resistant.

Several different species of rodgersia are commonly available, varying in size as well as flower and foliage colour. They are often sold as "rodgersia," with no species or cultivar name listed. The biggest of the species is *R. aesculifolia*, the fingerleaf rodgersia, which can top 6 feet in height and has creamy-white flowers; *R. pinnata* is commonly called the featherleaf rodgersia and is a little shorter in height, reaching to 4 feet and having red flowers. *R. sambucifolia*, the elderberry rodgersia, is the shortest of the species and the earliest to bloom, with white to pink flowers in late spring or early summer.

However, if you like unusual foliage colour, look for *R. pinnata* 'Chocolate Wings,' which is commonly available (although quite pricey) at some nurseries. As the name suggests, the foliage is cocoa-bronze in colour, especially in the spring, turning more bronze-green as the season progresses. Its flowers are deep pink, but I actually had to look this up—I so love the foliage texture and colour of my rodgersias, I rarely pay attention to the flowers!

Rudbeckia

rudbeckia, gloriosa daisies, black-eyed Susan, orange coneflower

Family: Asteraceae
Hardy to: varies with species
Bloom period: midsummer to autumn
Growing requirements: full sun, moist but well-drained soil
Height: 12 inches to 8 feet

Where best used: wildlife and pollinator plantings, native plantings, dry gardens
Propagation: division or seed
Problems: Crown rot in too-wet conditions.
Notes: Some rudbeckias are overenthusiastic spreaders. All are attractive to butterflies.

Mention the name black-eyed Susan and you'll see some gardeners roll their eyes. Maybe they don't like the colour of these plants, which are often a golden yellow or yellow-orange colour, a hue that can be challenging to blend into perennial borders. Perhaps they've had an attack of "familiarity breeds contempt," in which they were so used to seeing the wild rudbeckias that grow throughout Atlantic Canada that they thought all rudbeckias were the same. I like rudbeckias because there is such variety in the genus, with species that are good for front of border, and others that are massive, attention-commanding plants best suited at the back of a planting.

'Prairie Sun'

Rudbeckias are stars of the late summer or early autumn garden, putting on a big display of colour when many other perennials have wound down for the season. They are magnets for butterflies, so they're a staple in any pollinator-friendly garden. They tend to be quite trouble-free provided they are planted in well-drained soil with full sun to light shade. They're often recommended for dry plantings, but they really do best with adequate moisture; on too-dry sites, they tend to look straggly and tired very quickly. If you're growing the taller species and want to encourage shorter, bushier growth, pinch out the growing tips or shear the plants back by one-third their height in June.

'Goldsturm'

Rudbeckia fulgida: Back in 1999, this species's cultivar, 'Goldsturm,' was the perennial of the year, and I couldn't see what the fuss was about until I grew it myself. It's a dependable, trouble-free plant, producing masses of cheery, brown-eyed, orange-yellow flowers. It does spread by creeping roots but is easily contained. Zone 3.

R. hirta: The Gloriosa daisies are short-lived perennials but are nice additions to the late-summer border. Cultivars include 'Irish Eyes,' which has a green central disc; 'Cherokee Sunset,' with double daisies in variegated browns, golds, reds, and oranges; 'Autumn Colours,' in rich russets and reds; and 'Cherry Brandy,' which is the first red rudbeckia. Some of these varieties may self-seed, and all are easily grown from packaged seed. Zone 5.

R. laciniata: 'Hortensia' is also known as golden-glow or the outhouse plant: it can easily reach 7 feet tall and spreads out from its roots. Plants may require staking in windy sites. Zone 2.

R. maxima: Another giant of a rudbeckia, this species has unusual powder-blue leaves and yellow flowers, each bearing a central cone that can be as much as 6 inches tall. The plant sometimes goes by the endearing common name 'Dumbo's ears.' Zone 4.

R. nitida: Shining coneflower is a showstopper if you have the room for it: it routinely reaches 8 feet tall in my garden, with brilliant green cones surrounded by clear yellow petals. 'Herbstsonne' has a cumbersome cultivar name but is a remarkable plant; although it is said to self-seed freely, I've never experienced this in my garden. I have, however, shared it with gardeners around Atlantic Canada. Zone 4.

'Herbstsonne'

R. occidentalis 'Black Beauty': For the collector looking for something different, this cultivar is variously called the black or green coneflower. Its flowers are composed of dark brown, nearly black, cones but don't have the ring of bright-coloured florets around the cone. 'Green Wizard' is similar, but with green cones that turn dark brown in autumn. Zone 4.

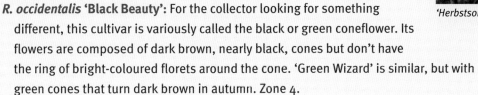

Salvia

salvia, sage

Family: Lamiaceae
Hardy to: varies with species
Bloom period: early summer to fall
Growing Requirements: full sun to light shade, good drainage
Height: 10–36 inches

Where best used: cutting gardens, pollinator gardens, herb plantings
Propagation: division, stem cuttings, seed
Problems: Whitefly or aphids may be present.
Notes: Many types of salvia are deer- and rabbit-resistant.

The salvias, or sages if you prefer, comprise the largest genus in the mint family, Lamiaceae. The best-known species is the culinary sage used in stuffings and with poultry, but there are literally hundreds of species of salvia, some used as perennials, others only grown as annuals in Atlantic Canada. Check labels closely at nurseries, because I've found a red-flowered salvia that is only hardy to zone 8 sold as a perennial in our region.

If there is a secret to growing salvia successfully, whether kitchen sage or an elegant ornamental-leafed variety like silver sage, it's to provide excellent drainage. I battled with salvias for a number of years before determining that they were not suited for the heavy clay in our back garden. I moved them around to the front beds where the drainage is better, and they've been performing well ever since. Once established, they tend to be drought-resistant, although Atlantic Canada isn't known for having true drought so much as occasional dry spells that last several weeks. Deadheading sages will usually promote more growth, and bees, hummingbirds, and other pollinators enjoy the flowers, which can be white, blue, purple, pink, or red.

'Eveline'

We cherish culinary sage for its fragrant foliage, which lends flavour to our cooking, but other salvias have pungent—even unpleasant—scented foliage. The good news is that this trait helps to deter deer, rabbits, and even some insect pests. Just don't assume that the neighbour's cat has been spraying your plants when you're growing salvias in the border.

One of the more unusual salvias is grown for its foliage rather than its flowers. Silver sage (*S. argentea*) acts as a biennial or short-lived perennial, and has large leaves covered in silky silvery "hair." It puts up stalks of small white flowers, which some gardeners prefer to cut off in the same way they remove hosta blooms, but I like the flowers almost as much as the foliage. Silver sage may be difficult to locate in garden centres and is only hardy to zone 5, but is worth trying if you can get an inexpensive plant or a division from a friend.

Some of the more commonly found salvias are cultivars or hybrids, and may be sold simply as *Salvia* x, followed by the cultivar name. Note that hardiness to zone 3 is contingent upon excellent drainage.

Recommended cultivars

***Salvia* x *sylvestris* 'Blue Hill':** Deep purple-blue flowers; grows to 20 inches. Zone 3.

***S.* 'May Night' ('Mainacht'):** Even deeper purple flowers; grows to 24 inches. Zone 3.

***S.* x 'Rose Queen':** Lovely rose pink flowers make an interesting change from the more common purple varieties; grows to 24 inches. Zone 4.

***S.* 'Snow Hill':** Pure white flowers and a long bloom period. Zone 3

***S. verticillata*:** The whorled sages have flower heads with obvious whorls of flowers spaced regularly up their stems, rather than the more spiky appearance of some of the others. 'White Rain' has small white flowers and grows to 24 inches; 'Purple Rain' is a little shorter, with dusky purple flowers. Zone 4.

'May Night'

'Snow Hill'

Scabiosa

scabious, pincushion flower

Family: Dipsacaceae

Hardy to: zone 3 or 4

Bloom period: early summer until fall, especially with deadheading

Growing requirements: full sun to light shade, well-drained soil

Height: 12–72 inches

Where best used: pollinator gardens, mixed perennial borders

Propagation: Division of plants every couple of years. Some may self-seed.

Problems: Slugs often attack foliage of young plants.

Notes: Very important butterfly and bee plants.

If you've ever seen a collection of pincushion flowers, happily blooming in the midsummer sun, you know why this is a plant that can sell itself. Its foliage is ordinary looking, as the plants produce basal rosettes of toothed leaves in a nondescript grey-green, but the flowers begin to show up in late spring or early summer and will continue until frost stops the plant's growth. And such appealing flowers they are, with pincushion-like central disks surrounded by longer, ray-like petals in shades of blue, lavender, pink, or white. Beloved by butterflies, scabiosa is an essential flower for a pollinator garden, and also makes an attractive cut flower.

It's possible that their genus and one common name may have deterred some gardeners from trying these plants in the past—scabiosa was formerly used as a home remedy to (reputedly) control itching caused by scabies and other skin irritations.

Scabiosa does best planted in full sun, although it can tolerate light shade (but may not flower as profusely). Taller species may need to be staked in shady or windy sites to keep their blooms upright. This plant needs evenly moist soil that drains well; winter wet

blue scabiosa

will take these plants out of commission very quickly, but they don't like to be dried out either.

'Butterfly Blue' is probably the most common cultivar of scabiosa available in nurseries, with near-continuous bloom producing pale lavender-blue flowers. 'Pink Mist' has pale pink blooms, and you may also find plants with no cultivar name but simply labelled as Scabiosa/Pincushion flower. Avoid *C. atropurpurea* unless it is sold as an annual, because it is only hardy to zone 9; you may grow it from seed because of its bright red or deep wine flowers and fragrance, but it is not hardy and doesn't self-seed reliably well.

If you have the space and like plants with attitude, try growing the giant scabious, *Cephalaria gigantea*, also sometimes listed as *Scabiosa gigantea*. This perennial can easily reach 8 feet tall. Its foliage is somewhat coarse, larger than that of other scabious species and cultivars, but its flowers are borne on tall, slender stems, giving the plant a rather airy look. Its flowers are a lovely pale yellow and the seed heads are interesting. Don't deadhead all the blooms and the plant should self-seed, or else divide the plants every couple of years to keep them flourishing. If you want a yellow-flowered species but don't have room for such a large plant, look for *S. ochroleuca* (also sold as *S. columbaria* var. *ochroleuca*), which is more compact and grows only to 3 feet tall.

Another pincushion flower

As if there weren't enough descriptive common names for plants, there's another ornamental genus that goes by the name pincushion flower. *Knautia macedonica* does resemble *Scabiosa*, although it tends to grow taller than all but the yellow species. Its flowers are smaller and are usually purple, reddish magenta, or pink. One type, called 'Mars Midget,' is a terrific bloomer with deep wine flowers and a shorter growth habit than most of the forms sold at nurseries. *Knautia* has the same growth requirements as *Scabiosa*.

giant scabious

a mixture of Knautias

Sedum

stonecrop, sedum

Family: Crassulaceae

Hardy to: zone 3

Bloom period: midsummer to early autumn

Growing requirements: average, well-drained soil

Height: 4–6 inches for creeping types; up to 3 feet for border species

Where best used: alpine gardens, dry gardens, edging borders

Propagation: division or cuttings

Problems: Rots possible if soil too wet. Overly fertile soil can lead to flopping plants in taller varieties.

Notes: Deer- and drought-resistant. Very attractive to pollinators. Excellent foliage colour.

The first sedums I ever grew were non-hardy, indoor houseplant varieties—such as burro's-tail sedum—in my residence room at college. A few years later, during a summer hike to Cape Split in Nova Scotia, I saw what looked like sedum growing from crevasses in the rocks near the cliff edge. These turned out to be hardy sedum, of which there are several species that grow wild in Atlantic Canada. Their versatility of forms and tolerance of poor soil and tough growing conditions explain why sedums are increasing in popularity as garden plants.

Although there are some three hundred species of sedums worldwide, many of which are highly ornamental, I have divided them into two categories. The ground cover, or creeping sedums, such as *S. rupestre* 'Angelina' or *S.* 'Dragons Blood,' rarely grow taller than 6 inches but spread out in carpet-like formations across the soil. The border sedums grow in a more upright, clump-forming habit, some as much as 3 feet tall but most between 12–20 inches. Perhaps the most well loved of sedums is the border variety, 'Autumn Joy'; it's well named, as it erupts into a blaze of rose-red blooms in late summer and retains its flower colour until well into fall.

'Frosty Morn'

'October Daphne'

Because there are so many species and varieties of sedums available, I've divided them into the two categories mentioned above.

Creeping/ground covers:

Sedum reflexum: Blue spruce stonecrop. Yellow flowers over blue-green, with needle-like foliage.

S. rupestre 'Angelina': A personal favourite, as described above, for fall colour as well as summer performance. Yellow flowers seem inconsequential compared to foliage. Excellent in containers as well as borders.

S. spurium 'Dragon's Blood': Two-row sedums. Deep rose-red flowers over green foliage that turns reddish in cool weather. Variations include 'Tricolor' which has white-edged leaves tipped in pink with matching pale pink flowers.

S. 'Bertram Anderson': Perhaps the darkest-leafed of the ground cover sedums, with burgundy black leaves and purple flowers.

'Angelina'

S. 'Capo Blanco': A dainty charmer with grey-green rosettes of foliage and starry, yellow flowers.

S. kamschaticum 'Variegatum': Russian stonecrop has bright orange-yellow flowers and green leaves edged and splashed with creamy white accents.

Tall/border selections:

'Autumn Joy': The quintessential favourite has huge heads of rose-red flowers over cool green foliage.

'Chocolate': For the chocoholic-plant fan, this variety has salmon flowers and chocolate bronze leaves.

'Red Cauli': I like this one for its blue-grey foliage and deep red, ball-like clusters of flowers.

'Matrona': Grey-green leaves, reddish-purple stems, and mauve flowers make this an unusual and attractive specimen.

'Purple Emperor': Deep purple leaves provide lovely contrast for dusty-rose flowers that turn to bronze seed heads in winter.

'Mediovariegatum': Green foliage has eye-catching blotches of pale yellow in the centre of each leaf; white to pale-pink flowers.

'Frosty Morn': Delicate green foliage is edged in snow-white with pale pink flowers.

While bees and butterflies adore the flowers of many sedums, I am taken primarily with their foliage. The first varieties I saw, including the wild species, had green or bluish green foliage, but today you can find sedums with red, pink, purple, cream, yellow, white, blue, and near-black tones in their fleshy leaves. In the spring, when my collection is waking up, the bed where they are planted is a patchwork quilt of colours. The most amazing cultivar, by

'Purple Emperor'

far, has to be 'Angelina,' which behaves somewhat like a heath or heather, turning amazing copper, gold, and bronze colours in the fall and over winter. Its spring colour settles down to more of a gold-and-lime-green shade, which is also impressive.

The main thing to remember about sedums is to site them with as much sun as possible, and to give them excellent drainage. Although some varieties are more tolerant of moist soil than others, they are definitely stars of the dry or alpine garden. With the taller border species, you may wish to pinch their shoots back in early June to keep the plants from growing too tall and floppy.

variegated Russian stonecrop

Stachys

lamb's-ears, betony

Family: Lamiaceae
Hardy to: zone 4
Bloom period: late June to mid-August
Growing Requirements: full sun to light shade, average soil with good drainage
Height: 24 inches when in bloom

Where best used: edging, pollinator garden, sloped areas, rock gardens
Propagation: division
Problems: Slugs and snails may chew young foliage.
Notes: Deer- and rabbit-resistant, drought-tolerant, great bee plant.

One of the first "pass-along plants" I was given when I moved back to the Canning area was a nice clump of *Stachys byzantina*, commonly known as lamb's-ears. I have no idea how many times I've shared divisions of that plant in the years since, but it's been quite a few. Lamb's-ears seems to be a plant that gardeners either adore or dislike immensely. I'm very fond of it for its silvery, softly furred foliage, and although the flowers aren't exactly showy, I never cut them off my plants because bees flock to them constantly.

lamb's-ears in flower

This is an easy perennial with a variety of uses in the garden, providing it has good drainage and a generous amount of sunlight. Mine are at the edge of my rock garden, where there's rather poor soil and very good drainage, along with full sun. Go easy on the fertilizer, because stachys tends to flop in too rich a soil. Without the flower stalks, the plants are only 6–12 inches tall, making them nice edging plants or a good choice for a rock garden.

Although in warmer, humid climates stachys can develop root rot and other rot-related problems, in Atlantic Canada the plants do well so long as they have good drainage. If you need to water them, avoid getting moisture on the leaves, which can lead to leaf spotting in much the same way as water affects the leaves of African violet houseplants.

Lamb's-ears is a perennial that will die out in the centre of the crown after a few years, so divide your plants every couple of years to keep them looking great. Some gardeners find that their plants self-sow a little too much for their liking, but this has never been a problem in my experience because the plant tends to spread very slowly.

Several cultivars of lamb's-ears are available, including two varieties that very seldom bloom: 'Silver Carpet' and the larger-leafed 'Big Ears.' For something quite different, look for 'Primrose Heron,' which has yellow-green foliage in the spring, turning silver-green in summer; it's not to everyone's taste, but it reminds me of the gold- or gold-and-green foliaged annual licorice plant (*Helichrysum*), and is an interesting addition to a perennial collection.

Another member of the *Stachys* genus that is well worth growing is big betony (*S. macrantha*); as its name suggests, it's a taller plant, growing to 2 feet tall, and its foliage is not silver or fuzzy but rather rich, dark green. It produces spikes of brilliant pink, purple, or violet flowers that are beloved by bees and other pollinators, and is hardy to zone 3. Wood betony (*S. officinalis*) is a smaller, less showy species with similar magenta or pink flowers, and has been used in herbal medicine for centuries.

seedlings of lamb's-ears

betony flowers

Thalictrum

meadow rue, king-of-the-meadow

Family: Ranunculaceae

Hardy to: zones 3–5

Bloom period: late spring to midsummer

Growing requirements: full sun to partial shade; compost-rich, moist, but well-drained soil

Height: 2–5 feet

Where best used: shade gardens, wildflower meadows, woodland or butterfly gardens

Propagation: division or seedlings

Problems: No serious pests or diseases.

Notes: Attractive pollinator plant. Taller varieties may need staking.

It's easy to mistake many thalictrum plants for those of the related columbine, at least before they bloom. Both have lacy leaves composed of multiple leaflets that are somewhat similar to maidenhair fern (*Adiantum*) foliage. The flowers of meadow rue are quite different from the tubular, very showy flowers of columbines; they are subtler in their way, and also tend to bloom later than columbines, beginning in late June and going on into August.

T. rochebruneanum *'Lavender Mist'*

You may see one species of meadow rue, *Thalictrum pubescens*, growing along roadsides in wet areas such as marshes, along rivers and streams, or in damp ditches throughout Atlantic Canada. You can't miss this plant, as it is quite tall, easily reaching 8 feet, with tufts of creamy white flowers at the end of tall, slender stems. Some meadow rues are dioecious, having both male and female plants, but this is not something that you'll generally need to think about because you're not usually worrying about producing seed, unlike with dioecious shrubs or trees. What is intriguing is that most species of thalictrum don't have any petals on their flowers, and the showy flowers are in fact stamens, sometimes surrounded by a ring of modified leaves or sepals.

Meadow rues are easy to care for; they don't need to be divided (unless you want more of them), they are pretty well oblivious to diseases and pests, and they are interesting even when not blooming. Taller species may need to be staked so that their flowering stalks aren't beaten down by summer winds or rains. Some gardeners will trim their plants back later in the summer, particularly if it's been a dry season, but I simply let mine do their thing, growing happily in the moist shade garden or the sunny, moist front garden, and enjoy their blossoms for weeks on end.

A bit of a botanical oddity, a little plant called rue-anemone (sometimes classified as *Thalictrum thalictroides* and sometimes as *Anemonella thalictroides*) is a spring ephemeral, meaning it blooms in spring and then disappears. It is a delightful little plant, less than 4 inches tall. Whether it is classified as a tiny thalictrum or as a close relative of anemones, if you can find rue-anemone, purchase it for your moist shade garden—it's tiny, but it won't disappoint you with its lovely little flowers.

'Black Stockings' thalictrum has dark stems

Recommended species and hybrids

Thalictrum aquilegifolium: Columbine meadow rue has blooms described as cotton candy-like, in white, cream, or shades of lilac and pink. 3–5 feet tall. Zone 3.

T. flavum ssp. *glaucum*: Dusty meadow rue is an unusual species and subspecies in the genus, with bright yellow flowers and striking, blue-green foliage. Grows to 6 feet. Zone 4.

T. rochebruneanum: It may have a cumbersome species name, but there's nothing cumbersome about this plant, with its lavender, starry flowers that last throughout late spring and well into summer. This species has obvious, showy sepals that can be mistaken for petals. 'Lavender Mist' is a popular cultivar. Zone 4.

T. 'Black Stockings': Grown as much for its stems, which are nearly black, as for the lavender powder-puff flowers. Matures at 6 feet tall, hardy to zone 5.

T. ichangense 'Evening Star': Plant breeders love to tease us by releasing new varieties of plants on a yearly basis. In 2010, Terra Nova Nurseries of Oregon launched this showy new thalictrum, which features colourful foliage that is somewhat like an *Epimedium*, with each leaflet featuring a silver star pattern. Although not yet available in Atlantic Canada, it should be here in a year or so; it's registered as hardy to zone 4 and grows only to a foot tall.

Tiarella

foamflower

Family: Saxifragaceae

Hardy to: zone 4

Bloom period: late spring to midsummer

Growing requirements: shade, moist but well-drained, humus-rich soil

Height: 12–18 inches with flower stalks

Where best used: woodland gardens, shade gardens

Propagation: division of clumps

Problems: Powdery mildew may appear in too-dry conditions.

Notes: Rabbit- and deer-resistant.

If you have moist, shady sites with humus-rich soil in your garden, you ought to try growing tiarella, or foamflowers. These are so-named because they send up sprays of delicate white or pink flowers that look like foam. *Tiarella cordifolia* is native to eastern North America, although it is rare in Nova Scotia woodlands. It and a similar wildflower from the same family, *Mitella nuda*, the mitrewort, are sometimes confused for one another and grow in similar rich woodlands.

Tiarella flowers

My first attempts at growing tiarella were less than successful; it takes several years to establish a plant or plants, which spread by rhizomes and make a useful ground cover in moist shade. My plants were choked out by the taller-growing and overzealous Canada anemone, *Anemone canadensis*. I finally created a site where the foamflowers could compete with less aggressive plants, and now enjoy several cultivars growing in my shade garden.

As noted above, foamflowers need humus-rich, moist soil in order to thrive. Mulching around the plants will keep the soil cool and help to preserve moisture, but if foamflowers are planted under trees where they have to compete for moisture, they may need to be watered in the heat of summer. Once they have finished flowering, clip off the spent flower stems to keep the plants looking tidy, and they may even throw up a few more flowers. Generally foamflowers are untroubled by pests or diseases, and are seldom damaged by deer or rabbits.

Plant breeders have created numerous hybrids of foamflowers, some of which are more clump-forming in nature than spreading, and many feature striking patterns in the foliage. The species sold as *T. wherryi* or sometimes *T. cordifolia* var. *collina* do not spread, but with the hybrids it isn't always possible to tell what the parent species are, so you may need to experiment. Some foamflowers will display even prettier foliage colours in cool weather, making them attractive perennials whether they are blooming or not. The only possible drawback is in sourcing more than a couple of cultivars locally, but as more gardeners embrace the species, local nurseries ought to grow and offer more varieties.

'Pink Skyrocket' foliage

Recommended cultivars

'Butterfly Wings': Highly cut foliage, almost like the finer-leafed cranesbills, accented with maroon. Pale pink flowers.

'Crow Feather:' White flowers over bright green leaves accented with chocolate feathering. Winter foliage colour (in milder areas) bronze, pink, purple.

'Iron Butterfly': Burgundy to black markings in the centre of large, lobed leaves. White flowers with a tinge of pink.

'Neon Lights': Brilliant green leaves heavily accented with burgundy-black markings, white flowers.

'Pink Skyrocket': Profuse spikes of pink flowers over finely cut leaves veined with burgundy-red.

'Skeleton Key': Deeply cut green leaves with green-bronze veining, white flowers.

Tradescantia

widow's tears, spiderwort

Family: Commelinaceae
Hardy to: zone 3
Bloom period: late spring through summer
Growing requirements: full sun to light shade; average, moist to wet soil
Height: up to 3 feet

Where best used: front of border, sloped areas, woodland plantings
Propagation: division in spring or autumn
Problems: No serious pests or diseases.
Notes: Deer-resistant. Nectar source for pollinators.

'Blue and Gold'

The tradescantias that many people grow are the tropical houseplant varieties that spill from hanging containers. However, the species that we plant in our gardens are native to North America, although not to Atlantic Canada. The genus is named after two botanists and gardeners of the seventeenth century: John Tradescant the Elder, and his son, John Tradescant the Younger, both of whom were plant collectors and head gardeners to Charles I.

Tradescantias do yeoman's service in my garden: they aren't the biggest flower showoffs, but they are consistent, hardworking perennials, requiring little care. They have grass-like foliage, with small, tri-petalled flowers appearing in clusters at the top of short stems emerging from the leaves. Each individual flower lasts only a day, and as they fade, they turn into a gelatinous liquid, hence the sometimes-used common name "widow's tears." They do particularly well in moist soil, but will also grow in average soil that's a little on the dry side—they tend to flower less in drier soil, and grow a little less vigorously. I've had several varieties of them in my 'soggy bed' for years, and they've flourished nicely.

After the first big flush of flowers, the foliage of spiderworts tends to become somewhat straggly, especially if the plant is in a particularly hot and dry location. The late, great British gardener Christopher Lloyd said spiderworts look "sleazy" when they start to falter, a hilarious yet accurate description. If your plants start looking sleazy, take your grass shears

'Concorde Grape'

'Osprey'

and cut the stems and foliage back to about half their height, and they'll regenerate a nice fresh crop of foliage and another flourish of flowers.

Depending on the cultivar, some spiderworts will sprawl if it's very hot or if they've been over-fertilized. To avoid this, cut them back by one-third in late spring; they'll be later to bloom, but they should also be bushier and less inclined to fall over. Other than that midsummer pruning, spiderworts are carefree, and are not troubled by pests or diseases.

The most common species of tradescantia to be offered at nurseries is a hybrid of the native Virginia spiderwort, *Tradescantia virginiana*. You may see these plants labelled as *Tradescantia Andersoniana* group or *T.* x *andersonii*. To make it even more confusing, a dizzying number of cultivars are now available, and sometimes they aren't named but only sold by flower colour.

Recommended cultivars

'Bilberry Ice': White flowers with a tinge of lavender-purple to the petals and stamens.

'Osprey': White flowers with noticeable blue stamens.

'Blue and Gold' (also labelled 'Sweet Kate'): My personal favourite, because it looks good in bloom or out. Chartreuse to gold foliage, bright blue flowers. Not as vigorous as some.

'J. C. Weguelin': Large china-blue flowers and enthusiastic growth habit.

'Concorde Grape': Grape-purple blooms.

'Snowcap': Pure white flowers, very showy.

'Purple Dome': Dark purple flowers.

Trollius

globeflower

Family: Ranunculaceae
Hardy to: zone 3
Bloom period: late spring to early summer
Growing requirements: partial shade to full sun with moist to wet soil
Height: up to 36 inches

Where best used: shade garden, mid-back of mixed border, wet area
Propagation: division
Problems: Powdery mildew on occasion.
Notes: Rabbit- and deer-resistant.

Think of giant orange, yellow, or cream-coloured buttercups, but with a much better growth habit and ornamental value, and you're got globeflowers. Globeflowers are great plants for wet areas, and while I hesitate to call any plant care-free, in all the years I've had globeflowers I've never done anything to them except deadhead them when their flowers are finished. Deer and rabbits avoid them, slugs and other insect pests leave them alone, and they're largely disease-free.

'Golden Queen'

Globeflowers are a great plant for a wet site, and in fact may sulk if the soil isn't moist enough. They're happily tolerant of heavy clay soil, which I have in abundance, so I grow them in several different sites from mostly sun to very shady, and they all thrive due to consistently moist soil. If you have drier conditions, mulch the plants well. If they get too dry, they may develop powdery mildew, in which case cut back and destroy damaged foliage and keep the soil around the plants consistently moist in future years.

Don't be concerned if globeflowers don't show up first thing in the spring—they're a little later to emerge from the soil than some perennials. If you're new to growing them you might want to mark the site where you planted yours so you won't accidentally dig the plants up thinking they have expired. The foliage of globeflowers very much resembles that of a large buttercup, so be careful not to weed it out like I am pretty sure I did the first time I planted one.

Unlike buttercups, which spread rampantly by runners and seed, globeflowers are tidy clump-forming perennials. The hybrids don't self-seed, so if you want more plants from your existing globeflowers, divide them in spring. Another charming trait of globeflowers is that their blooms last for three or four weeks, and are borne on long stems that work beautifully as cut flowers.

Most of the globeflowers that you will see offered for sale will be sold as *Trollius* hybrids with just the cultivar name. If you want a different variety for the front of your border, look for *T. pumilus*, the dwarf globeflower, which only grows to about a foot in height and produces miniature flowers only about an inch in diameter.

'Lemon Queen': The quintessential globeflower, with bowl-shaped, buttercup yellow blossoms.

'Orange Princess': Brilliant orange, globe-shaped flowers and deep green foliage.

'Golden Queen' (Goldkonigen): Another orange variety but with a more open flower shape and a strong, crest-like display of its central stamens.

'Cheddar': My personal favourite, this globeflower has creamy-white flowers that resemble an uncoloured cheddar or Stilton cheese. I've found it a little slower to develop and later to bloom than others.

'Cressida': I don't know what botanical wag created this cultivar, but obviously that individual was a fan of Shakespeare's play *Trollius and Cressida*. This cultivar is a paler yellow than most of the yellow-flowered globeflowers, and worth seeking out for its unique colouring.

'Lemon Queen'

'Cheddar'

Vernonia

ironweed

Family: Asteraceae
Hardy to: zone 3
Bloom period: late summer to early autumn
Growing requirements: full sun; rich, moist to wet but well-draining soil
Height: 4–7 feet

Where best used: pollinator gardens, back of border, naturalized (meadow) plantings
Propagation: division, seedlings
Problems: No serious pests or diseases. May require staking.
Notes: Excellent late-season bloomer, loved by butterflies.

It's one thing to read about a particular plant in a book; it's quite another to see the plant growing in a garden. Once you see this plant and its masses of tiny, deep purple flowers glowing at the tops of its tall stems, happy pollinators swarming all around it, you can't help but be smitten.

I first saw ironweed growing in a friend's garden in Greenwood, Nova Scotia, as a complement to many tall grasses, its rich purple flowers dotted with bees and butterflies. That gorgeous colour is especially appealing as the plant blooms in late summer, when many of the flower

prairie ironweed

colours are in autumnal shades of gold, russet, orange, bronze, and yellow. Ironweed both contrasts with such colours and harmonizes with them, in the same way that late-summer asters provide a welcome change in the flower colour palette. The sturdy stems of ironweed also mean they work well as a cut flower for indoor bouquets.

A member of the aster family, ironweed is related to and somewhat resembles Joe-Pye weed (*Eupatorium* spp.) and has a similar growth habit and requirements. Full sun and plenty of moisture in compost-rich soil will keep this plant growing nicely. It will take partial shade but is apt to not grow as large or as strong-stemmed. Even in full sun, you may wish to provide stake supports if your ironweed plant is located in a windy spot. For those who don't want their plants quite so tall, you can cut them back by about one-third in late spring: they'll be shorter and bushier, but may also be later flowering.

Vernonia is a long-lived perennial and doesn't require regular division unless you want to make more plants (although you may find seedlings are a better option). This plant does self-seed fairly freely, so if you don't want many seedlings, mulch well around the plants to reduce seed germination.

The one drawback to vernonia is that it may be hard to locate at nurseries, perhaps because some are less than impressed by the common name. However, I do know that Lloyd Mapplebeck of Hillendale Perennials carries ironweed, because he gave me one to get them started in my garden. Late in the summer of 2010, I also discovered the marvelous *V. crinita* 'Purple Bowl,' which has showy flowers. Seed sources are also available, including the wonderful Wildflower Farm, a mail-order company in Ontario that specializes in native plants. They carry two species: New York ironweed (*V. novaboracensis*), and prairie ironweed (*V. fasciculata*), the latter of which normally grows to 4 feet tall. My hope is that more local nurseries will start carrying vernonia as soon as gardeners start asking for it.

V. crinita *'Purple Bowl'*

New York ironweed showing foliage and impression of height

Veronica

veronica, speedwell

Family: Plantaginaceae

Hardy to: zone 2–4

Bloom period: spring–summer

Growing requirements: full sun to light shade, moist but well-drained soil

Height: 8–36 inches

Where best used: front of border, mixed borders, rockeries, cutting gardens

Propagation: division, seedlings

Problems: Mildew may occur in humid weather.

Notes: Good pollinator plants. Deer- and rabbit-resistant.

The genus *Veronica* has been moved from the Scrophulariaceae, or figwort family (which includes the mulleins, *Verbascum*), to the plantain family. The genus name comes from a minor character in the Christian New Testament and several books of the Apocrypha. Veronica was a woman who had suffered many years from menstrual hemorrhaging, but when she touched the hem of the teacher Jesus, she was healed and eventually canonized as St. Veronica. Several speedwells, including the common wild speedwell, *V. officinalis*, have played a role in ancient and modern herbal medicines.

Speedwells are an essential part of any mixed or perennial border, performing diligently with minimal care. They require good drainage and prefer full sun or very light shade, but are tolerant of most soils given those two requirements. I've learned

'Aztec Gold' creeping speedwell

'Royal Candles'

to plant speedwells in the better-drained parts of my garden, because standing water and excessive winter wetness will kill them promptly.

Speedwells have two very different growth habits: creeping varieties spread by rhizomes and usually have larger individual flowers, while most of the taller varieties are clump formers with spikes composed of many small flowers. All are quite rabbit- and deer-resistant and generally untroubled by disease, other than occasional mildew if weather is hot and humid. Good spacing between plants can help reduce possible mildew outbreaks.

'Red Fox'

Recommended species and cultivars

Veronica gentianoides: Gentian speedwell is an early bloomer (late May in my garden) with white to pale blue flowers, marked with deeper blue and having green throats. Striking and lovely. Zone 2.

V. incana: As its common name suggests, woolly or silver speedwell has grey green, fuzzy leaves and silvery stems. Flowers are violet blue. 'Silver Sea' is a nice cultivar. Zone 3.

V. prostrata (sometimes V. peduncularis): Creeping speedwells have cobalt-blue flowers. Keep a close eye on them as they will spread. 'Georgia Blue' is a popular cultivar with bronze-green foliage.

V. 'Aztec Gold': Brilliant gold foliage is a perfect compliment to the periwinkle-blue flowers. Although this is a creeping form, its gold foliage keeps it from being overly ambitious about spreading.

V. 'Sunny Border Blue': One of the most popular of speedwells, with a long bloom period and deep violet blue flower spikes. A cultivar derived from this plant, 'Royal Candles,' has a shorter growth habit and even more brilliant flowers. Zone 3.

V. spicata 'Red Fox': There are several spike speedwells with vibrant rose-pink flowers, this being one of the more readily available ones.

V. 'Purplicious': Just as I was finishing up the profiles for this book, I discovered this new cultivar for sale at a local nursery. It boasts a new colour for speedwells, a vibrant lavender-purple somewhere between the blue and pink varieties, and features longer spikes than many of the tall speedwells.

drift of white Veronicastrum

Veronicastrum roseum

Veronicastrum *or Culver's root*

Culver's root, *Veronicastrum virginicum*, used to be classified with the speedwells but is now in its own genus. This tall, striking native of North America is an excellent choice for the back of sunny borders or for naturalizing in a wildflower meadow or garden. It will tolerate some shade but is inclined to be a bit floppy and not as floriferous. Hardy to zone 3, Culver's root does best in moist to wet soil, and is very tolerant of clay provided it is enriched with compost.

Culver's root has a different growth habit from its relatives the speedwells. Whorls of narrow leaves grow all around the tall stems, until the spikes of white, blue, lavender, or pinkish flowers appear at the tips. You may wish to stake plants to keep them upright, especially if your site is prone to winds, or they can be trimmed back by one-third in late spring or early summer. It may take several years for newly planted specimens to fill out into nice clumps, but once they do they are architecturally pleasing plants, deer- and rabbit-resistant, with flowers that are very attractive to pollinators. *V.* 'Erica' has red buds that open to soft pink flowers; 'Fascination' has lavender flowers.

V. gentianoides

'Georgia Blue' creeping speedwell

Achillea
Aconitum
Actaea
Alchemilla
Amsonia
Anemone
Aquilegia
Artemisia*
Asclepias
Aster
Astilbe
Baptisia
Bergenia*
Brunnera*
Chelone
Dianthus
Dicentra
Dictamnus
Digitalis
Echinacea

Epimedium
Eupatorium
Euphorbia
Ferns (Athyrium,
    Dryopteris,
    Matteucia,
    Osmunda,
    Polystichum)
Galium (sweet
    woodruff)*
Geranium
Grasses
    (Calamagrostis,
    Carex,
    Miscanthus,
    Panicum)
Helleborus
Heuchera
Heucherella
Iris

Lamiastrum*
Lamium*
Lavendula
Liatris
Lychnis coronaria
Monarda
Oenothera
Paeonia
Papaver
Perovskia*
Polemonium
Pulmonaria
Rudbeckia
Sedum
Solidago*
Stachys
Tanacetum*
Thymus*
Tiarella
Veronica
Yucca*

Shrubs and trees
Aesculus
Amelanchier
Berberis
Betula
Buxus
Cornus sericea
Chamaecyparis
Fagus
Hippophae
Pieris japonicus
Picea pungiens
Pinus sylvestris
Sambucus
Syringa

Appendix B
Plants for pollinators

Achillea
Actaea
Agastache*
Aquilegia
Aruncus
Asclepias
Aster
Astilbe
Baptisia
Campanula
Centaurea
Chelone
Chrysanthemum*
Coreopsis
Digitalis
Echinacea

Echinops
Eryngium
Eupatorium
Filipendula
Gaillardia*
Geranium
Helenium
Helianthus*
Hypericum*
Lavendula
Liatris
Lupinus
Monarda
Nepeta
Phlox
Ratibida*

Rudbeckia
Salvia
Sanguisorba*
Scabiosa
Sedum
Solidago*
Tanacetum*
Tradescantia
Vernonia
Veronica
Veronicastrum

Shrubs and Trees
Acer
Aesculus
Amelanchier

Aronia
Cornus
Hamamelis
Hydrangea
Ilex
Magnolia
Myrica
Pieris
Physocarpus
Rhus
Rosa
Salix
Sambucus
Spirea
Viburnum

Appendix C
Salt- and drought-resistant plants

Aubretia or *Arabis**
Armeria
Centaurea hypoleuca
Centranthus ruber, red valerian*
Cichorium, chicory*
Crambe, sea kale*
Dianthus
Echinacea
Eryngium
Euphorbia
Gypsophila, perennial baby's breath*

Hemerocallis
Hypericum, St. John's wort, both perennials and shrubby forms*
Nepeta
Potentilla
Pulsatilla, prairie crocus*
Salvia
Sedum
Tradescantia
Veronica

Shrubs and Trees
Aesculus
Amelanchier
Crataegus
Caragana, Siberian pea shrub*
Ginkgo
Ilex verticillata
Larix, larch or tamarack*
Magnolia
Myrica
Philadelphus, mock orange*

Picea
Pinus
Rhus
Robinia, honey locust*
Symphoricarpus, snowberry*
Syringa
Vaccinium, highbush and wild blueberries*

Appendix D
Plants for moist or wet soil

Anemone
Aquilegia
Aruncus
Astilbe
Carex (sedges)
Dicentra
Eupatorium
Filipendula
Helenium
Hemerocallis
Hosta
Hypericum (St. John's wort)*
Iris ensata
Iris sibirica
Lamium (deadnettle)*

Lobelia
Lysimachia (loosestrife)*
Mertensia (Virginia bluebells)*
Monarda
Myosotis (forget-me-not)
Sanguisorba (burnet)*
Solidago (goldenrods)*
Thalictrum
*Trillium**
Trollius
Vernonia

Shrubs and trees
Acer
Aesculus
Aronia
Catalpa (bean tree)*
Cercidiphyllum
Clethra (summersweet)*
Cornus alba
Cornus sericea
Fothergilla (fothergill)
Fraxinus (ash)*
Hydrangea
Ilex verticillata
Larix (larch)*

Metasequoia
Myrica
Picea
Platanus (London plane tree)*
Quercus (oak)*
Salix
Sambucus canadensis
Spirea
Thuja occidentalis
Viburnum nudum var. *cassinoides*
Viburnum trilobum

This list is by no means exhaustive, but it includes links to professional trade associations as well as some horticultural societies available on the Internet.

New Brunswick:

Brunswick Nurseries. 308 Model Farm Road, Quispamsis, NB. 506-847-8244. brunswicknurseries.com

Cedarcrest Garden Centre. 1050 Sandy Point Road, Saint John, NB. 506-658-1112. cedarcrestgardens.com

Dooryard Greenhouse. 4 Welch Street, Florenceville-Bristol, NB. 506-392-5918.

Farmer Brown's Greenhouse. 371 Osborne Corner Road, Dawson Settlement, NB. 506-734-1908. farmerbrowns.ca

Green Pig Country Market. 2927 Fredericton Road, Salisbury, NB. 506-372-5640. greenpigmarket.com

Halifax Seed. 664 Rothesay Avenue, Saint John, NB. 506-633-2032. halifaxseed.ca

Hillcrest Nurseries and Greenhouses. 86 Hillcrest, Perth-Andover, NB. 506-273-9859.

Hope Seeds. 365 Knowlesville Road, Knowlesville, NB. 506-375-6434. hopeseed.com

Kingsbrae Garden's Plant Centre. 220 King Street, St. Andrews, NB. 506-529-9026. kingsbraegarden.com/Services/pc.html

Landscape New Brunswick. nbhta.ca

MacArthur's Nurseries. 232 McLaughlin Drive, Moncton, NB. 506-859-2727.

Mr. Tomato. 11015 rue Principale, Rogersville, NB. 506-775-6042.

Scotts Nursery. 2192 Route 102, Lincoln, NB. 506-458-9208. scottsnursery.nb.ca

Sun Nurseries. 47 Morrow Avenue, Sussex, NB. 506-432-1100.

Newfoundland and Labrador:

Bickerstaffe Farms and Nurseries. 131 Witch Hazel Road, Portugal Cove/St. Phillips, NL. 709-895-3417.

Holland Nurseries. 401 Torbay Road, St. John's, NL. 877-726-1283. flowersnewfoundland.com

Humber Nurseries. 137-141 West Valley Road, Corner Brook, NL. 800-565-3241. www.humbernurseriescornerbrook.com

Landscape Newfoundland and Labrador. landscapenf.org

Murrays Garden Centre. 1525 Portugal Cove Road, Portugal Cove, NL. 709-895-2800. murraysgardens.com

Nuthatch Nursery. Lethbridge, NL. 709-467-1309.

O'Neill's Gardenland and Landscape Construction. Spaniard's Bay, NL. 709-798-9533.

Traverse Gardens. 12 Byrnes Lane, Torbay, NL. 709-437-5539. traversegardens.com

Nova Scotia:

Baldwin Nurseries. 500 Mines Road, Falmouth, NS. 902-798-9468. baldwinnurseries.com

Bloom Greenhouse. 1421 Hammonds Plains Road, Hammonds Plains, NS. 902-832-9268.
    bloomgreenhouse.com

Briar Patch Farm and Nursery. 4568 Highway 1, South Berwick, NS. 902-538-9164. briarpatchnursery.com

Bunchberry Nurseries. 2779 Highway 1, Upper Clements, NS. 902-532-7777. bunchberrynurseries.ca

Canning Daylily Gardens. 165 Pereau Road, RR # 1, Canning, NS. 902-582-7966.
    canningdaylilygardens.com

Den Haan's. 12688 Highway 1, Middleton, NS. 902-825-4722. denhaansgardenworld.com

Greenhouse Nova Scotia. greenhousenovascotia.com

Halifax Seed. 5860 Kane Street, Halifax, NS. 902-454-7456. halifaxseed.ca

Lowland Gardens. Highway 2, Great Village, NS. 902-668-2309. lowland-gardens.com

Ocean View Garden Centre and Landscaping. 4392 Highway 3, Chester, NS. 902-275-2505. plantcrazy.ca

Ouest-Ville Perennials. Argyle Sound Road, West Pubnico, NS. 902-762-3198. ouestvilleperennials.com

Pleasant Valley Nurseries. Church Street Extension, Antigonish, NS. 902-863-1072.
    pleasantvalleynurseries.com

West River Greenhouses. 509 Hwy 376, Central West River, Pictou County, NS. 902-925-2088.

Prince Edward Island:

Doiron's Landscaping and Garden Centre. 2 Day Avenue, Charlottetown, PEI. 902-368-1666.
    doironslandscaping.com

Island Pride Garden Company. 19905 Route 2, Hunter River, PEI. 866-962-2044. islandpride.ca

Jewell's Country Market and Garden Centre. 394 York Road, York, PEI. 902-629-1900.
    jewellscountrymarket.com

Kool Breeze Farms. 231 Read Drive, Summerside, PEI. 866-536-1900. kookbreezefarms.com

Red Lane Gardens (Daylilies and Japanese Irises). RR3, Belfast, PEI. 902-659-2478. redlanegardens.com

Van Kampen's Greenhouses. 58 Allen Street, Charlottetown, PEI. 902-894-5146.

York Greenhouses. 618 York Road, York, PEI. 902-566-1503. yorkgreenhouses.ca

Clubs/Societies:

Atlantic Rhododendron and Horticultural Society. atlanticrhodo.org

Newfoundland Horticultural Society. nfldhort.dhs.org/page2.htm

Nova Scotia Association of Garden Clubs. nsagc.com

Contacts for individual clubs not having umbrella organizations can be found at:
    icangarden.com/clubs.cfm

FURTHER READING

Armitage, Allan. *Armitage's Native Plants for North American Gardens*. Timber Press, 2006.

Anisko, Tomasz. *When Perennials Bloom*. Timber Press, 2009.

Bell, Adrian D. *Plant Form: An Illustrated Guide to Flowering Plant Morphology*. Timber Press, 2008.

Burrell, C. Colston. *Perennial Combinations*. Rodale Press, 1999.

Burrell, C. Colston, ed. *Wildflower Gardens*. Brooklyn Botanical Gardens, 1999, 2007.

Bloom, Adrian. *Gardening with Conifers*. Firefly Books, 2002.

Clarke, Graham. *Success with Shade-Loving Plants*. GMC Publications, 2007.

Deardorff, David and Kathryn Wadsworth. *What's Wrong with My Plant*? Timber Press, 2009.

Dirr, Michael A. *Manual of Woody Landscape Plants*. Stipes, 1998 (revised 2004, 2009).

Dirr, Michael A. *Viburnums*. Timber Press, 2007.

Harris, Marjorie. *Botanica North America*. HarperCollins, 2003.

Howell, Catherine Herbert. *Flora Mirabilis*. National Geographic Society and Missouri Botanical Garden, 2009.

Hinds, Harold R. *Flora of New Brunswick* (2nd edition). University of New Brunswick, 2000.

James Jr., Theodore and Harry Haralambou. *Seaside Gardening*. Abrams, 2006.

Kress, Stephen W., ed. *Hummingbird Gardens*. Brooklyn Botanical Gardens, 2007 (revised edition).

LaRue, Diane. *Common Wild Flowers and Plants of Nova Scotia*. Nimbus, 2004.

Lloyd, Christopher. *Christopher Lloyd's Garden Flowers*. Timber Press, 2005.

Lloyd, Christopher. *Color for Adventurous Gardeners*. Firefly Books, 2001.

Ondra, Nancy. *The Perennial Care Manual*. Storey Books, 2009.

Ondra, Nancy and Stephanie Cohen. *Fallscaping*. Storey Books, 2008.

Osborne, Robert. *Hardy Roses*. Key Porter Books, 2002 (revised edition).

Oudolf, Piet and Noel Kingsbury. *Planting Design: Gardens in Time and Space*. Timber Press, 2005.

Phillips, Roger and Martyn Rix. *The Botanical Garden. Volume 1, Trees and Shrubs, Volume 2, Perennials and Annuals*. Firefly Books, 2002.

Primrose, Mary and Marian Munro. *Wildflowers of Nova Scotia, New Brunswick and Prince Edward Island*. Formac, 1998, 2006.

Scott, Peter J. *Edible Plants of Atlantic Canada*. Boulder Publications, 2010.

Scott, Peter J. and Dorothy Black. *Wildflowers of Newfoundland and Labrador*. Boulder Publications, 2006.

Shepherd, Matthew, Stephen L. Buchmann, Mace Vaughn, and Scott Hoffman Black. *Pollinator Conservation Handbook*. The Xerces Society, 2003.

Turner, Roger. *Tall Perennials*. Timber Press, 2009.

Walker, Marilyn. *Wild Plants of Eastern Canada*. Nimbus Publishing, 2008.

Wells, Diana. *100 Flowers and How They Got Their Names*. Algonquin Books, 1997.

Zinck, Marian. *Roland's Flora of Nova Scotia, Volumes 1 and 2*. Nimbus Publishing and the Nova Scotia Museum, 1998.

INDEX

A

abscess root. See *Polemonium*

Acadia University 36

Acer 4–5, 242, 243

Acer palmatum 6–7

Acer shirasawanum 'Aureum'. See *Acer palmatum*

Achillea 91–92, 242

Aconitum 93–94, 242

Actaea 96–97, 242

Adiantum 36, 229

Aegopodium podegraria x, 30, 104, 106

Aesculus 8–9, 216, 242, 243

Agastache 242

Agavaceae 172

Ajuga 30, 31, 106, 109

Alchemilla 98–99, 242

all-heal. See *Achillea*

alpine gardening x, 109

alumroot. See *Heuchera*

Amelanchier 10–11, 242, 243

American beech. See *Fagus sylvatica*

American elder. See *Sambucus*

American Hosta Society 174

Amos, Tim 22

Amsonia 100–101, 242

Amur maple. See *Acer*

Anacardiaceae 68

Andromeda polifolia 59

Anemone 102–103, 231, 242, 243

Anemone canadensis 106

Anemonella thalictroides 230

Annapolis Royal Historic Gardens 175

anthocyanins 13

aphids 33, 57, 76, 84, 133, 186, 199, 212, 220

Apiaceae 120, 150

Apocyanaceae 100

Apocynum androsaemifolium 100

apple rust 32

Aquifoliaceae 44

Aquilegia 242, 243

Arabis 110, 243

arborvitae. See *Thuja occidentalis*

archangel. See *Lamiastrum*

Armeria maritime 107–108, 110, 243

Armitage, Allan 112, 129

Aronia 12–13, 242, 243

Artemisia 106, 242

Aruncus 111–112, 242, 243

Asarum 31

Asclepiadaceae 113

Asclepias 113–114, 242

ash 243

Aster 115–117, 242

Asteraceae 91, 115, 116, 126, 144, 146, 152, 175, 180, 182, 218, 237

Aster yellows disease 117

Astilbe 118–119, 242, 243

Astrantia 120–121

Athyrium 157, 242. See also ferns

Atlantic Rhododendron and Horticultural Society 64

Aubretia 243

avens. See *Geum*

Azalea. See *Rhododendron* (deciduous azalea)

B

bachelor button 126

bagworm 81

Baldwin, Rob 40, 58

balsam fir x

baneberry. See *Actaea*

Baptisia 122–123, 242

barrenwort. See *Epimedium*

basketflower 126

bastard pellitory. See *Achillea*

Bayport Plant Farm 58

bean tree 243

beautybush x

beebalm. See *Monarda*

beech bark disease 34

bellflower. See *Campanula*

Bells-of-Scotland 125

Berberidaceae 14, 148

Berberis 14–15, 242

bergamot. See *Monarda*

Bergenia 242

Bethlehem sage. See *Pulmonaria*

betony. See *Stachys*

Betula 16–17, 242

Betulaceae 16, 28

birch. See *Betula*

birch borer 17

bishop's cap. See *Epimedium*

bishop's hat. See *Epimedium*

bishop's weed. See Aegopodium podegraria

black alder. See *Ilex verticillata*

Black, Dorothy 107

black elder. See *Sambucus*

black-eyed Susan 218

blackspot 70

blazingstar. See *Liatris*

bleeding-heart. See *Dicentra*

bloodwort 214

blossom blight 79

blue aconite. See *Aconitum*

blue beech. See *Carpinus caroliniana*

blueberries 243

blueberry 11

blue false indigo. See *Baptisia*

Blue Lyme grass 106

blue poppy x

blue spruce. See *Picea*

bluestar. See *Amsonia*

bog myrtle. See *Myrica pennysylvanica*

bog rosemary. See *Andromeda polifolia*

boneset. See *Eupatorium*

Boraginaceae 214

Botanica North America 152

botrytis 7, 95, 196, 197

bottlebrush buckeye. See *Aesculus*

box. See *Buxus*
boxwood. See *Buxus*
brideflower. See *Achillea*
bride's feathers. See *Aruncus*
bristlecone pine. See *Pinus*
Brunnera 242
Bryson, Sharon 63
B.t. spray 57
buckeye. See *Aesculus*
Buddleia 113.
bugbane. See *Actaea*
bugleweed. See *Ajuga*
bunchberry. See *Cornus canadensis*
Bunchberry Nurseries 209
burnet 243
burning bush. See *Dictamnus albus*
butterfly bush x, 113
butterfly weed. See *Asclepias*
Buxaceae 18
Buxus 18–19, 52, 242

C

Calamagrostis 203, 242
Callitropsis 25
Calluna 20–21, 110
Campanula 110, 124–125, 242
Campanula rapunculoides 106
Campanula takesimana 106
Campanulaceae 124, 184
campion. See *Lychnis*
Canada holly. See *Ilex verticillata*
Canadian Rose Society 70
Canadian Wildlife Federation 88
candleberry. See *Myrica pennysylvanica*
canker 26
Canning Daylily Gardens 169
Caprifoliaceae 74, 86
Caragana 243
cardinal flower. See *Lobelia*
Carex 203, 242, 243
Carissa 100
carnation. See *Dianthus*
carotene 41
Carpinus caroliniana 35
Cartier, Jacques 81
Caryophyllaceae 135, 188
caryopteris x
Catalpa x, 243
catchfly. See *Lychnis*

catmint. See *Nepeta*
catnip. See *Nepeta*
cedar rust 32
Cedrus 81
Celastrus orbiculatus x
Centaurea 126–127, 242
Centaurea hypoleuca 243
Central Experimental Farm 79
Centranthus ruber 243
Cephalaria gigantea 223
Cerastium 109, 188
Cercidiphyllum 22–23, 243
Chamaecyparis 24–25, 242
Chamaepericlymenum canadense 129
chameleon plant. See *Houttuynia cordata*
Chelone 128, 242
Chicago Botanic Garden 123, 145
chickweeds 188
chicory 243
Clinton lanium 100
Chinese witch-hazel. See *Hamamelis*
chokeberry. See *Aronia*
chokecherry 12
Christmas rose. See *Helleborus*
Chrysanthemum 242
chuckly pear. See *Amelanchier*
Cichorium 243
Cimicifuga 96
cinquefoil. See *Potentilla*
Clethra 243
cohosh. See *Actaea*
Commelinaceae 233
common barberry. See *Berberis*
common box. See *Buxus*
common horse chestnut. See *Aesculus*
Compositeae 116
Consolida ambigua 134
copper beech. See *Fagus sylvatica*
coral bells. See *Heuchera*
coralberry. See *Ilex verticillata*
Coreopsis 242
corkscrew hazel. See *Corylus avellana* 'Contorta'
Cornaceae 26
Cornelian cherry. See *Cornus*
Cornhill Nursery 70
Cornus 26–27, 242, 243
Cornus canadensis 129–130
Cornus sericea 242
Cornus suecica 130

Corydalis 131–132
Corylus avellana 'Contorta' 28–29, 35
cowslip. See *Primula*
crackerberry. See *Cornus canadensis*
Crambe 243
cranesbill. See *Geranium*
Crassulaceae 224
Crataegus 10, 32–33, 243
creeping bellflower 104
creeping Jenny 106
crocosmia x
Culpeper's Complete Herbal 99
Culver's root 241
Cupressaceae 24, 46, 50, 81
currants 62
cut leaf maple. See *Acer palmatum*
Cyperaceae 201

D

daisies x
dawn redwood. See *Metasequoia glyptostroboides*
daylily. See *Hemerocallis*
dead men's fingers. See *Digitalis*
deadnettle 243. See *Lamium*
Delosperma 110
Delphinium 133–134
design (gardens) 90
deutzia x
devil's helmet. See *Aconitum*
Dianthus 110, 135–136, 242, 243
Dicentra 131, 138–139, 242, 243
Dictamnus albus 140, 141, 242
digitalin 142
Digitalis 142–143, 242
Dipsacaceae 222
Dipsacus 106, 146
Dirr, Michael 22, 24, 40, 46, 81, 84. See also *Manual of Woody Landscape Plants*
ditch lily. See *Hemerocallis fulva*
dittany. See *Dictamnus albus*
dogtooth daisy. See *Helenium*
dogwood. See *Cornus*
Dowdeswell, Terry 134
Dryopteris 157, 242. See also ferns
Dutchman's breeches. See *Dicentra*

spiderwort. See *Tradescantia*
Spirea 76–77, 242, 243
spreading dogbane 100
spruce. See *Picea*
spruce gall aphids 56
spurge. See *Euphorbia*
squirrel corn. See *Dicentra*
Stachys 227–228, 242
staghorn sumac. See *Rhus*
staking 2–3
Steele, Captain Richard (Dick) 50, 58
steeplebush. See *Spirea*
Stellaria 188
stem rust 14
St. John's wort 243
stonecrop 224
strawberry 211
sumac. See *Rhus*
summersweet 243
sundrop. See *Oenothera*
sunflowers x
Svejda, Felicitas 87
sweetroot. See *Polemonium*
sweet William. See *Dianthus*
sweet woodruff 243. See *Gallium odoratum*
Swiss stone pine. See *Pinus*
Symphoricarpus 243
Symphytotrichum 116
Syringa 78–80, 242, 243

T

tall perennials 104
tamarack 243
Tanacetum 242
Taxus xii
teasel 106, 146
Thalictrum 229–230, 243
The English Physician 99
Thermopsis 187
thimbleweed. See *Anemone*
thornapple. See *Crataegus*
Thuja occidentalis 81–82, 243
Thujopsis 82
thyme. See *Thymus*
Thymus 31, 110, 242
Tiarella 171, 231–232, 242
tiger lily. See *Hemerocallis fulva*
Toxicodendron radicans 68
Tradescantia 233–234, 242, 243
Trillium 243
triple-20 19
Trollius 235–236, 243
true larkspur 134
Tsusuji 63

tulip tree 48
turtlehead. See *Chelone*
tussock moths 57
twig blight 26

U

umbel 120
University of Illinois 13
University of Minnesota 64
U. S. National Arboretum 49

V

Vaccinium 243
Verbascum 239
Vernonia 237–238, 242, 243
Veronica 239–240, 241, 242, 243
   Veronica repens 106
Veronicastrum 241, 242
Viburnum 83–84, 242, 243
Vinca 30, 31, 100
Viola 106
violet 106
Virginia bluebells 243
vitamin C 11

W

Walker, Marilyn 130
Weigela 86–87
western red cedar 81
white cedar. See *Chamaecyparis*
whiteflies 220
white spruce. See *Picea*
white tussock moth 33
widow's tears. See *Tradescantia*
Wild About Gardening 88
wild ageratum. See *Eupatorium*
Wildflower Farm 181
Wildflowers of Newfoundland and Labrador 107
Wild Plants of Eastern Canada 130
wild raisin. See *Viburnum*
Wilgenhof, Bill 63
willow. See *Salix*
Wilmott, Ellen 151
windbreaks. See shelterbelts
windflower 106. See *Anemone*
winterberry. See *Ilex verticillata*
witches' gloves. See *Digitalis*
witch-hazel. See *Hamamelis*
witherod. See *Viburnum*
wolfsbane. See *Aconitum*

X

Xerces Society for Invertebrate Conservation 88
x *Heucherella* 171

Y

yarrow. See *Achillea*
yellow archangel 106
yellow false lupin 187
yellow loosestrife 106
yellow stonecrop 106
yew x
Young's weeping birch. See *Betula*
Yucca 242